CHAPTER ONE
GRUDGE

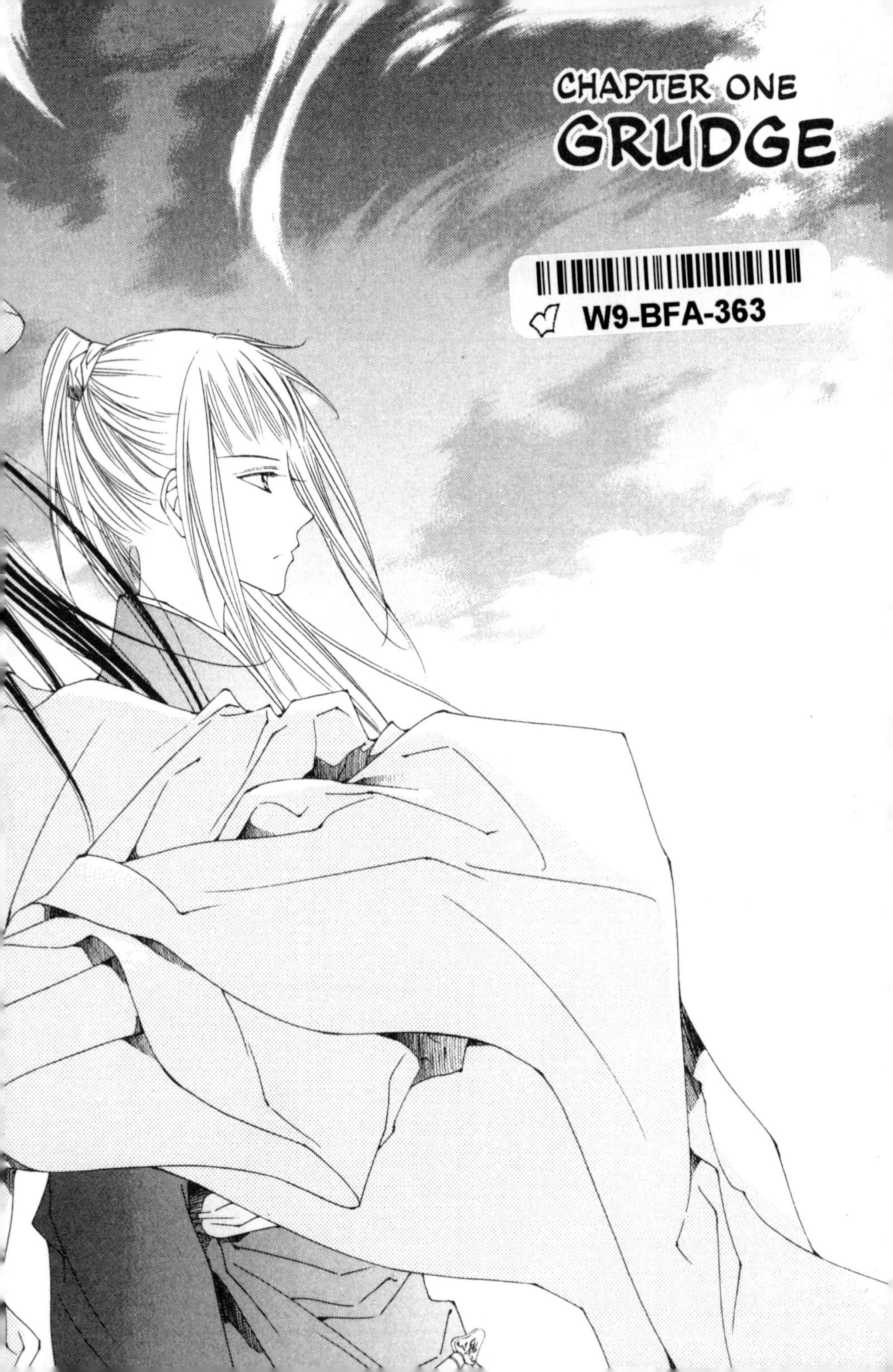

"THE SOUND OF A FLUTE
ONE SPRING NIGHT IN LUOYANG"
LI BAI

FROM WHOSE HOUSE SOARS THE JADE FLUTE'S SONG
LOST IN THE SPRING WIND THAT FILLS LUOYANG?
AS THE WILLOW SNAPS TO THE NIGHT'S NOCTURNE
WHO CAN HELP BUT TO LONG FOR THEIR HOME?

TIME
AND
AGAIN

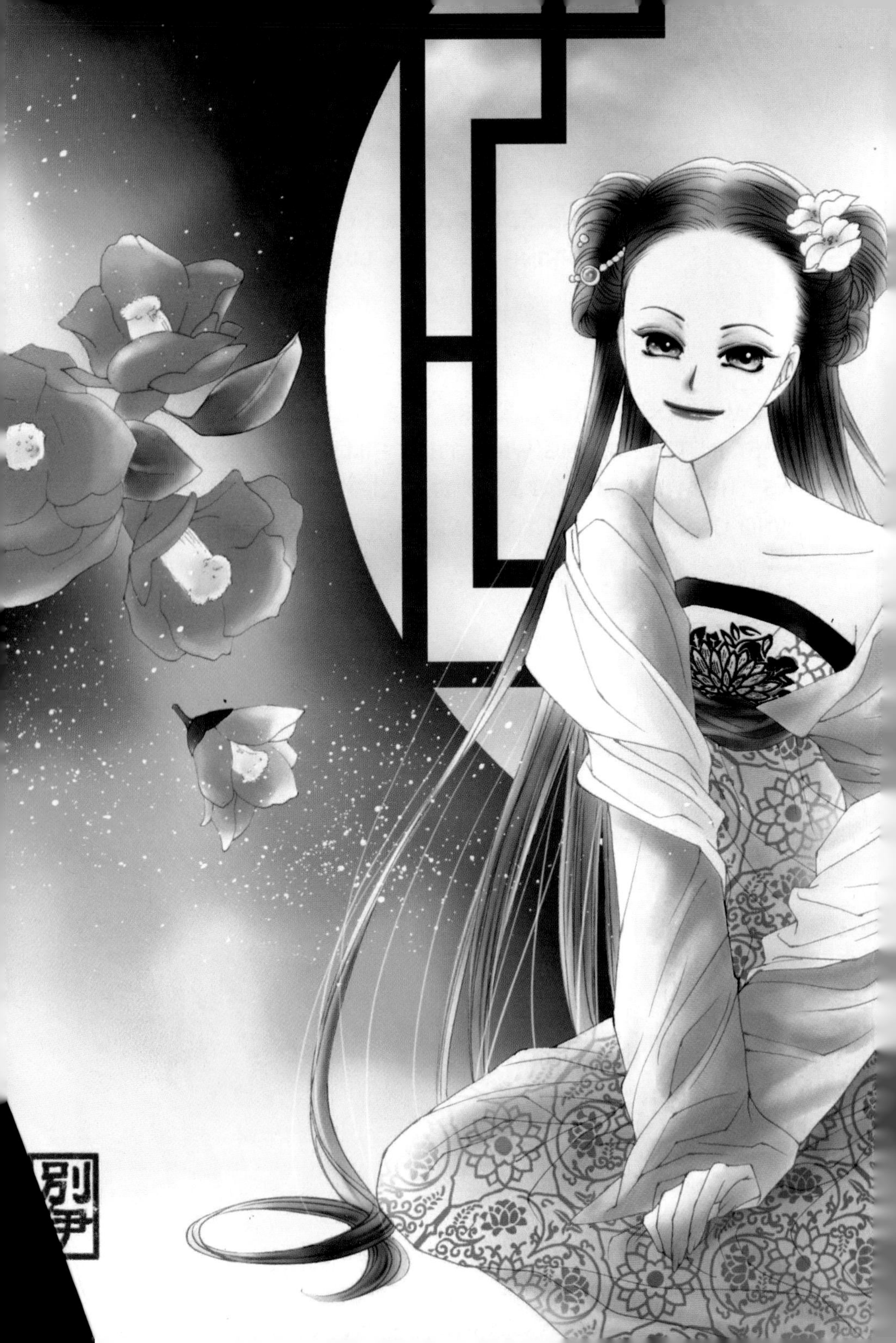
別

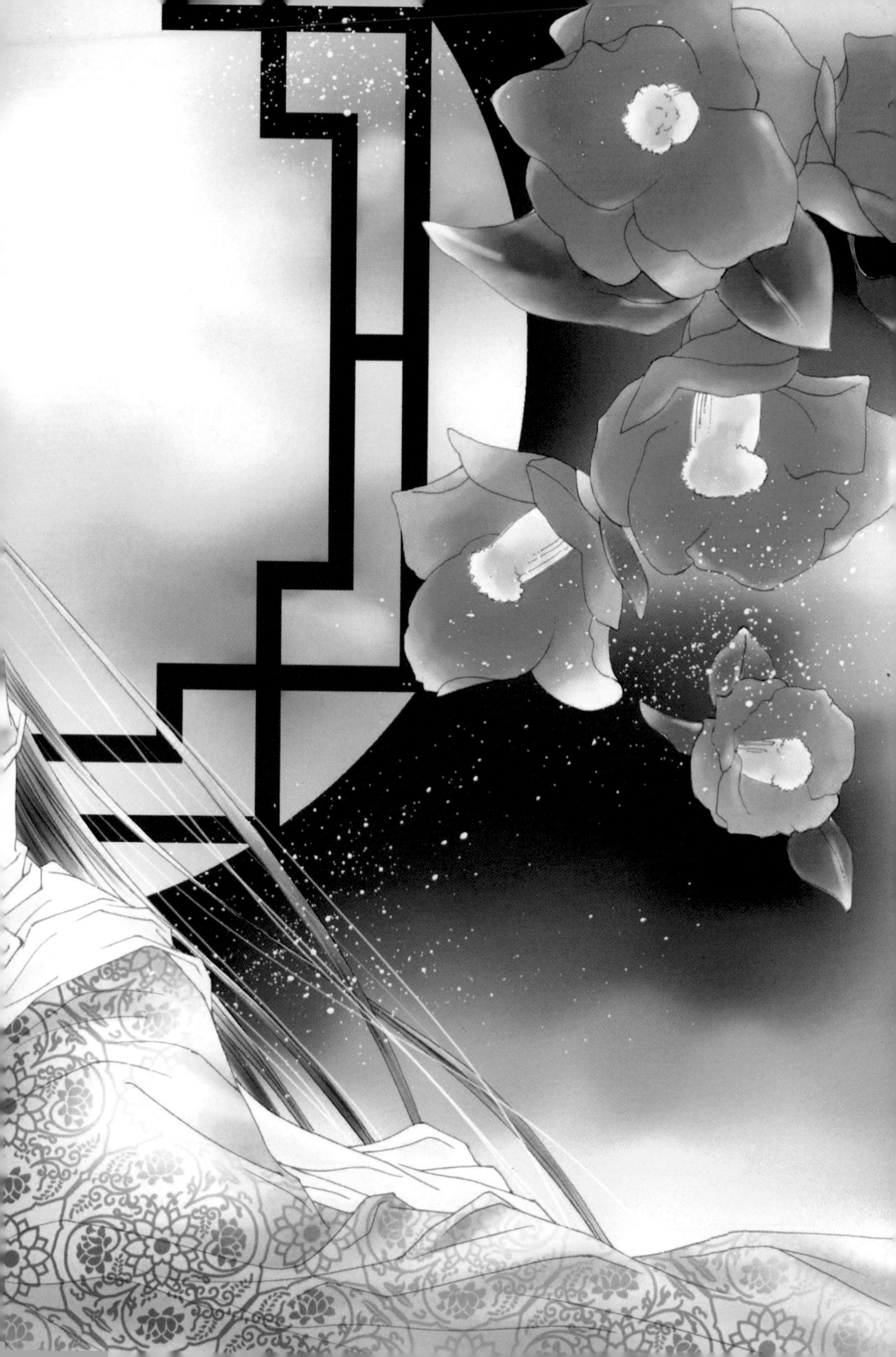

CONTENTS

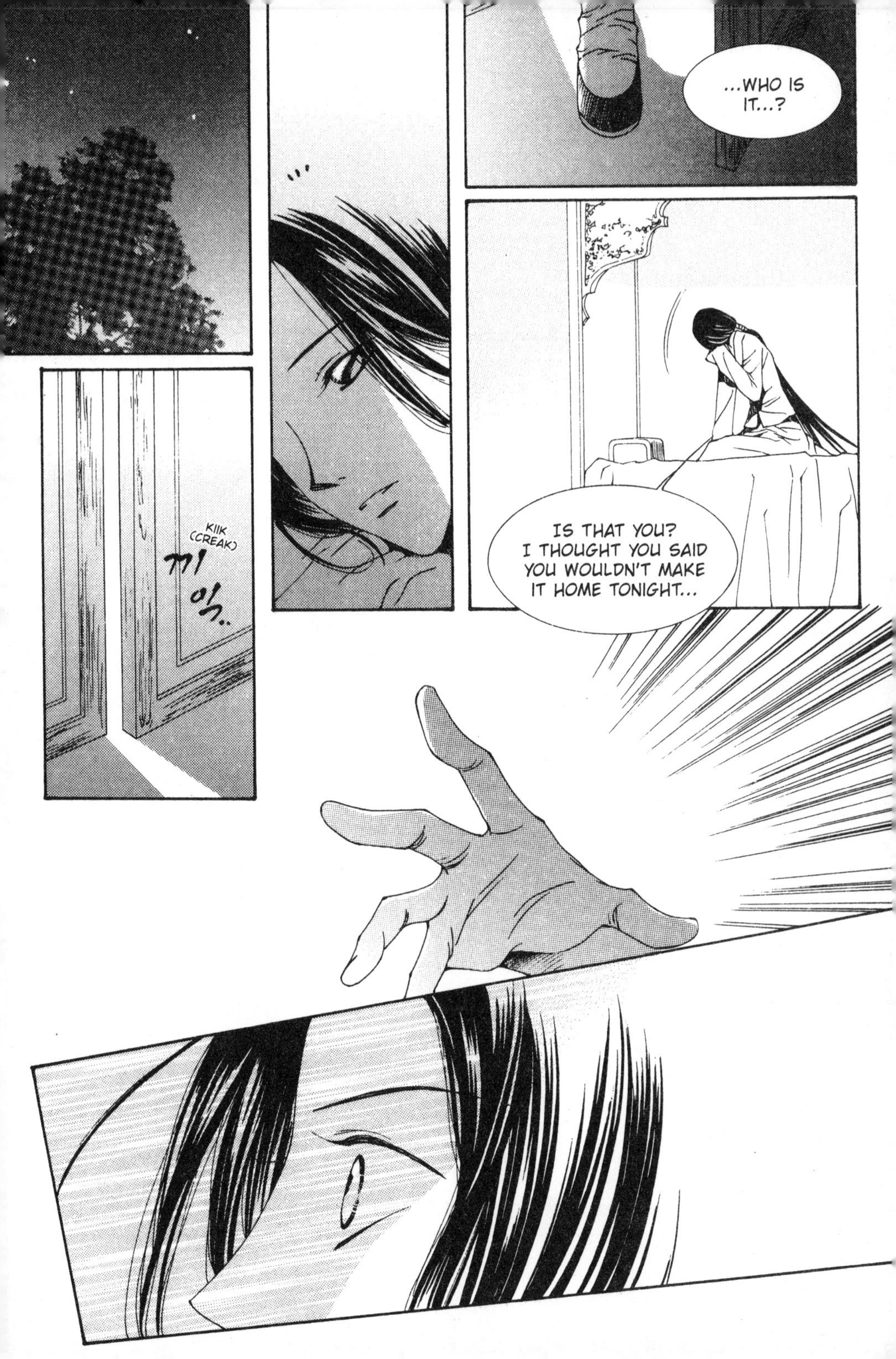
KIIK (CREAK)
끼익..
...
...WHO IS IT...?
IS THAT YOU? I THOUGHT YOU SAID YOU WOULDN'T MAKE IT HOME TONIGHT...

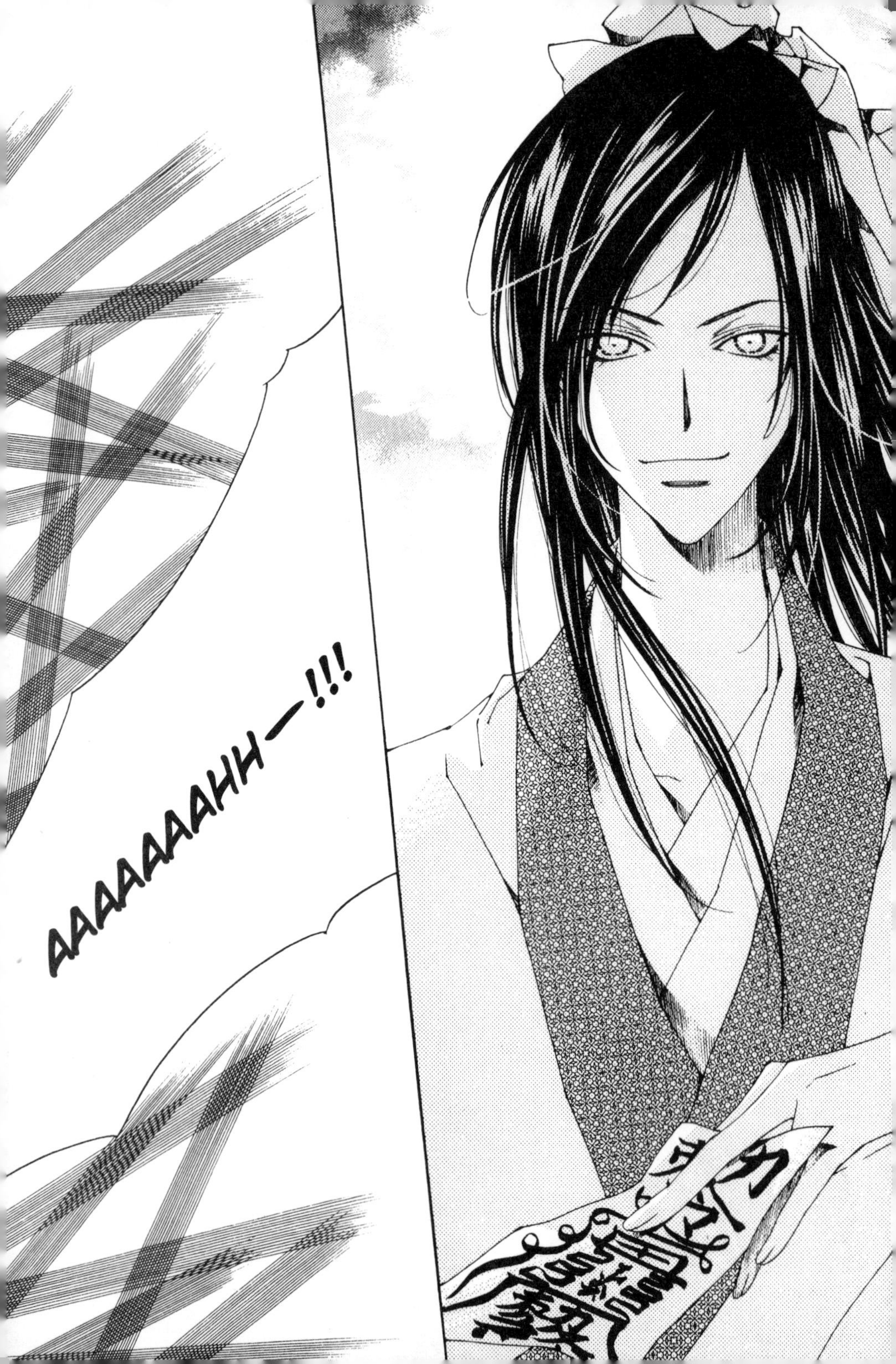
AAAAAAAHH—!!!

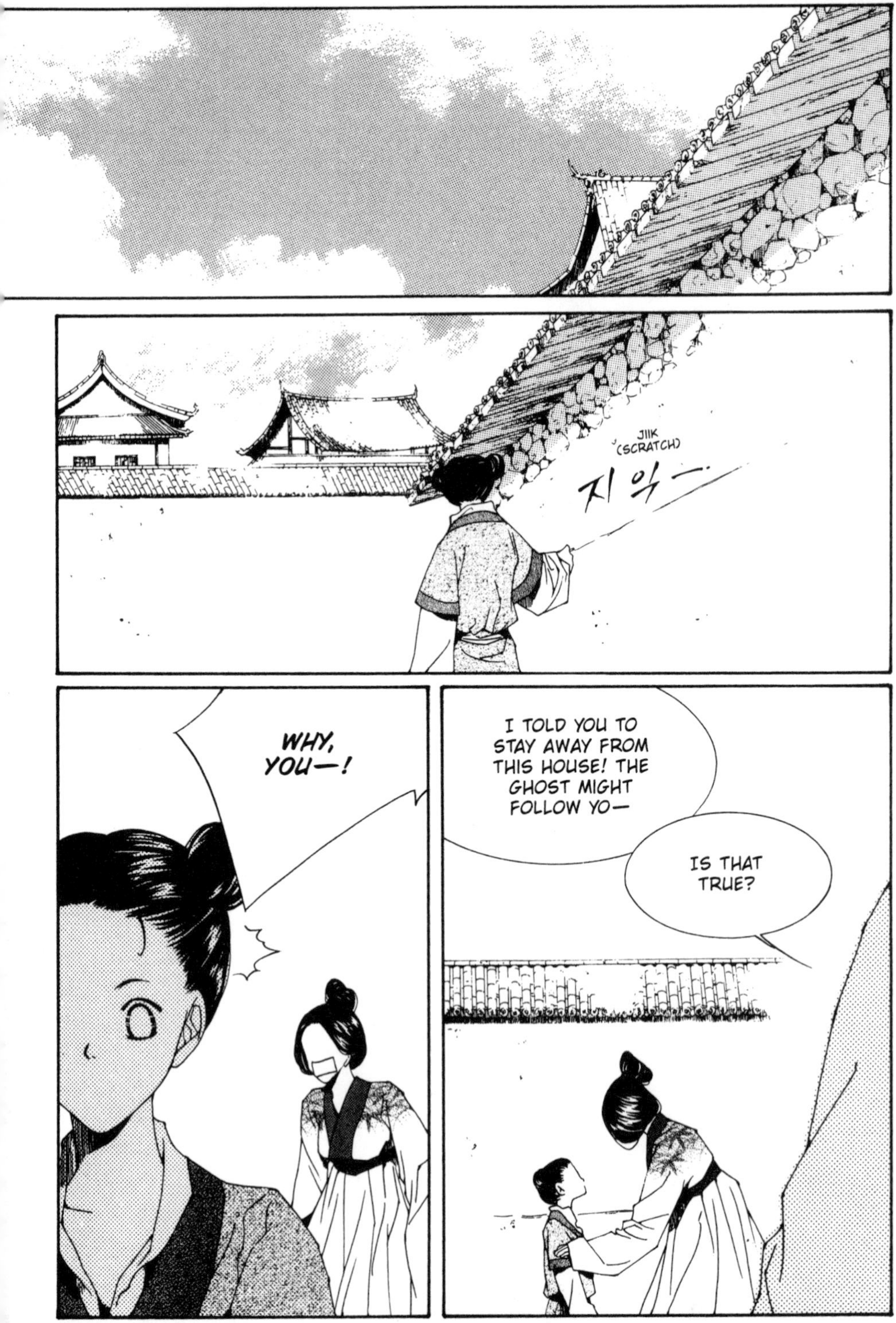
JIIK (SCRATCH)
지익—
WHY, YOU—!
I TOLD YOU TO STAY AWAY FROM THIS HOUSE! THE GHOST MIGHT FOLLOW YO—
IS THAT TRUE?

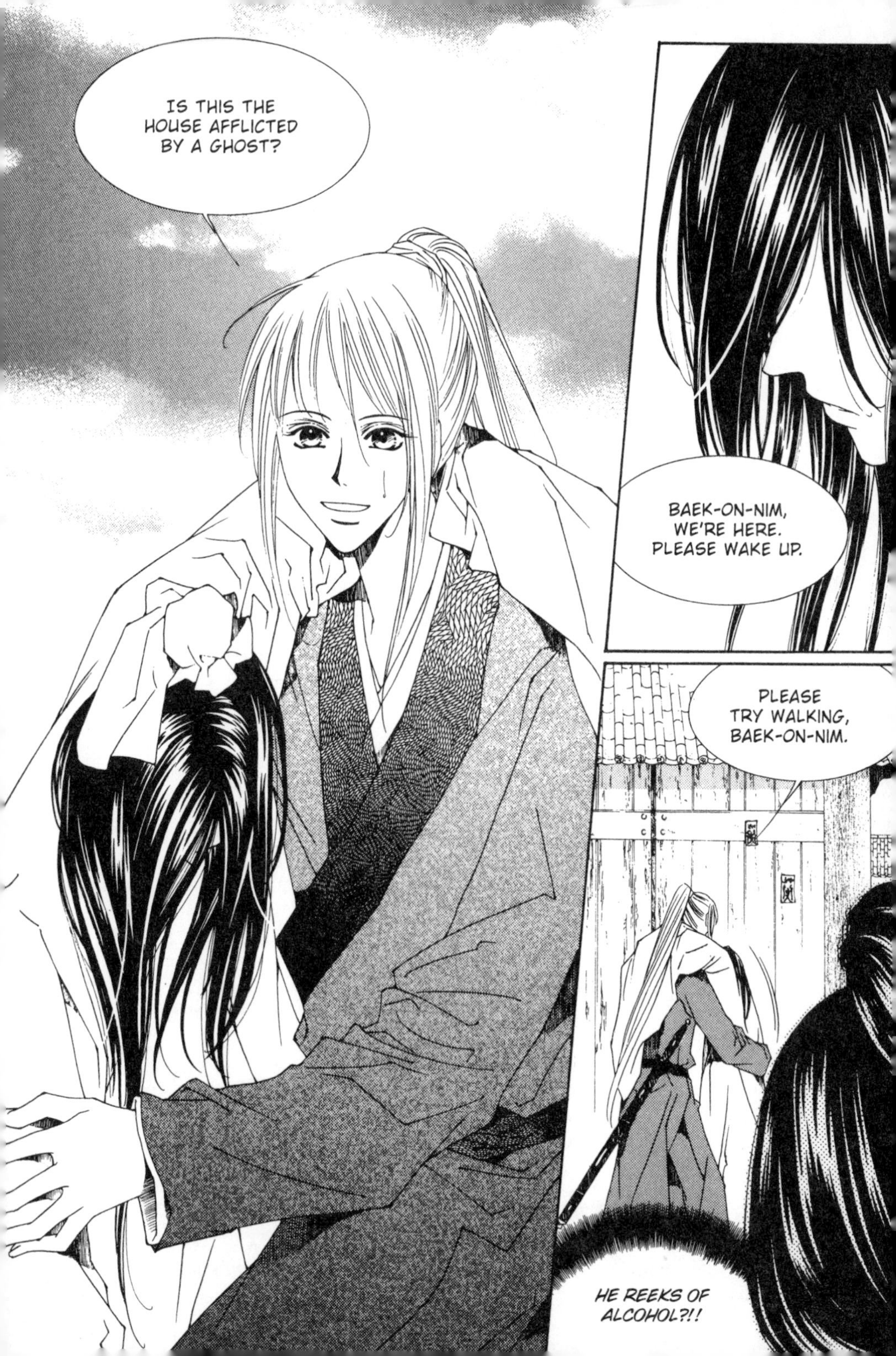
IS THIS THE HOUSE AFFLICTED BY A GHOST?
BAEK-ON-NIM, WE'RE HERE. PLEASE WAKE UP.
PLEASE TRY WALKING, BAEK-ON-NIM.
HE REEKS OF ALCOHOL?!!

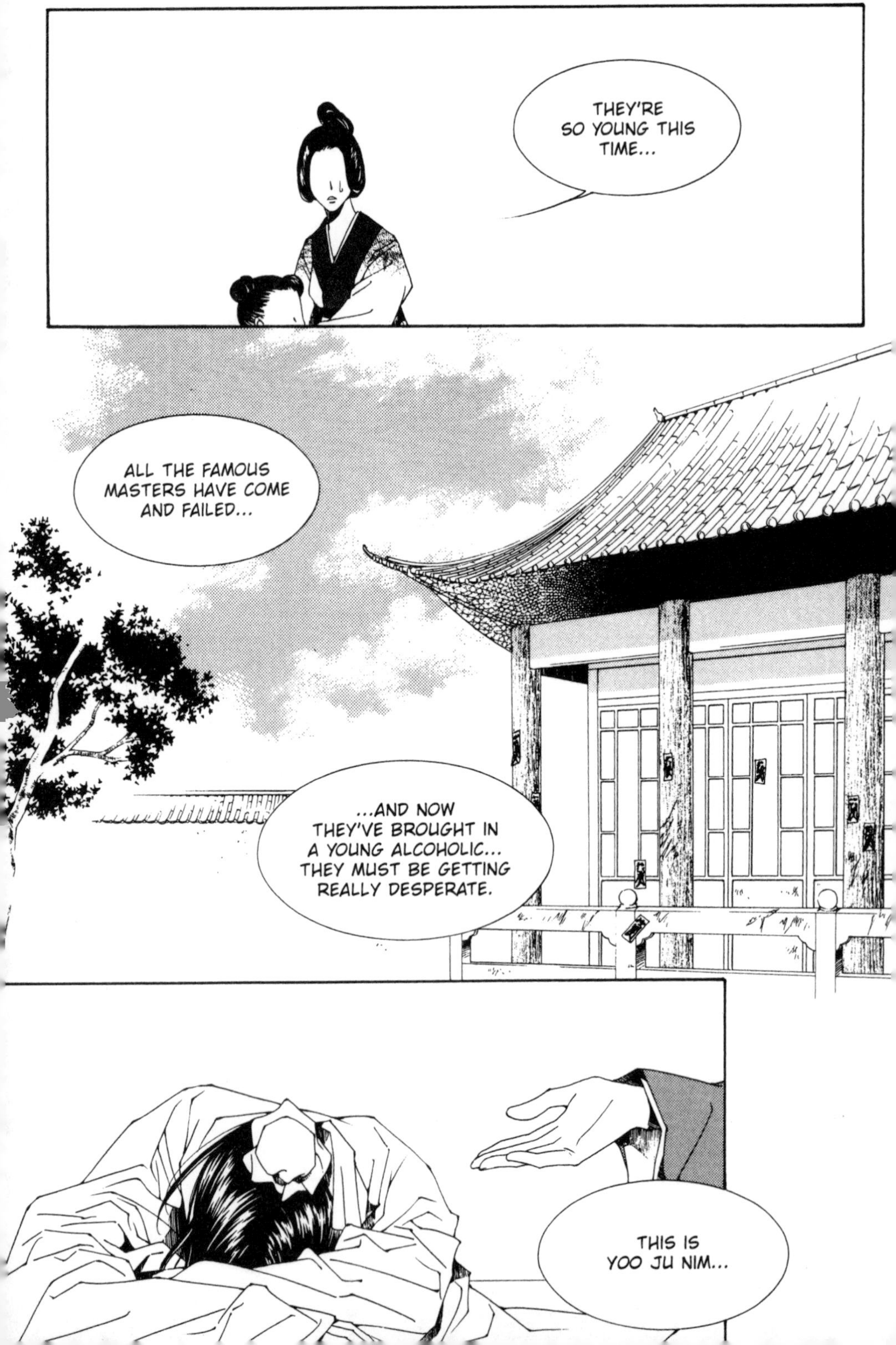
THEY'RE SO YOUNG THIS TIME...
ALL THE FAMOUS MASTERS HAVE COME AND FAILED...
...AND NOW THEY'VE BROUGHT IN A YOUNG ALCOHOLIC... THEY MUST BE GETTING REALLY DESPERATE.
THIS IS YOO JU NIM...

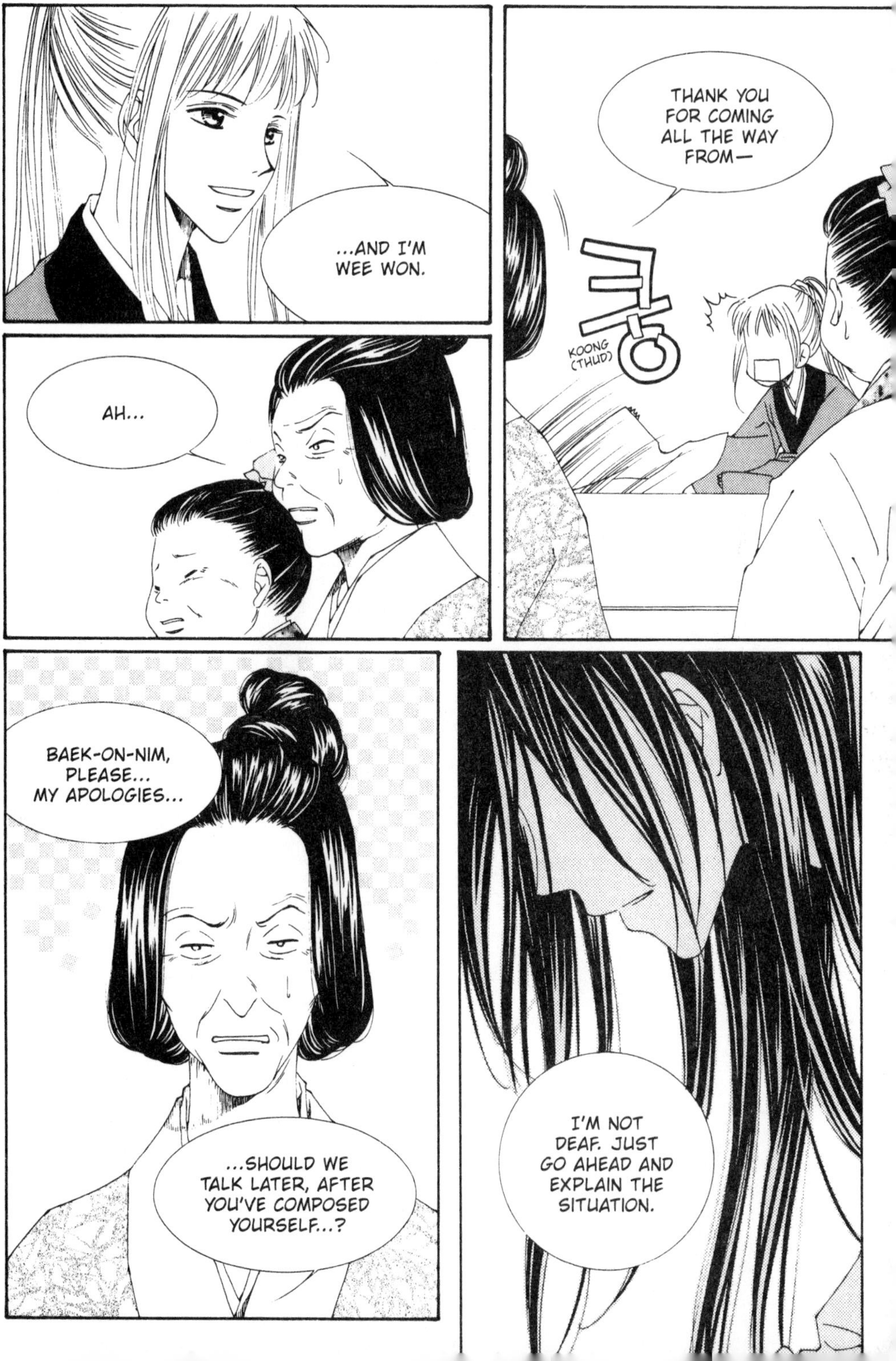
...AND I'M WEE WON.
AH...
THANK YOU FOR COMING ALL THE WAY FROM—
쿵
KOONG (THUD)
BAEK-ON-NIM, PLEASE... MY APOLOGIES...
...SHOULD WE TALK LATER, AFTER YOU'VE COMPOSED YOURSELF...?
I'M NOT DEAF. JUST GO AHEAD AND EXPLAIN THE SITUATION.

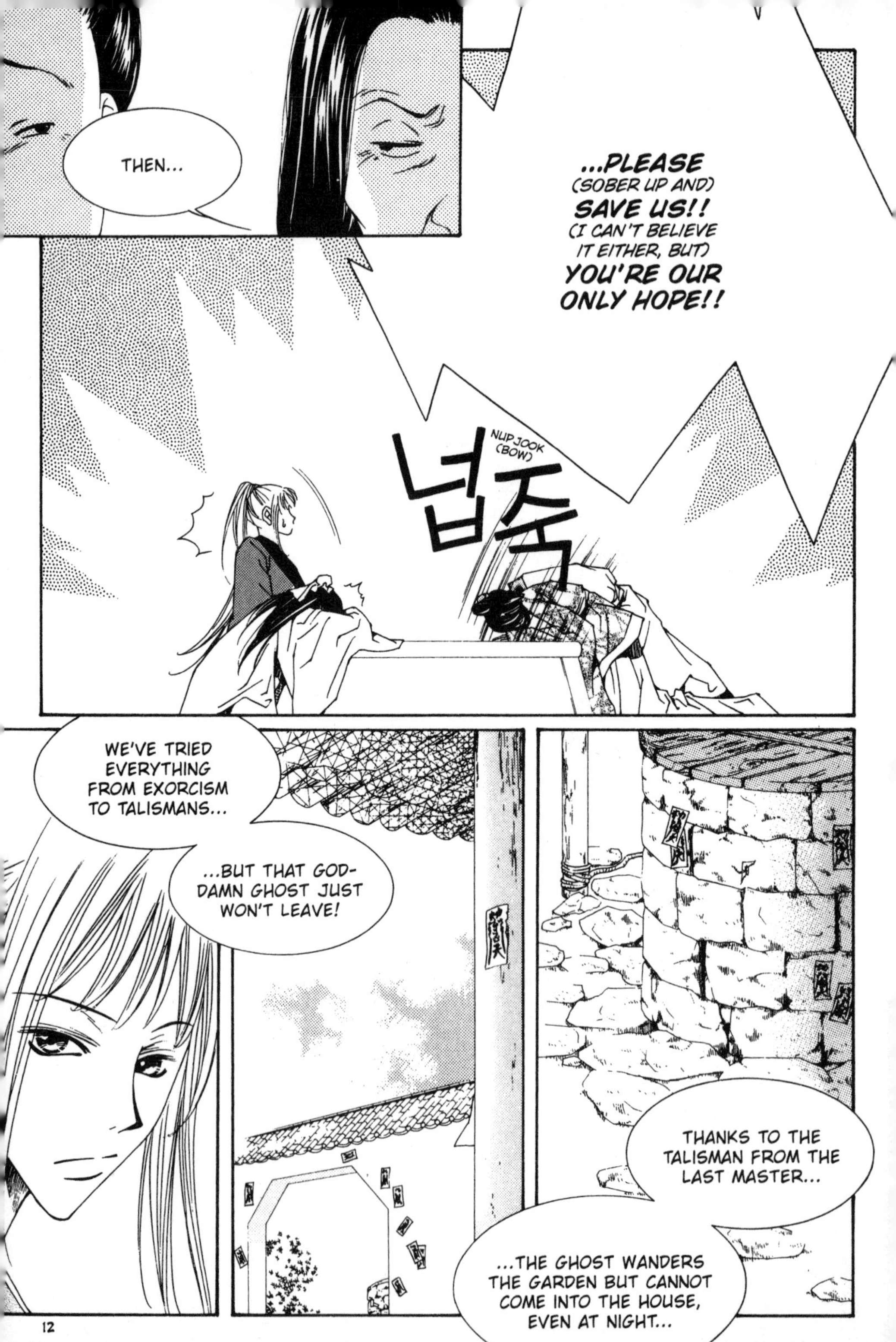
THEN...
...PLEASE (SOBER UP AND) SAVE US!! (I CAN'T BELIEVE IT EITHER, BUT) YOU'RE OUR ONLY HOPE!!
넙죽
NUP JOOK (BOW)
WE'VE TRIED EVERYTHING FROM EXORCISM TO TALISMANS...
...BUT THAT GOD-DAMN GHOST JUST WON'T LEAVE!
THANKS TO THE TALISMAN FROM THE LAST MASTER...
...THE GHOST WANDERS THE GARDEN BUT CANNOT COME INTO THE HOUSE, EVEN AT NIGHT...

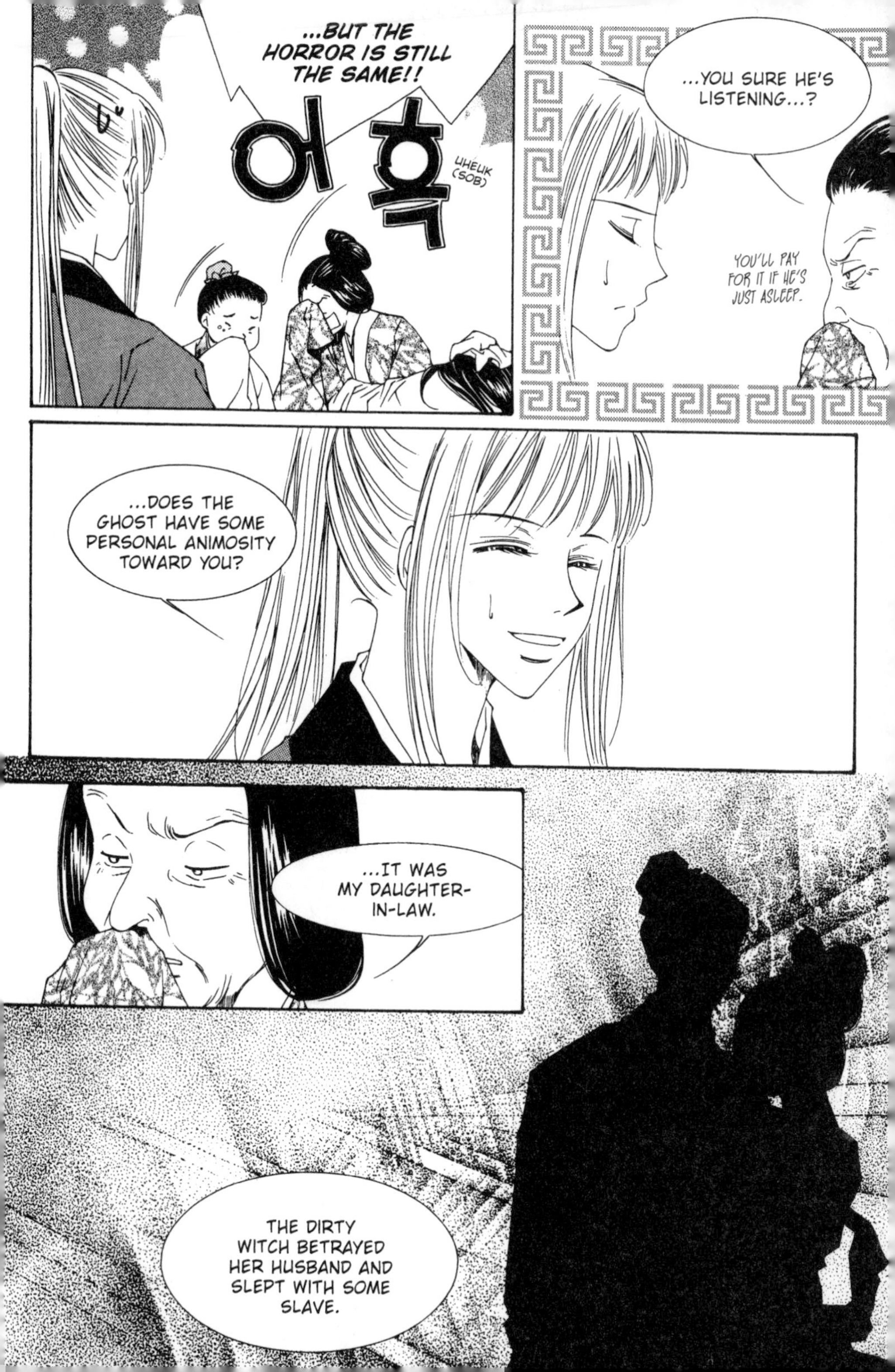
...BUT THE HORROR IS STILL THE SAME!!
어흑
UHEUK (SOB)
...YOU SURE HE'S LISTENING...?
YOU'LL PAY FOR IT IF HE'S JUST ASLEEP.
...DOES THE GHOST HAVE SOME PERSONAL ANIMOSITY TOWARD YOU?
...IT WAS MY DAUGHTER-IN-LAW.
THE DIRTY WITCH BETRAYED HER HUSBAND AND SLEPT WITH SOME SLAVE.

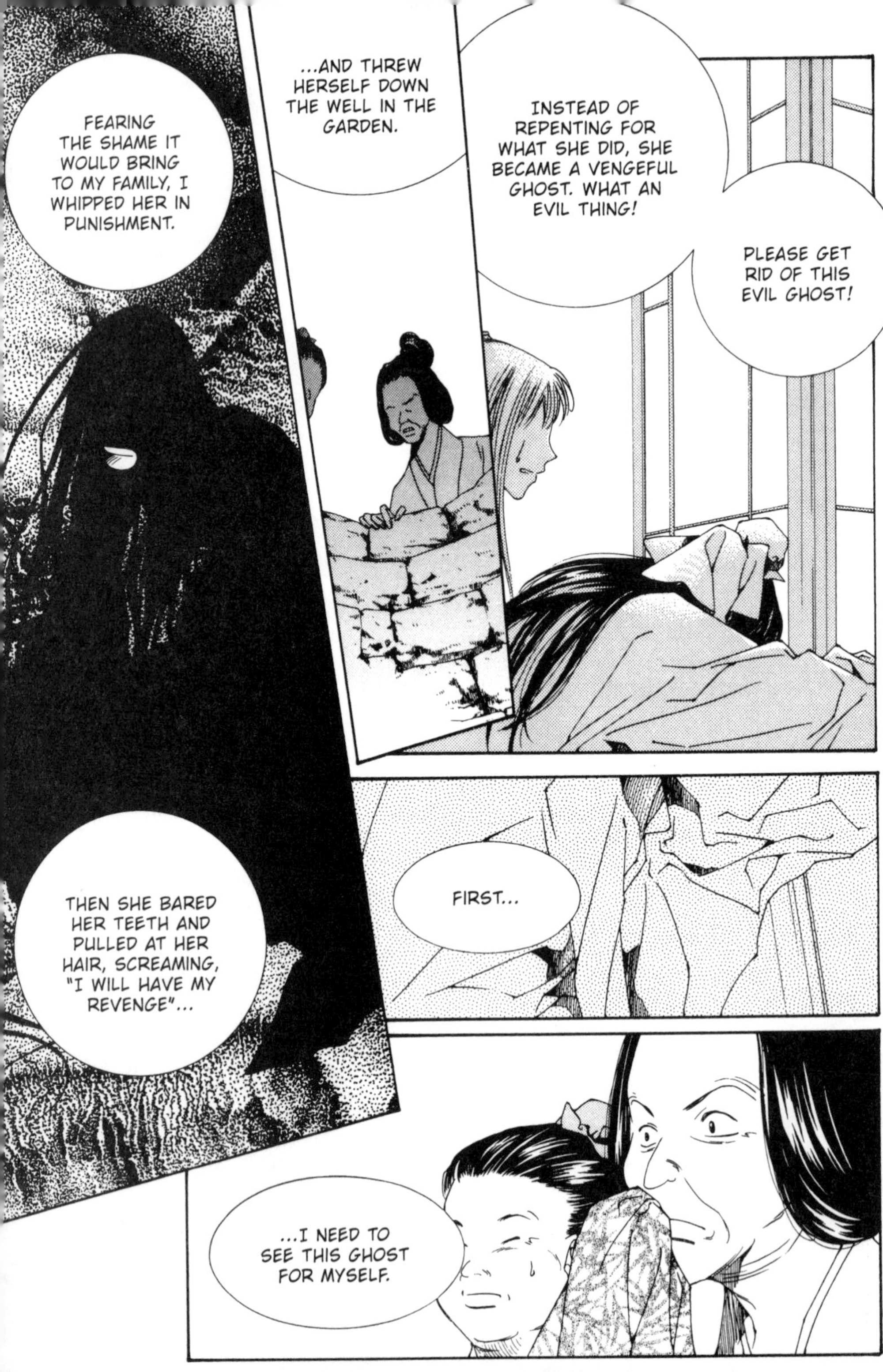
FEARING THE SHAME IT WOULD BRING TO MY FAMILY, I WHIPPED HER IN PUNISHMENT.
THEN SHE BARED HER TEETH AND PULLED AT HER HAIR, SCREAMING, "I WILL HAVE MY REVENGE"...
...AND THREW HERSELF DOWN THE WELL IN THE GARDEN.
INSTEAD OF REPENTING FOR WHAT SHE DID, SHE BECAME A VENGEFUL GHOST. WHAT AN EVIL THING!
PLEASE GET RID OF THIS EVIL GHOST!
FIRST...
...I NEED TO SEE THIS GHOST FOR MYSELF.

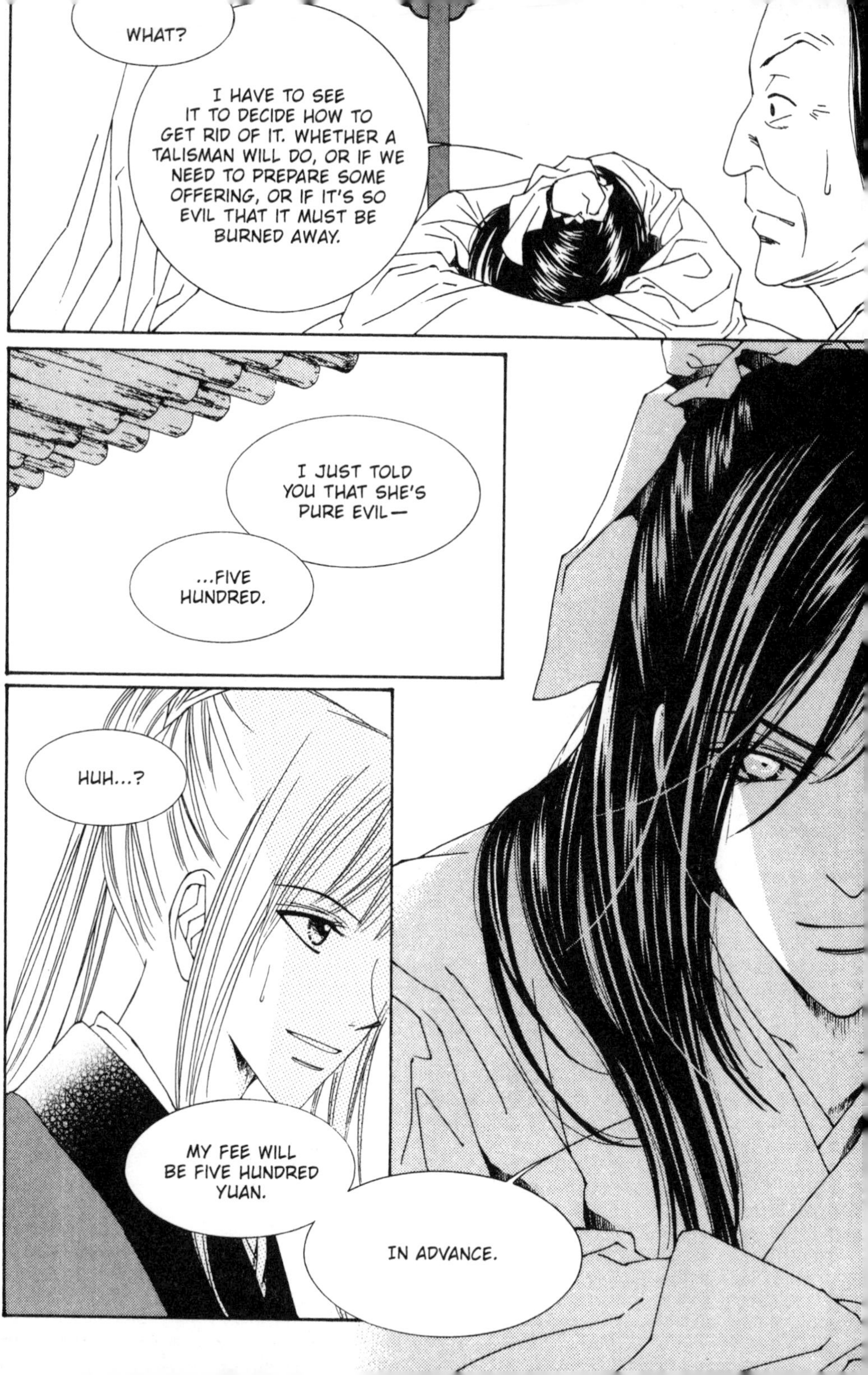
WHAT?
I HAVE TO SEE IT TO DECIDE HOW TO GET RID OF IT. WHETHER A TALISMAN WILL DO, OR IF WE NEED TO PREPARE SOME OFFERING, OR IF IT'S SO EVIL THAT IT MUST BE BURNED AWAY.
I JUST TOLD YOU THAT SHE'S PURE EVIL—
...FIVE HUNDRED.
HUH...?
MY FEE WILL BE FIVE HUNDRED YUAN.
IN ADVANCE.

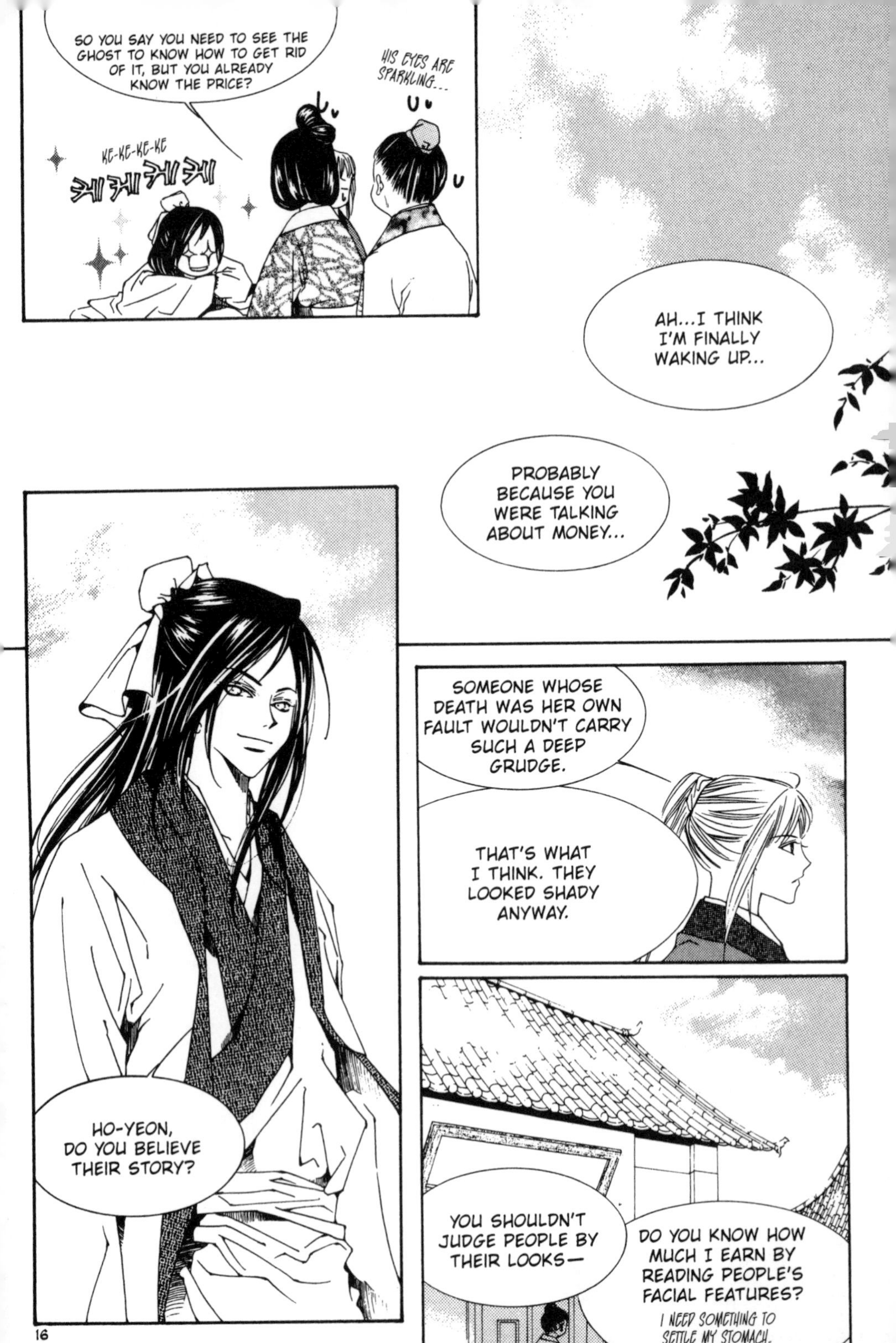

SO YOU SAY YOU NEED TO SEE THE GHOST TO KNOW HOW TO GET RID OF IT, BUT YOU ALREADY KNOW THE PRICE?
HIS EYES ARE SPARKLING...
KE-KE-KE-KE
케케케케
AH...I THINK I'M FINALLY WAKING UP...
PROBABLY BECAUSE YOU WERE TALKING ABOUT MONEY...
HO-YEON, DO YOU BELIEVE THEIR STORY?
SOMEONE WHOSE DEATH WAS HER OWN FAULT WOULDN'T CARRY SUCH A DEEP GRUDGE.
THAT'S WHAT I THINK. THEY LOOKED SHADY ANYWAY.
YOU SHOULDN'T JUDGE PEOPLE BY THEIR LOOKS—
DO YOU KNOW HOW MUCH I EARN BY READING PEOPLE'S FACIAL FEATURES?
I NEED SOMETHING TO SETTLE MY STOMACH.

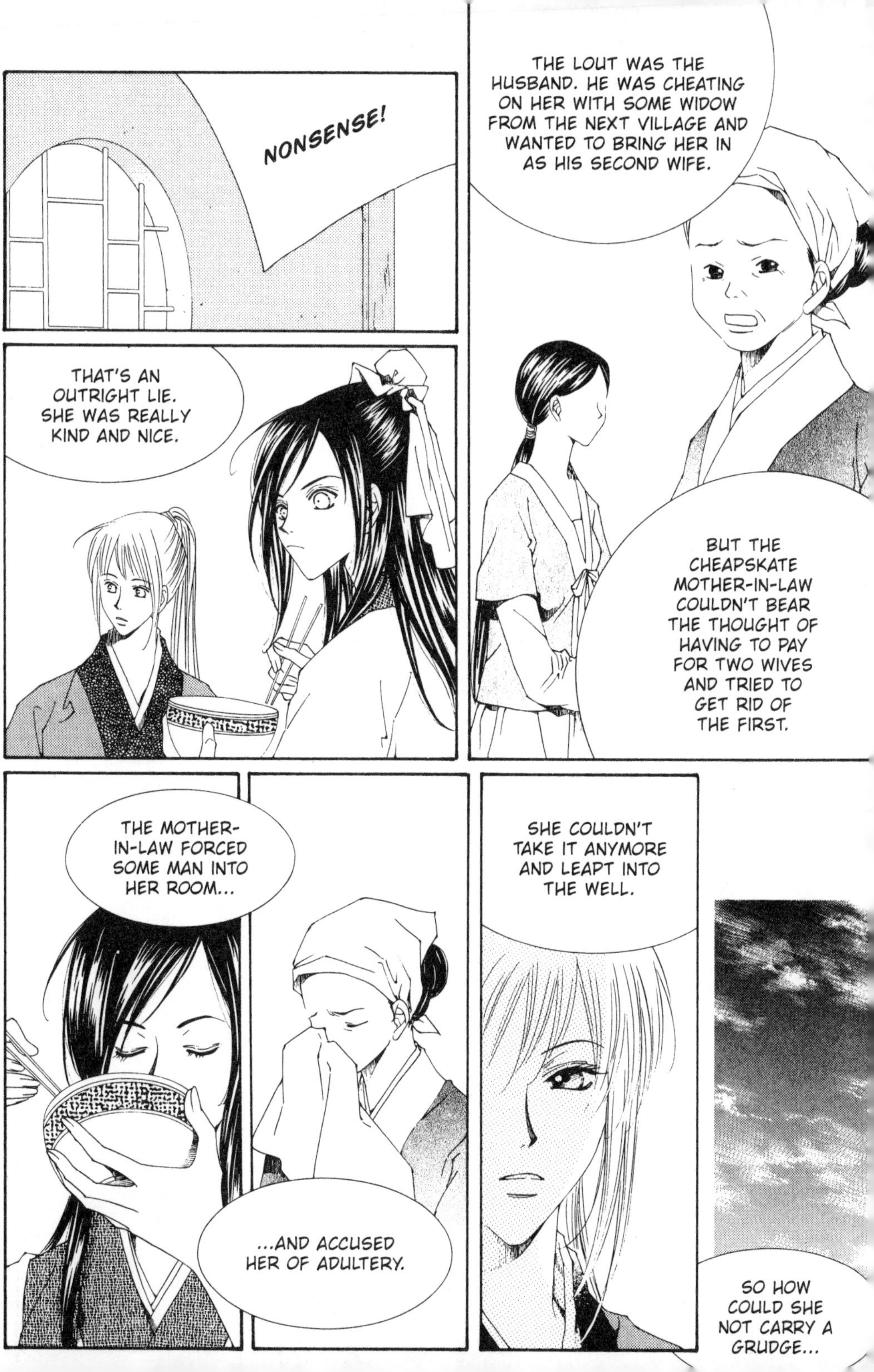
NONSENSE!
THAT'S AN OUTRIGHT LIE. SHE WAS REALLY KIND AND NICE.
THE LOUT WAS THE HUSBAND. HE WAS CHEATING ON HER WITH SOME WIDOW FROM THE NEXT VILLAGE AND WANTED TO BRING HER IN AS HIS SECOND WIFE.
BUT THE CHEAPSKATE MOTHER-IN-LAW COULDN'T BEAR THE THOUGHT OF HAVING TO PAY FOR TWO WIVES AND TRIED TO GET RID OF THE FIRST.
THE MOTHER-IN-LAW FORCED SOME MAN INTO HER ROOM...
...AND ACCUSED HER OF ADULTERY.
SHE COULDN'T TAKE IT ANYMORE AND LEAPT INTO THE WELL.
SO HOW COULD SHE NOT CARRY A GRUDGE...

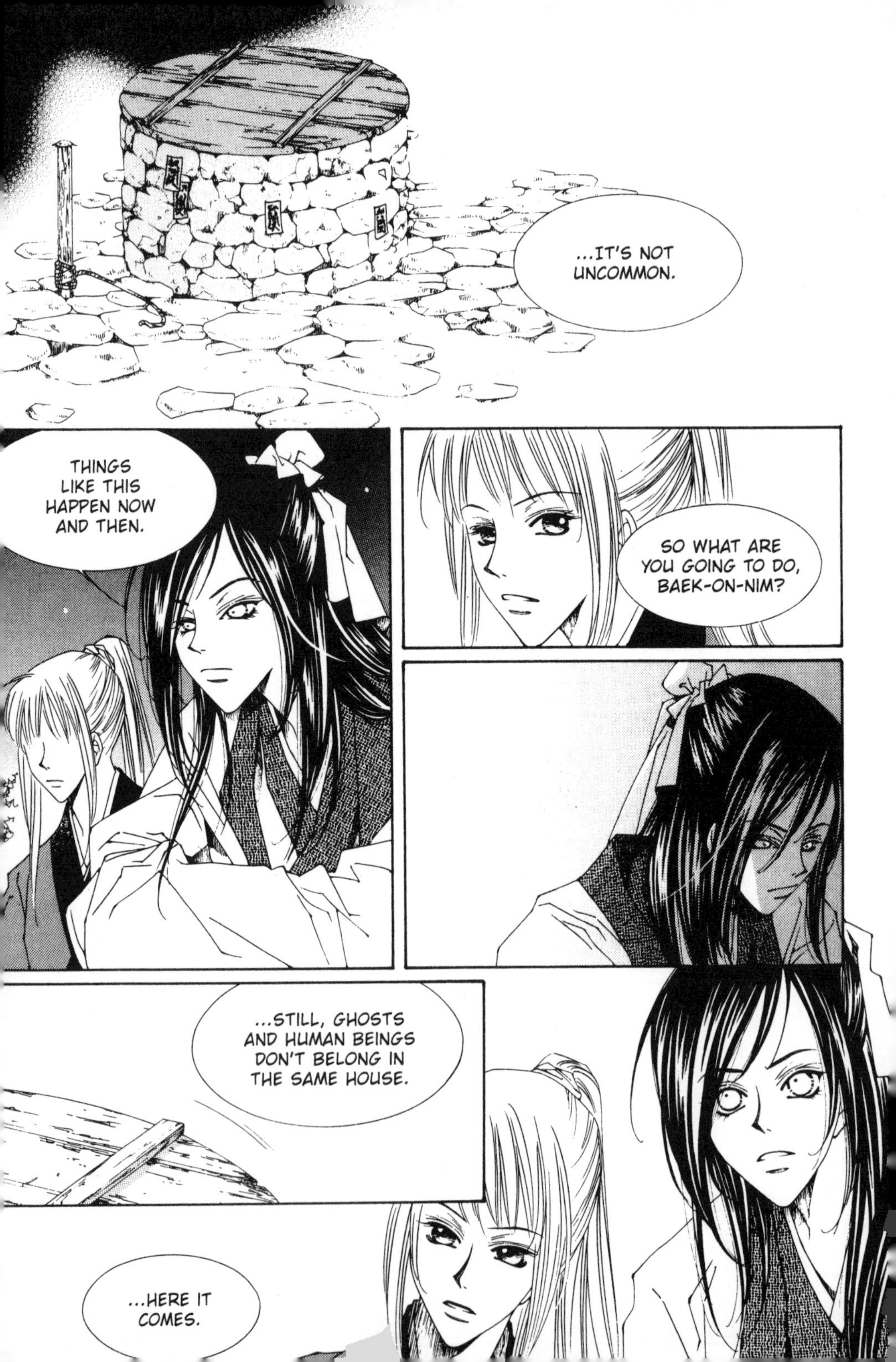
...IT'S NOT UNCOMMON.
THINGS LIKE THIS HAPPEN NOW AND THEN.
SO WHAT ARE YOU GOING TO DO, BAEK-ON-NIM?
...STILL, GHOSTS AND HUMAN BEINGS DON'T BELONG IN THE SAME HOUSE.
...HERE IT COMES.

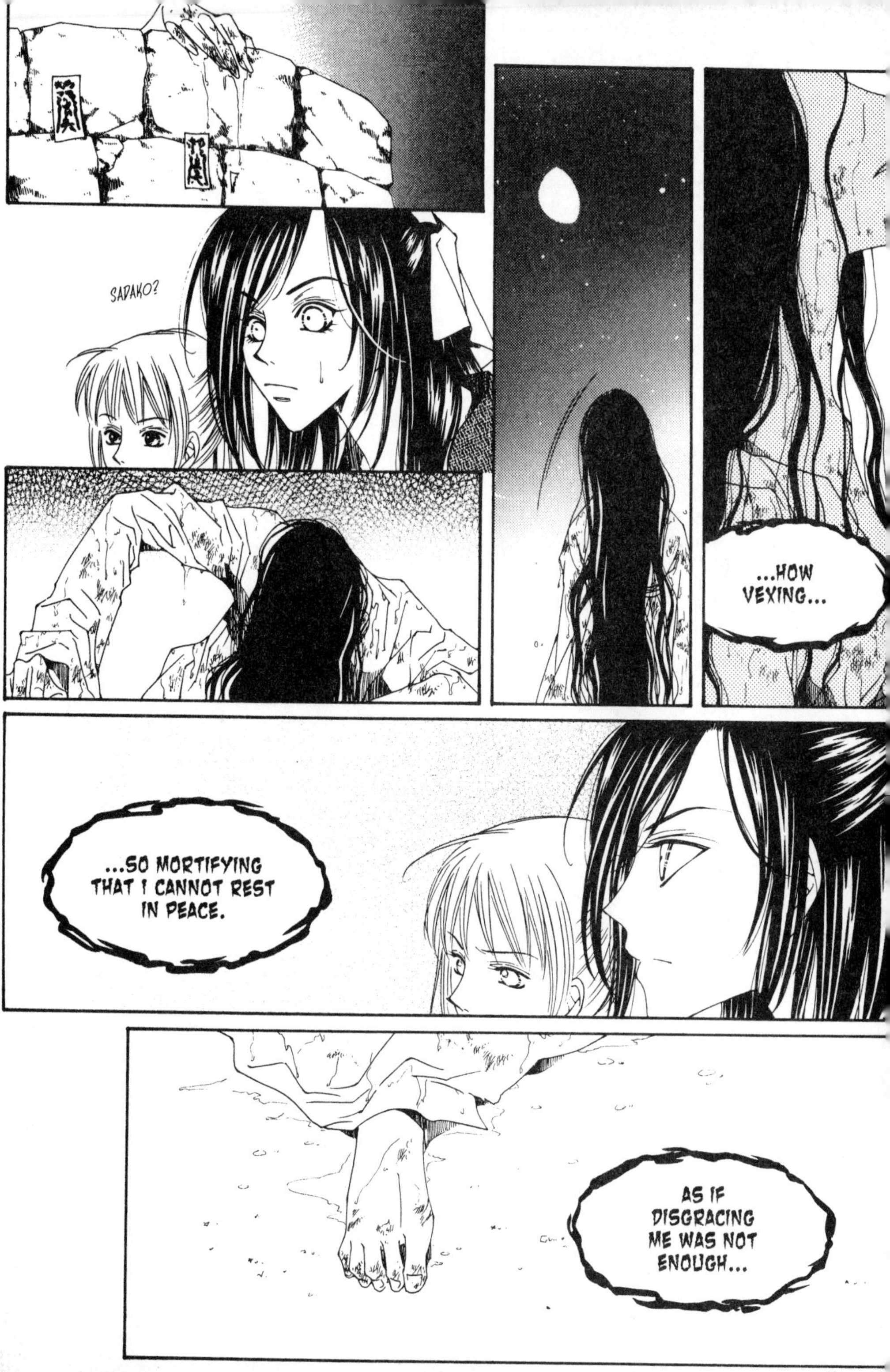
SADAKO?
...HOW VEXING...
...SO MORTIFYING THAT I CANNOT REST IN PEACE.
AS IF DISGRACING ME WAS NOT ENOUGH...

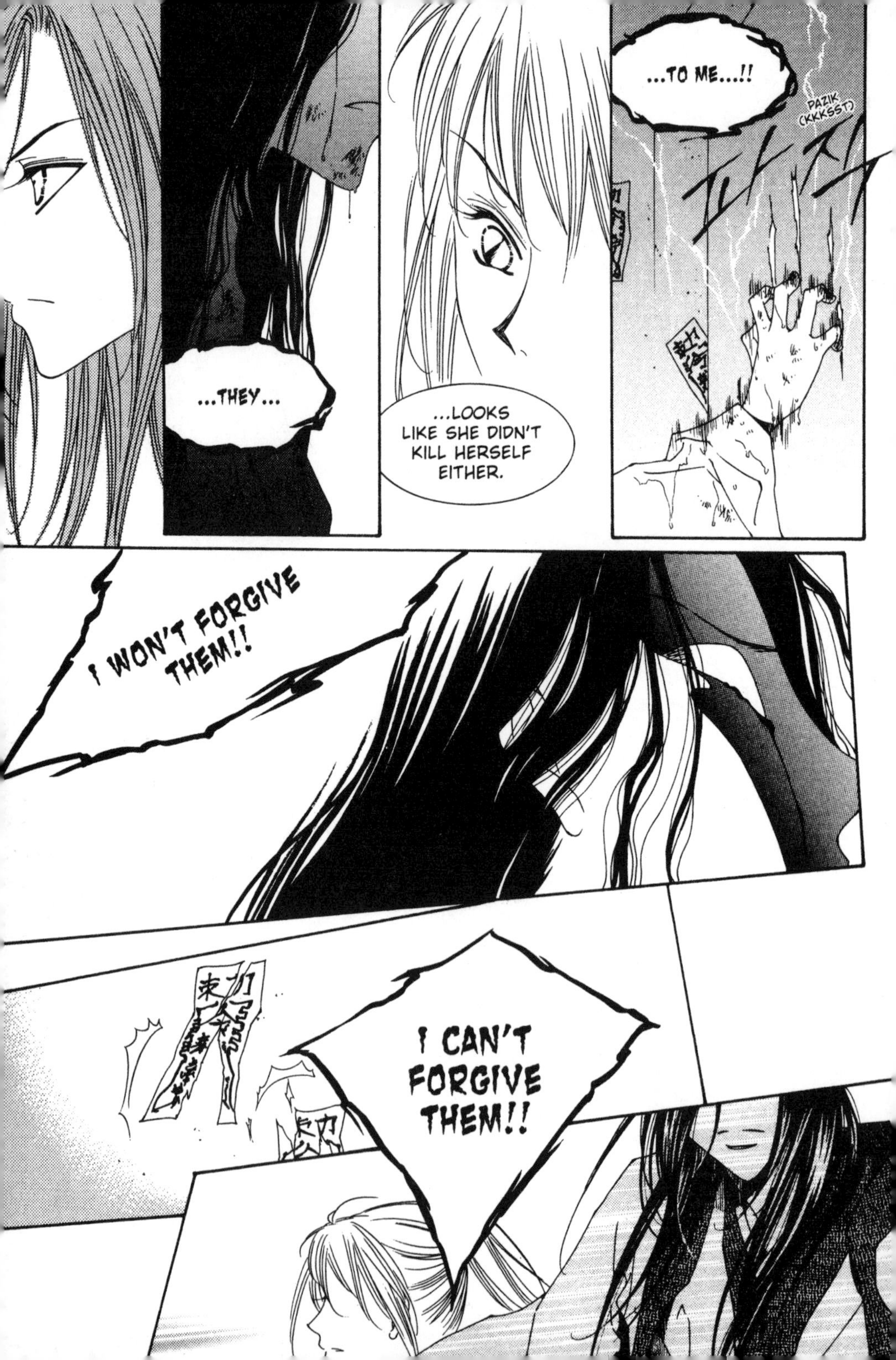
...THEY...
...LOOKS LIKE SHE DIDN'T KILL HERSELF EITHER.
...TO ME...!!
PAZIK (KKKSST)
I WON'T FORGIVE THEM!!
I CAN'T FORGIVE THEM!!

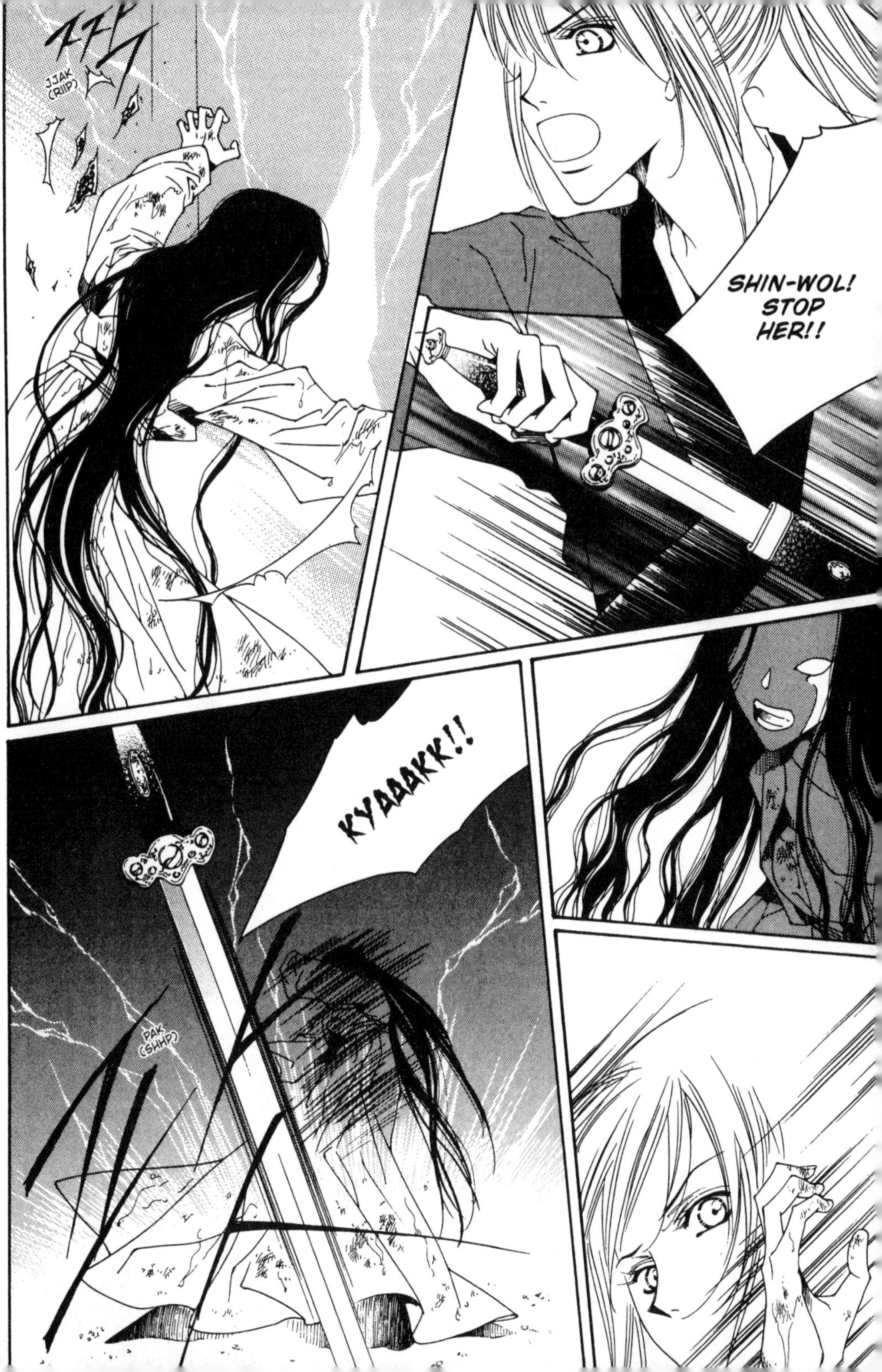

JJAK (RIIP)
SHIN-WOL! STOP HER!!
KYAAAKK!!
PAK (SHHP)

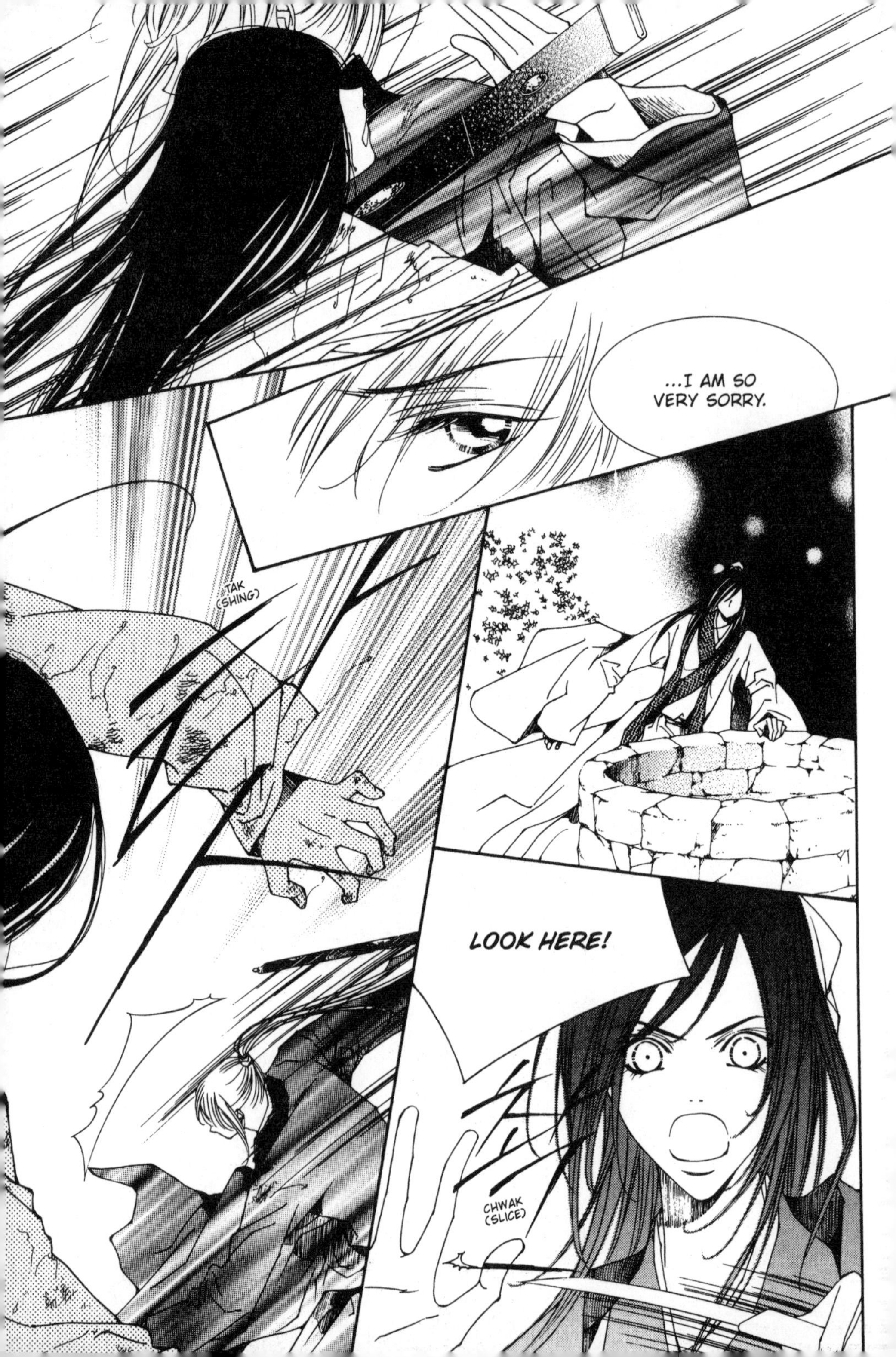
...I AM SO VERY SORRY.
TAK (SHING)
LOOK HERE!
CHWAK (SLICE)

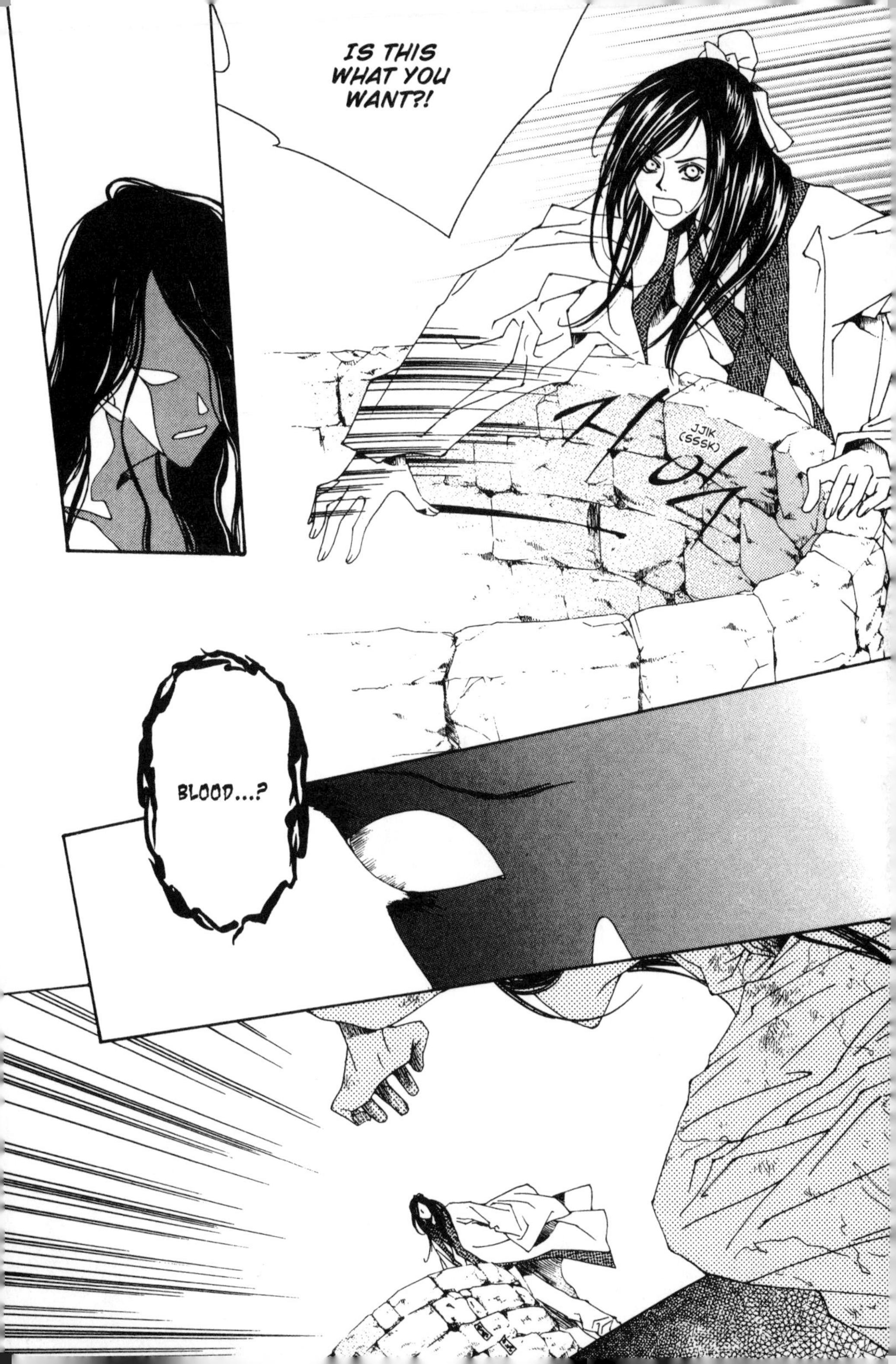
IS THIS WHAT YOU WANT?!
JJIK (SSSK)
BLOOD...?

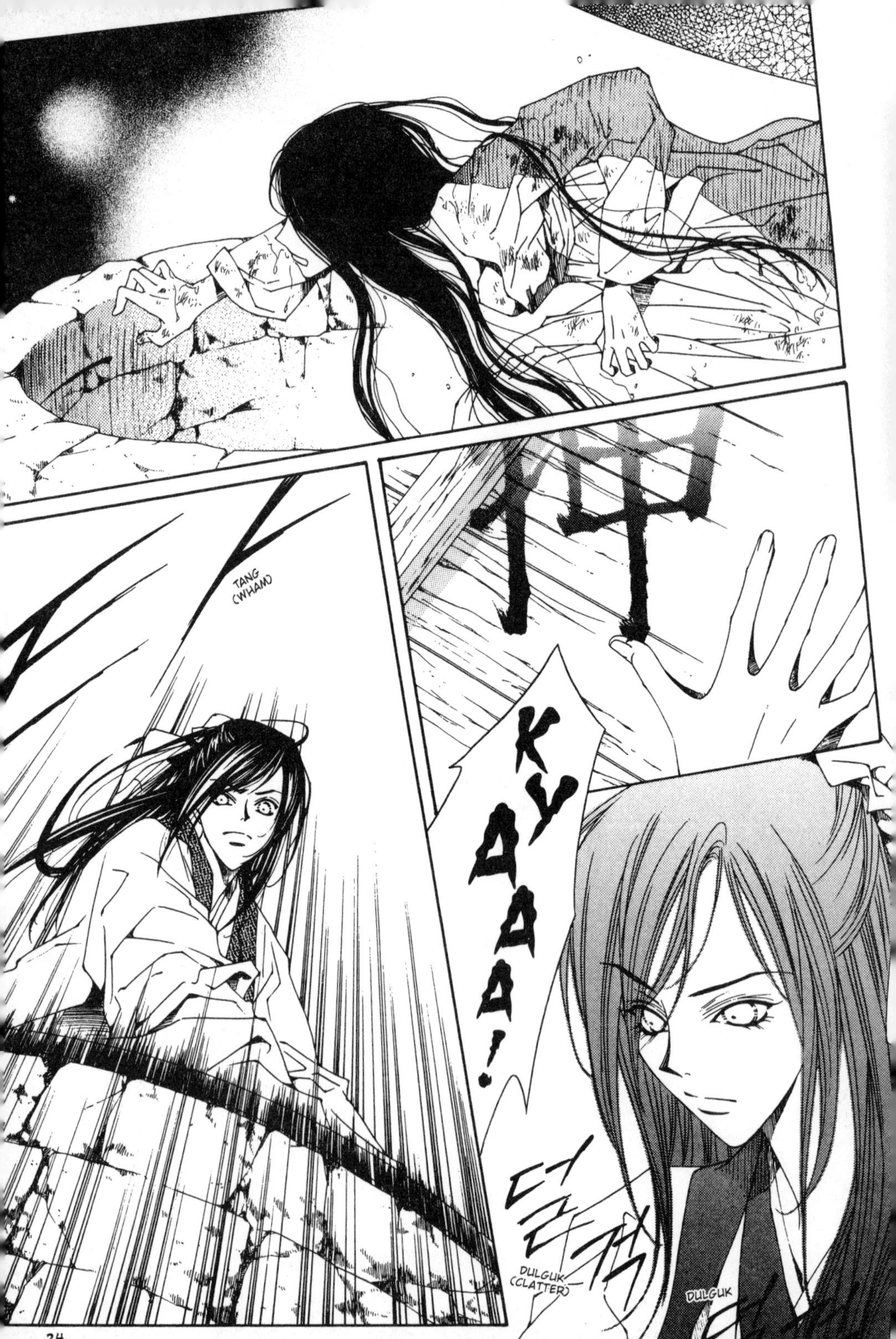
TANG
(WHAM)
KYAAA!
DULGUK
(CLATTER)
DULGUK

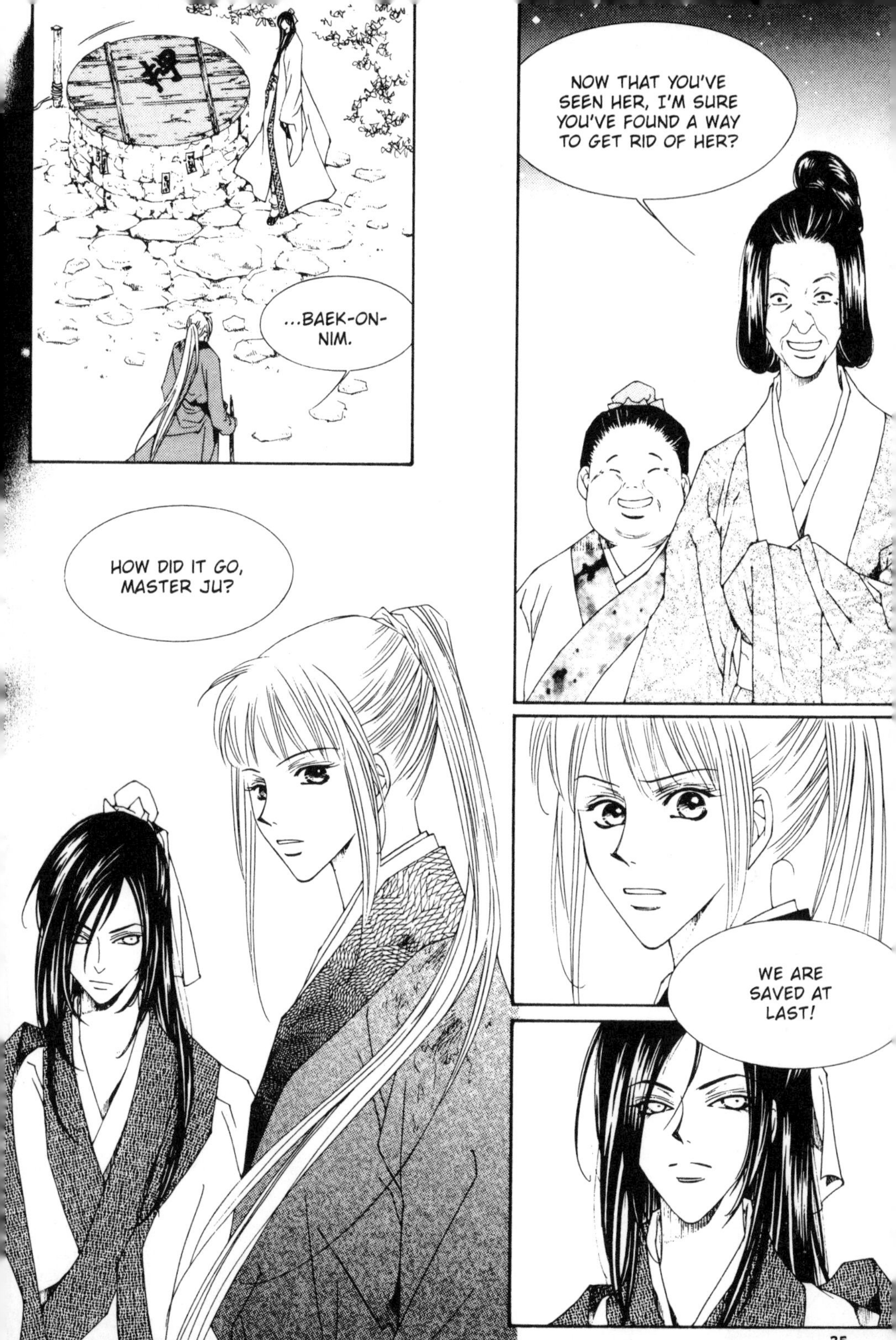
...BAEK-ON-NIM.
HOW DID IT GO, MASTER JU?
NOW THAT YOU'VE SEEN HER, I'M SURE YOU'VE FOUND A WAY TO GET RID OF HER?
WE ARE SAVED AT LAST!

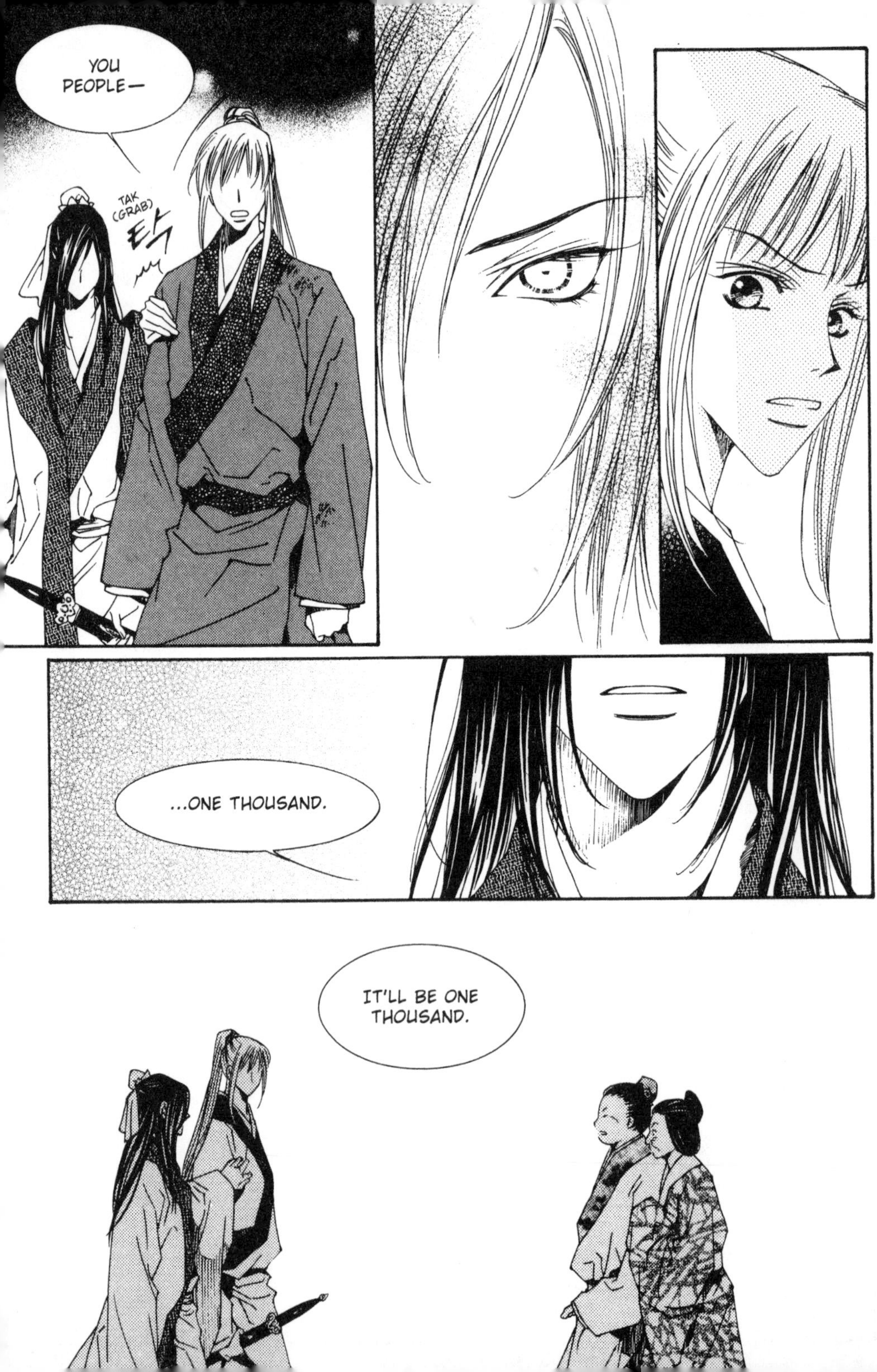
YOU PEOPLE—
TAK (GRAB)
...ONE THOUSAND.
IT'LL BE ONE THOUSAND.

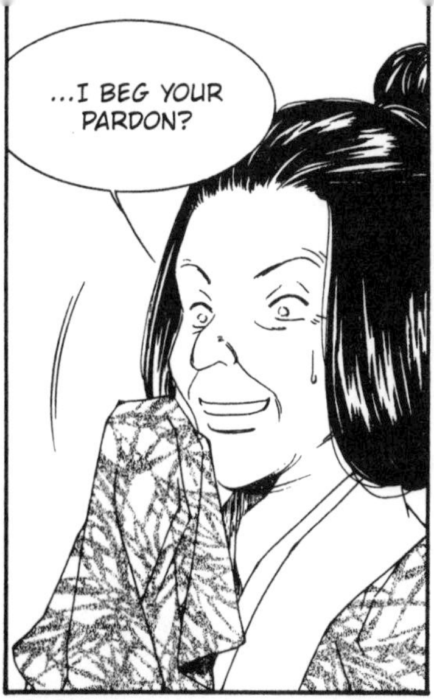
...I BEG YOUR PARDON?

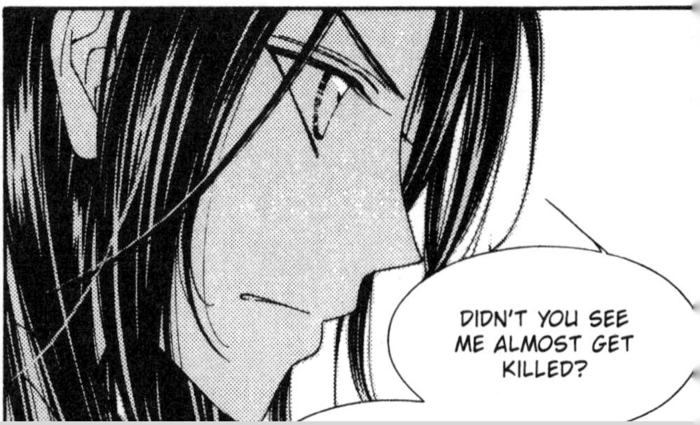
DIDN'T YOU SEE ME ALMOST GET KILLED?

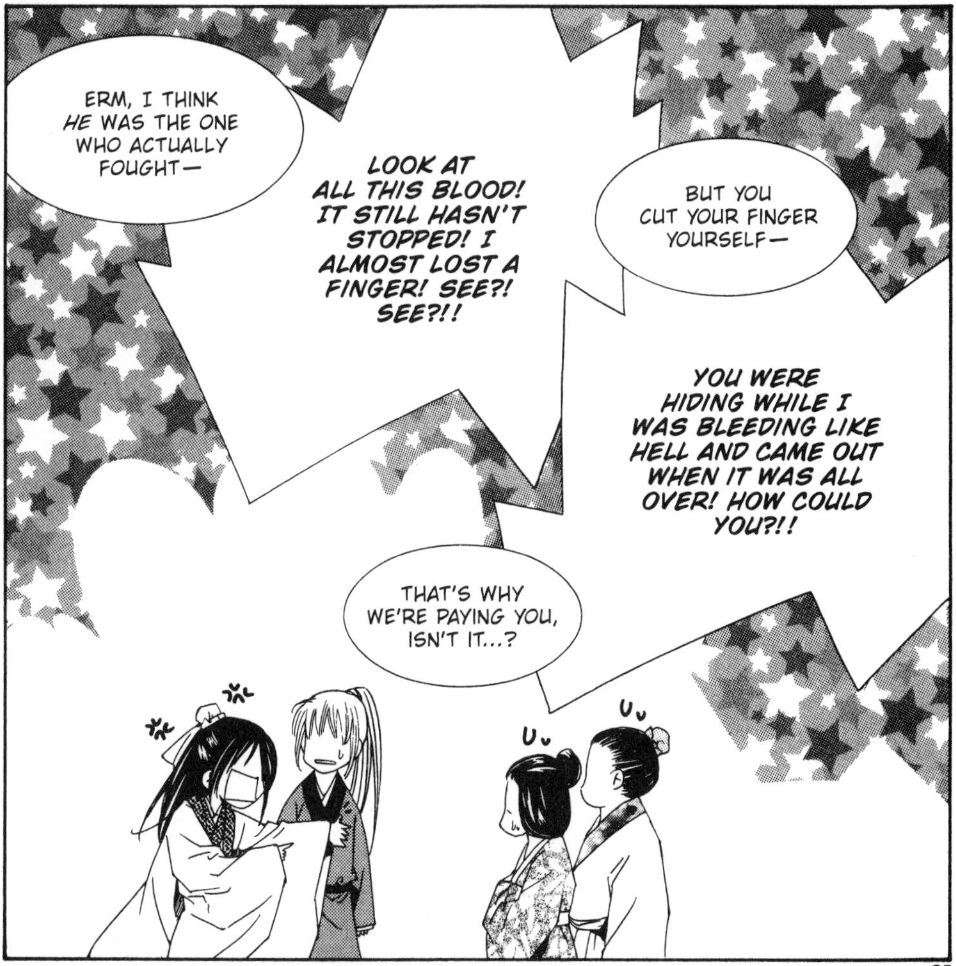
ERM, I THINK *HE* WAS THE ONE WHO ACTUALLY FOUGHT—
LOOK AT ALL THIS BLOOD! IT STILL HASN'T STOPPED! I ALMOST LOST A FINGER! SEE?! SEE?!!
BUT YOU CUT YOUR FINGER YOURSELF—
YOU WERE HIDING WHILE I WAS BLEEDING LIKE HELL AND CAME OUT WHEN IT WAS ALL OVER! HOW COULD YOU?!!
THAT'S WHY WE'RE PAYING YOU, ISN'T IT...?

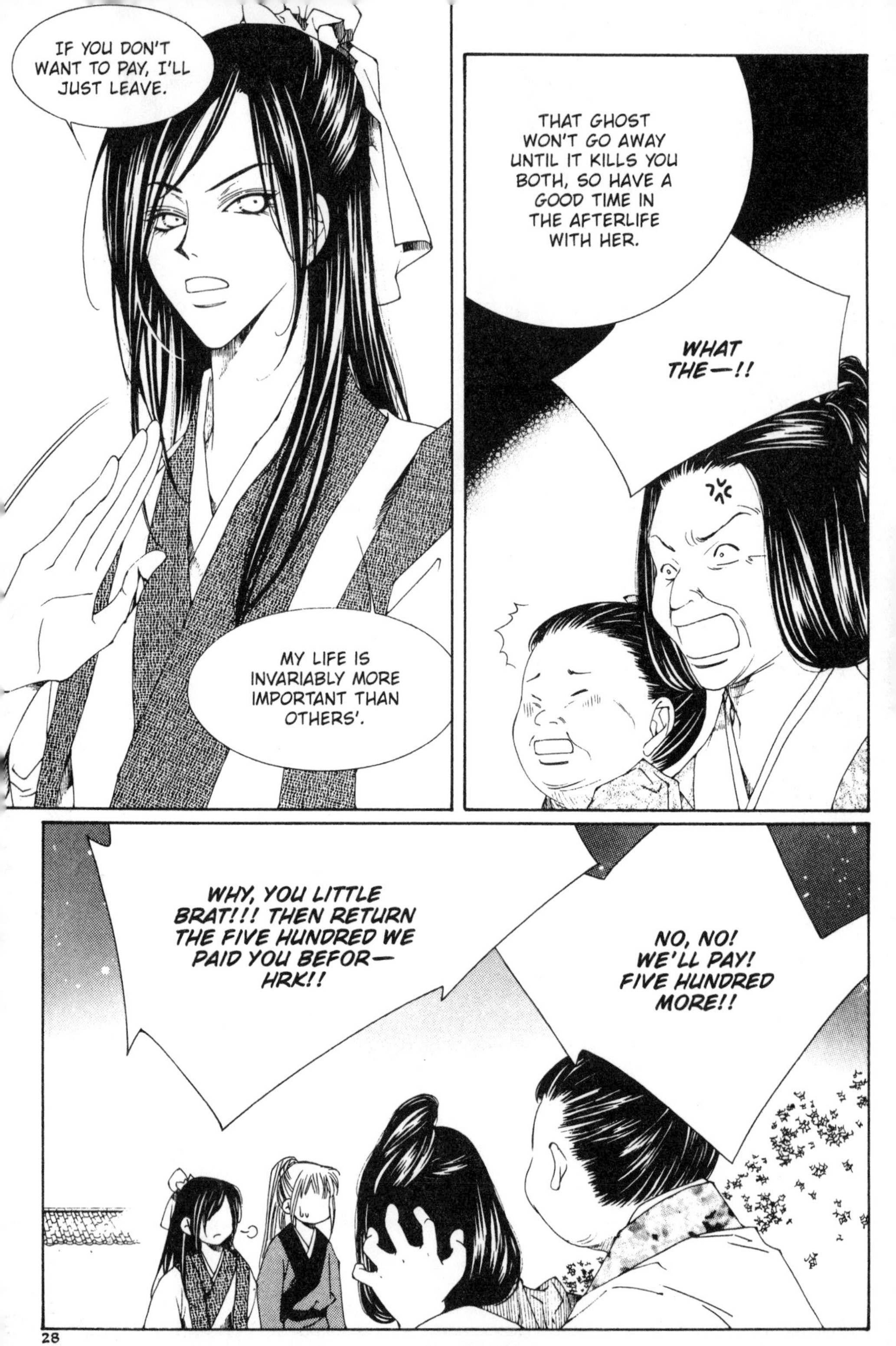
IF YOU DON'T WANT TO PAY, I'LL JUST LEAVE.
MY LIFE IS INVARIABLY MORE IMPORTANT THAN OTHERS'.
THAT GHOST WON'T GO AWAY UNTIL IT KILLS YOU BOTH, SO HAVE A GOOD TIME IN THE AFTERLIFE WITH HER.
WHAT THE—!!
WHY, YOU LITTLE BRAT!!! THEN RETURN THE FIVE HUNDRED WE PAID YOU BEFOR—HRK!!
NO, NO! WE'LL PAY! FIVE HUNDRED MORE!!

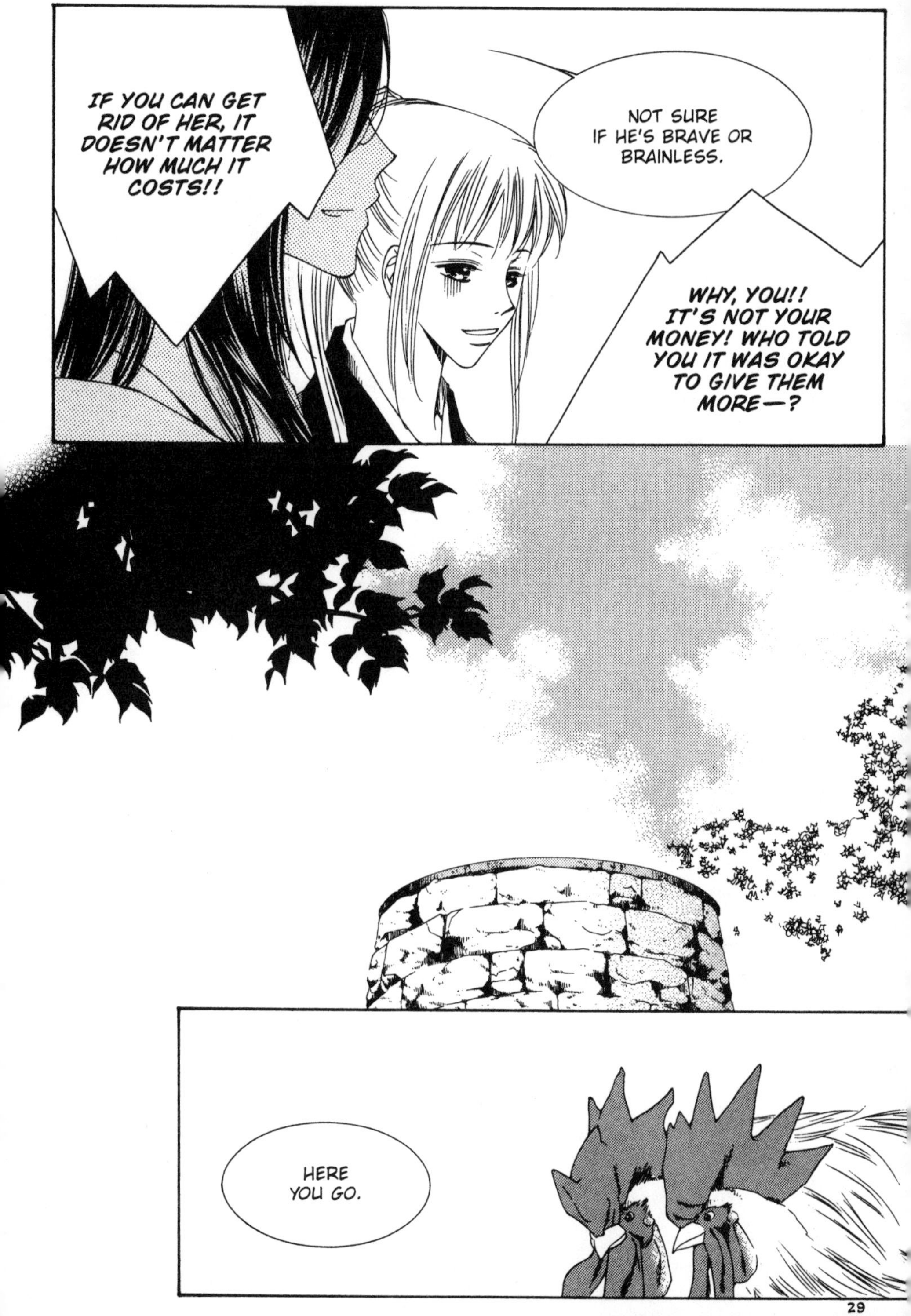
IF YOU CAN GET RID OF HER, IT DOESN'T MATTER HOW MUCH IT COSTS!!
NOT SURE IF HE'S BRAVE OR BRAINLESS.
WHY, YOU!! IT'S NOT YOUR MONEY! WHO TOLD YOU IT WAS OKAY TO GIVE THEM MORE—?
HERE YOU GO.

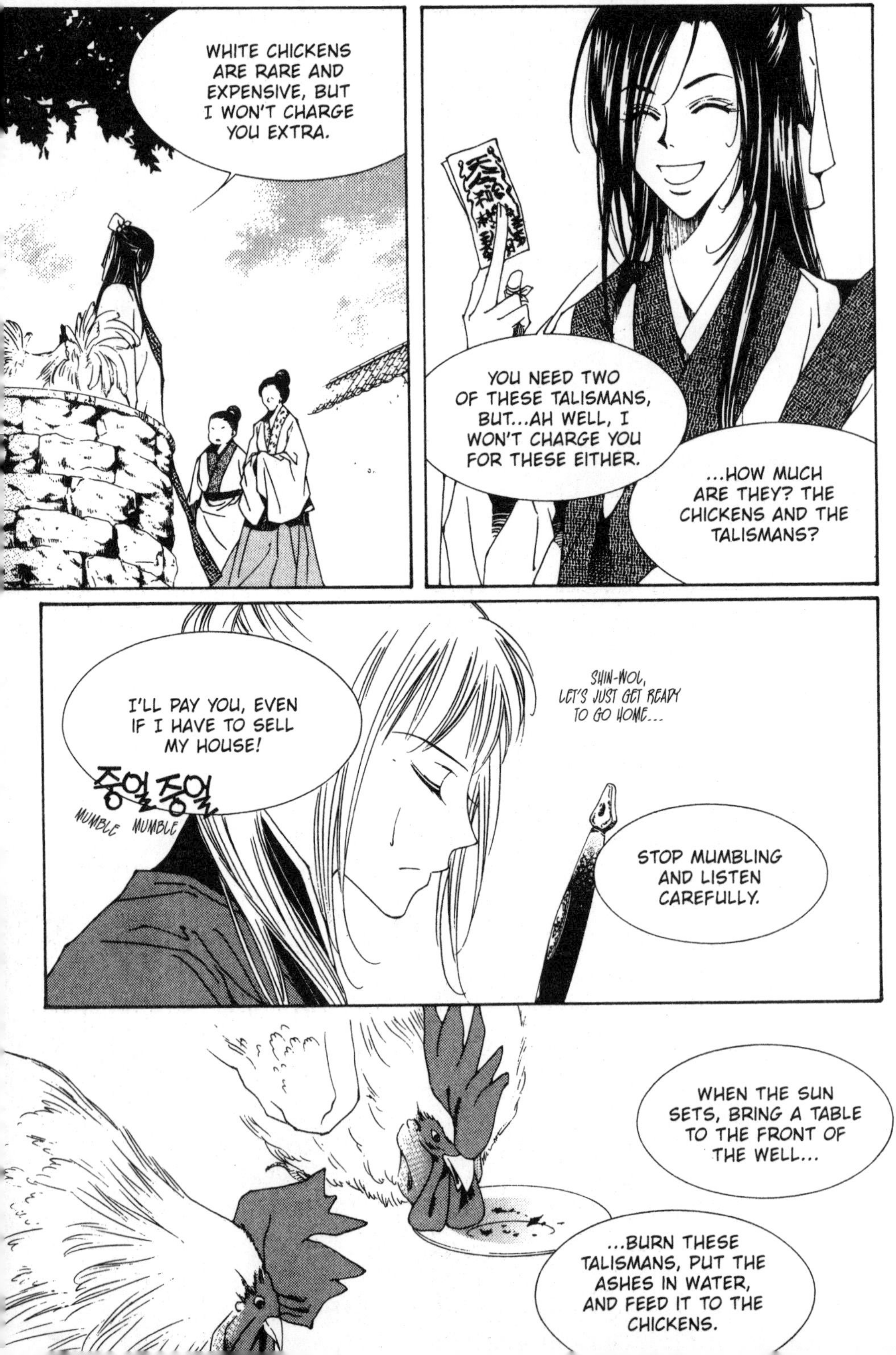
WHITE CHICKENS ARE RARE AND EXPENSIVE, BUT I WON'T CHARGE YOU EXTRA.
YOU NEED TWO OF THESE TALISMANS, BUT...AH WELL, I WON'T CHARGE YOU FOR THESE EITHER.
...HOW MUCH ARE THEY? THE CHICKENS AND THE TALISMANS?
I'LL PAY YOU, EVEN IF I HAVE TO SELL MY HOUSE!
중얼중얼
MUMBLE MUMBLE
SHIN-WOL, LET'S JUST GET READY TO GO HOME...
STOP MUMBLING AND LISTEN CAREFULLY.
WHEN THE SUN SETS, BRING A TABLE TO THE FRONT OF THE WELL...
...BURN THESE TALISMANS, PUT THE ASHES IN WATER, AND FEED IT TO THE CHICKENS.

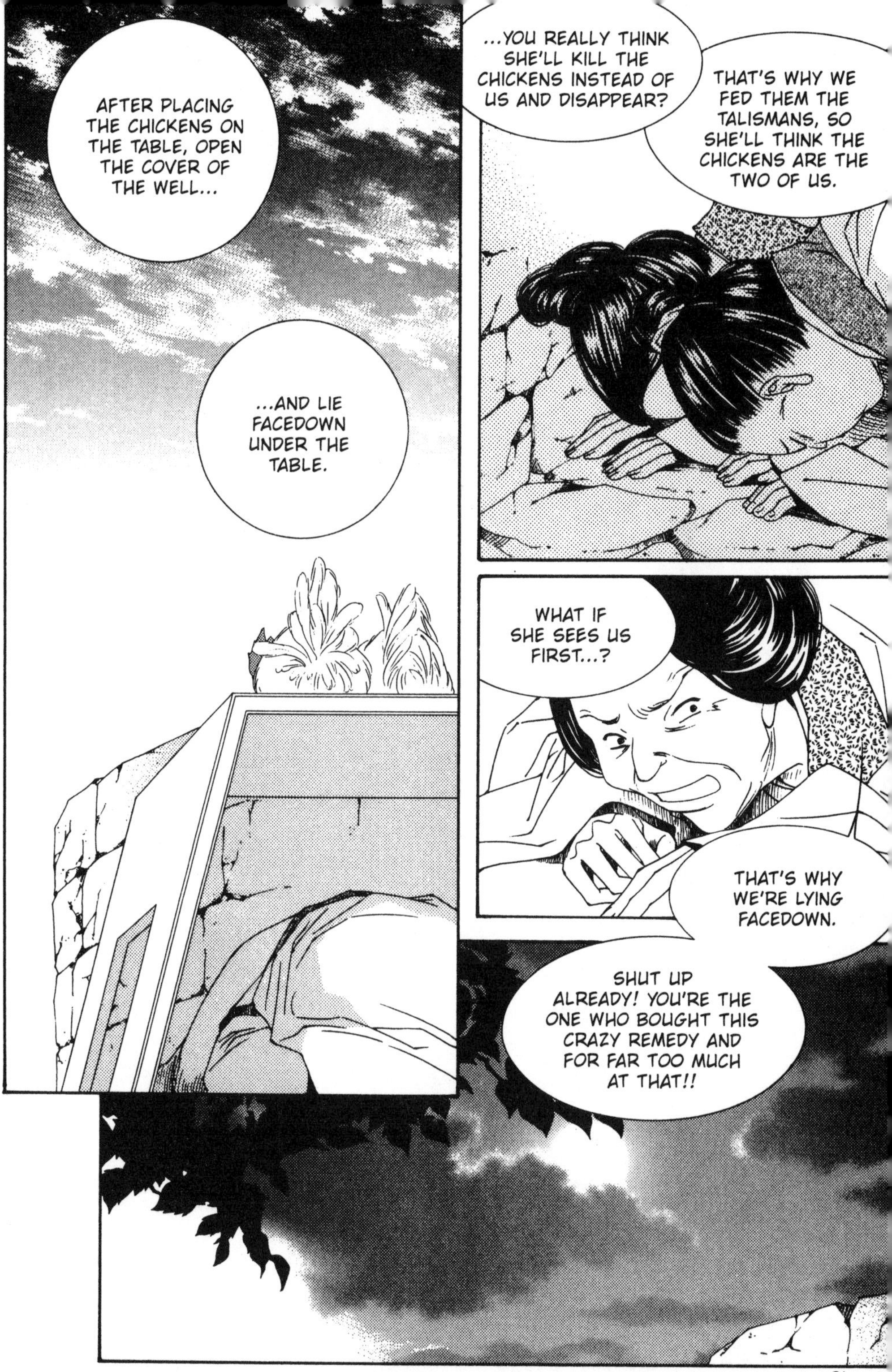
AFTER PLACING THE CHICKENS ON THE TABLE, OPEN THE COVER OF THE WELL...
...AND LIE FACEDOWN UNDER THE TABLE.
...YOU REALLY THINK SHE'LL KILL THE CHICKENS INSTEAD OF US AND DISAPPEAR?
THAT'S WHY WE FED THEM THE TALISMANS, SO SHE'LL THINK THE CHICKENS ARE THE TWO OF US.
WHAT IF SHE SEES US FIRST...?
THAT'S WHY WE'RE LYING FACEDOWN.
SHUT UP ALREADY! YOU'RE THE ONE WHO BOUGHT THIS CRAZY REMEDY AND FOR FAR TOO MUCH AT THAT!!

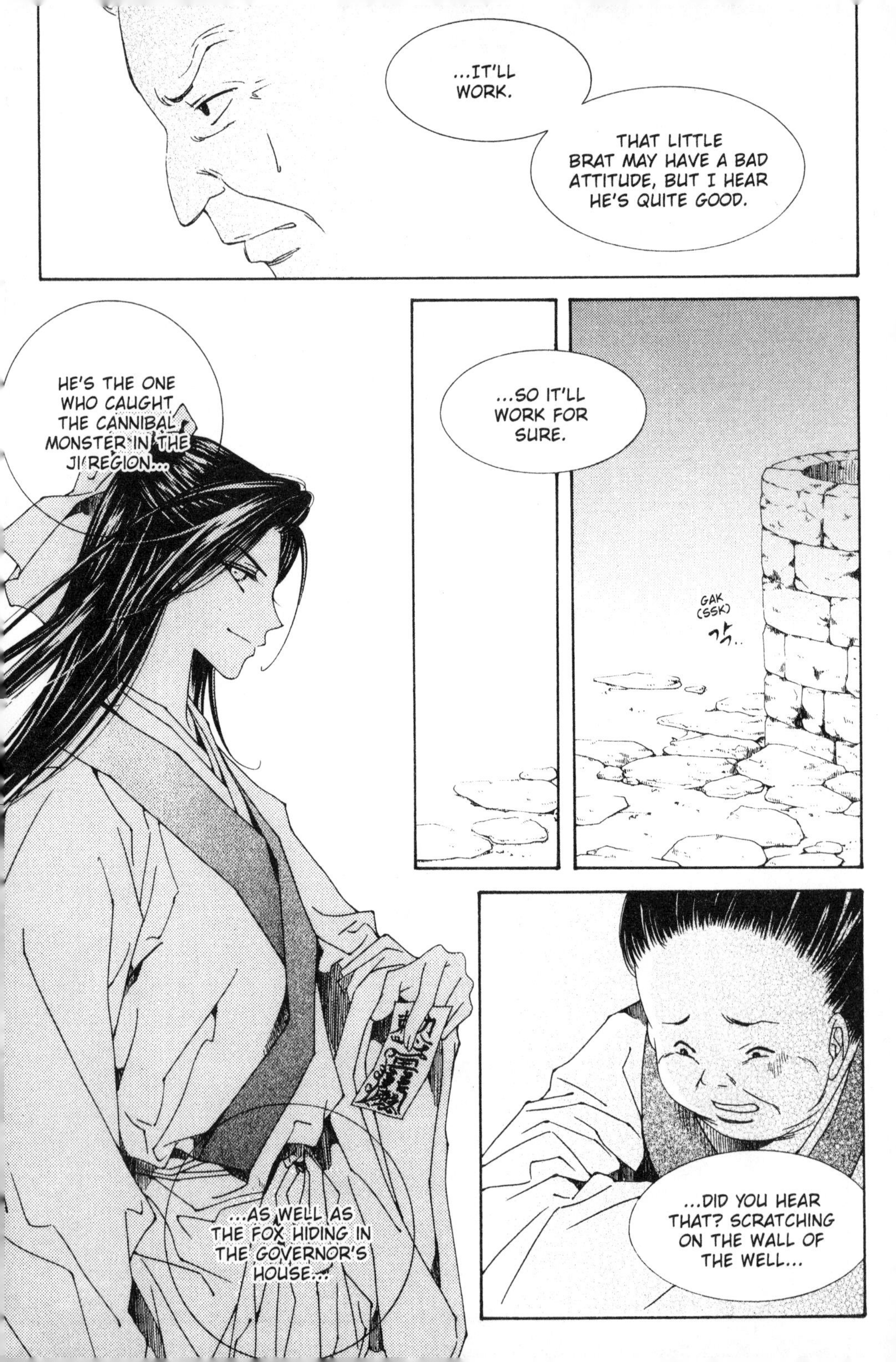
...IT'LL WORK.
THAT LITTLE BRAT MAY HAVE A BAD ATTITUDE, BUT I HEAR HE'S QUITE GOOD.
HE'S THE ONE WHO CAUGHT THE CANNIBAL MONSTER IN THE JI REGION...
...AS WELL AS THE FOX HIDING IN THE GOVERNOR'S HOUSE...
...SO IT'LL WORK FOR SURE.
GAK (SSK)
각..
...DID YOU HEAR THAT? SCRATCHING ON THE WALL OF THE WELL...

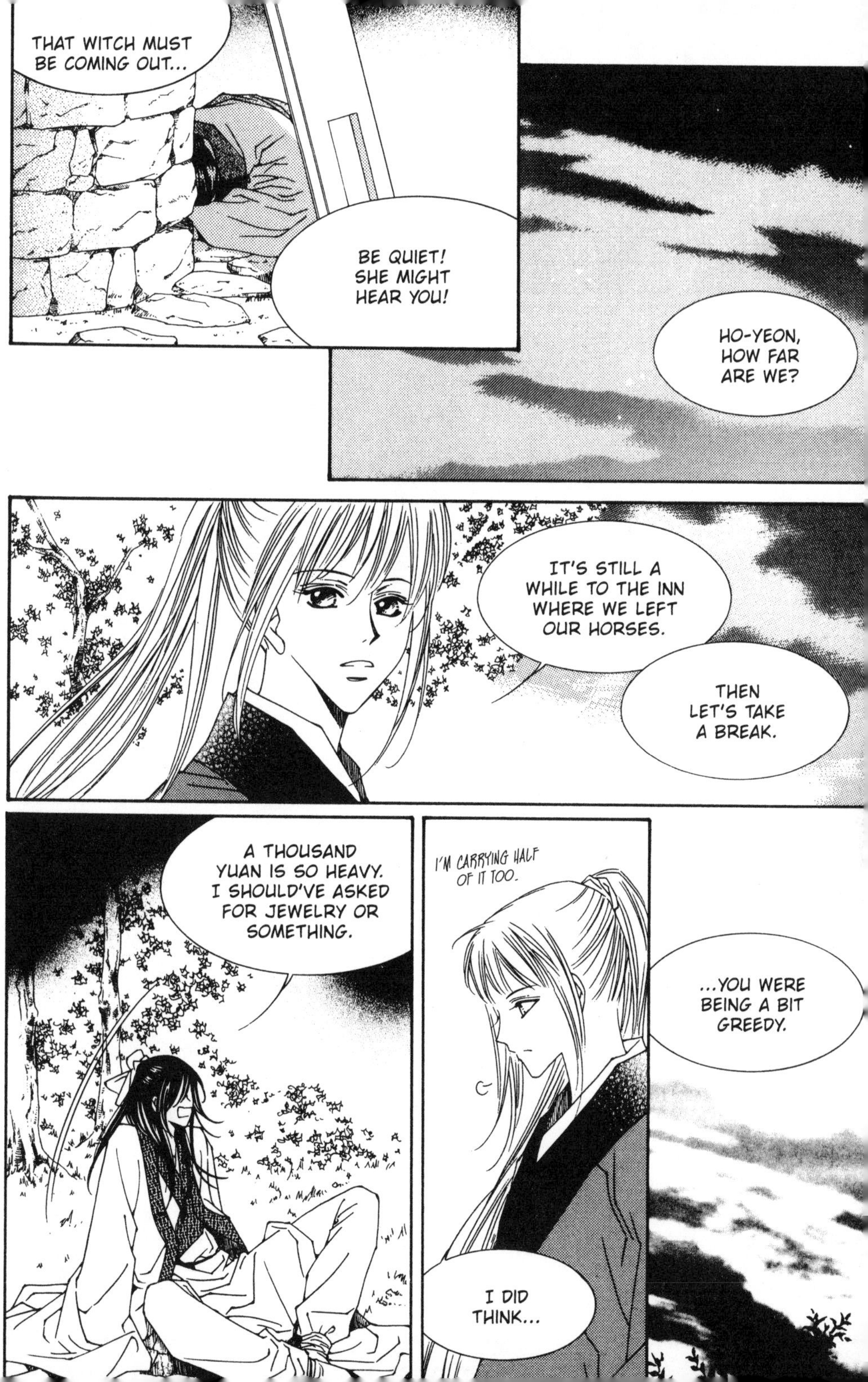
THAT WITCH MUST BE COMING OUT...
BE QUIET! SHE MIGHT HEAR YOU!
HO-YEON, HOW FAR ARE WE?
IT'S STILL A WHILE TO THE INN WHERE WE LEFT OUR HORSES.
THEN LET'S TAKE A BREAK.
A THOUSAND YUAN IS SO HEAVY. I SHOULD'VE ASKED FOR JEWELRY OR SOMETHING.
I'M CARRYING HALF OF IT TOO.
...YOU WERE BEING A BIT GREEDY.
I DID THINK...

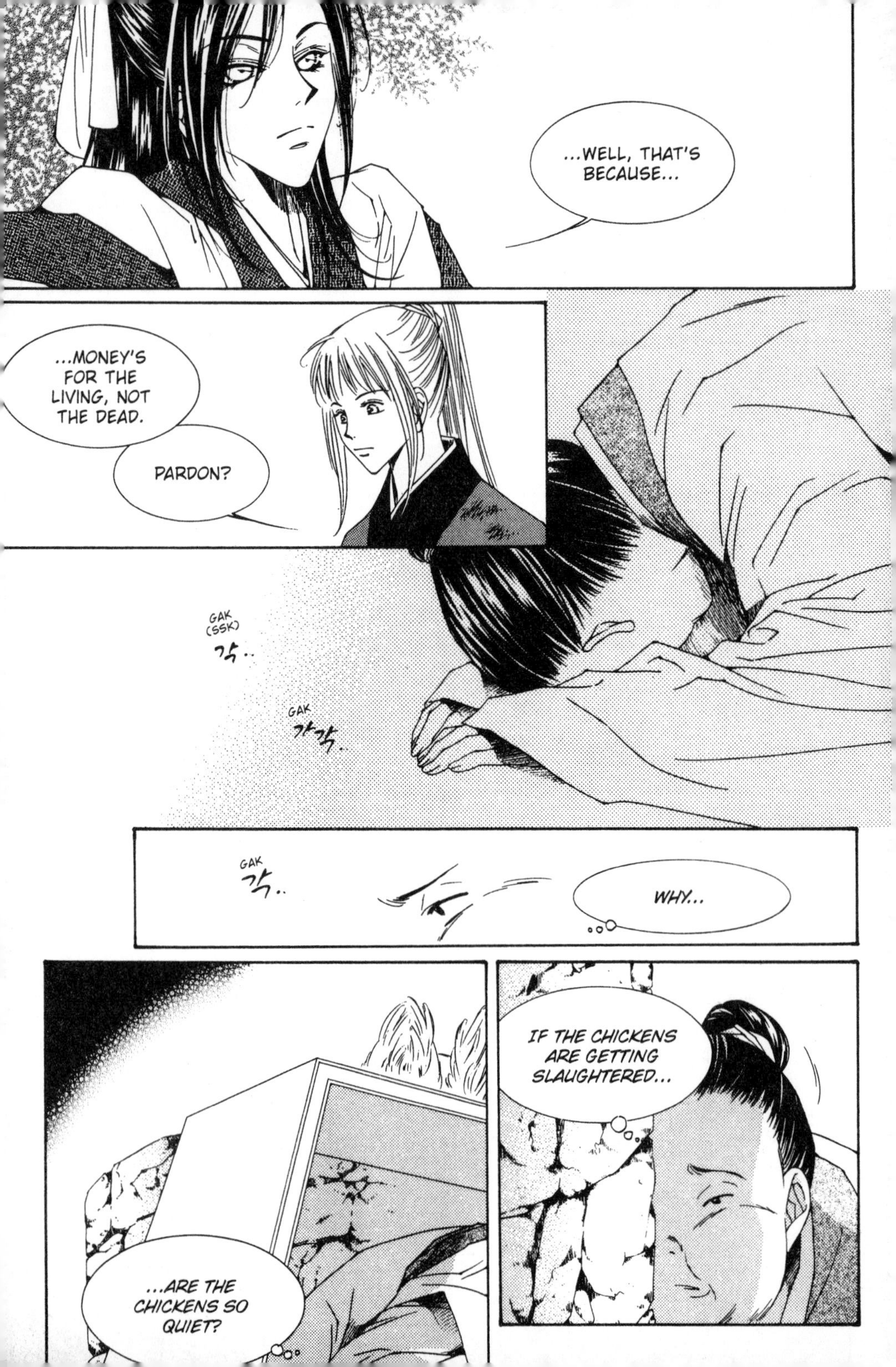
...WELL, THAT'S BECAUSE...
...MONEY'S FOR THE LIVING, NOT THE DEAD.
PARDON?
GAK (SSK)
각..
GAK
가각.
GAK
각..
WHY...
...ARE THE CHICKENS SO QUIET?
IF THE CHICKENS ARE GETTING SLAUGHTERED...

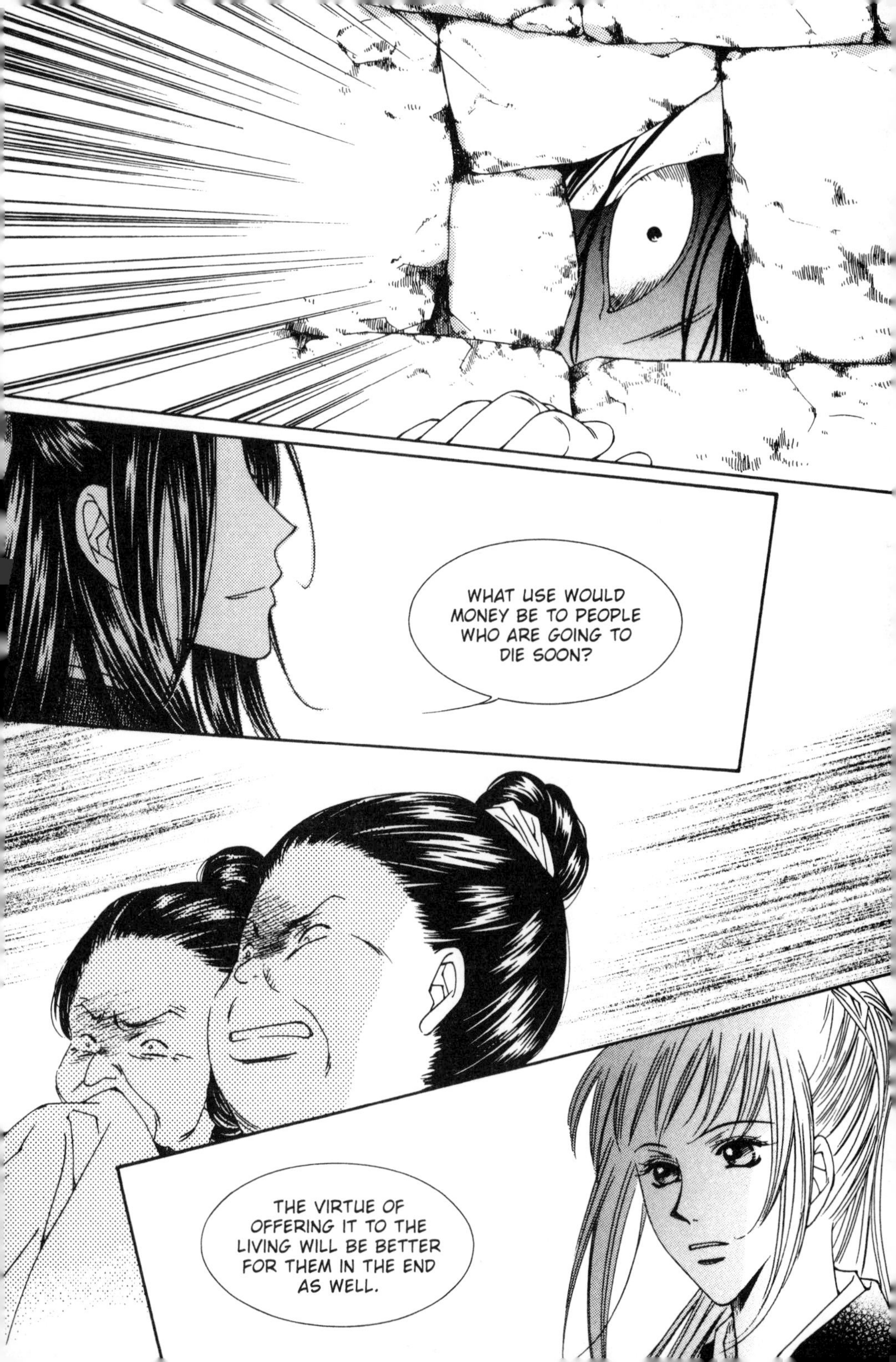
WHAT USE WOULD MONEY BE TO PEOPLE WHO ARE GOING TO DIE SOON?
THE VIRTUE OF OFFERING IT TO THE LIVING WILL BE BETTER FOR THEM IN THE END AS WELL.

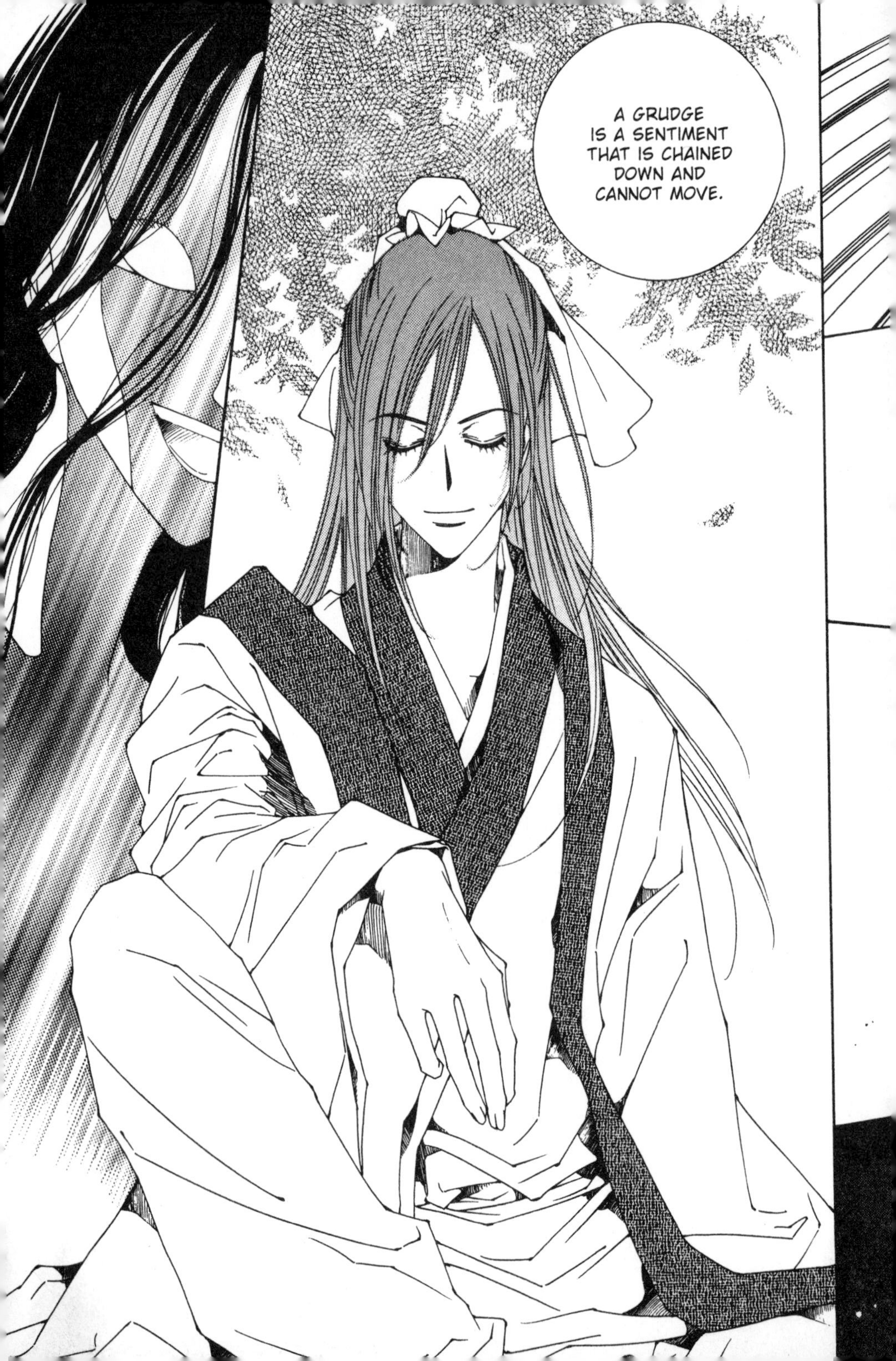
A GRUDGE IS A SENTIMENT THAT IS CHAINED DOWN AND CANNOT MOVE.

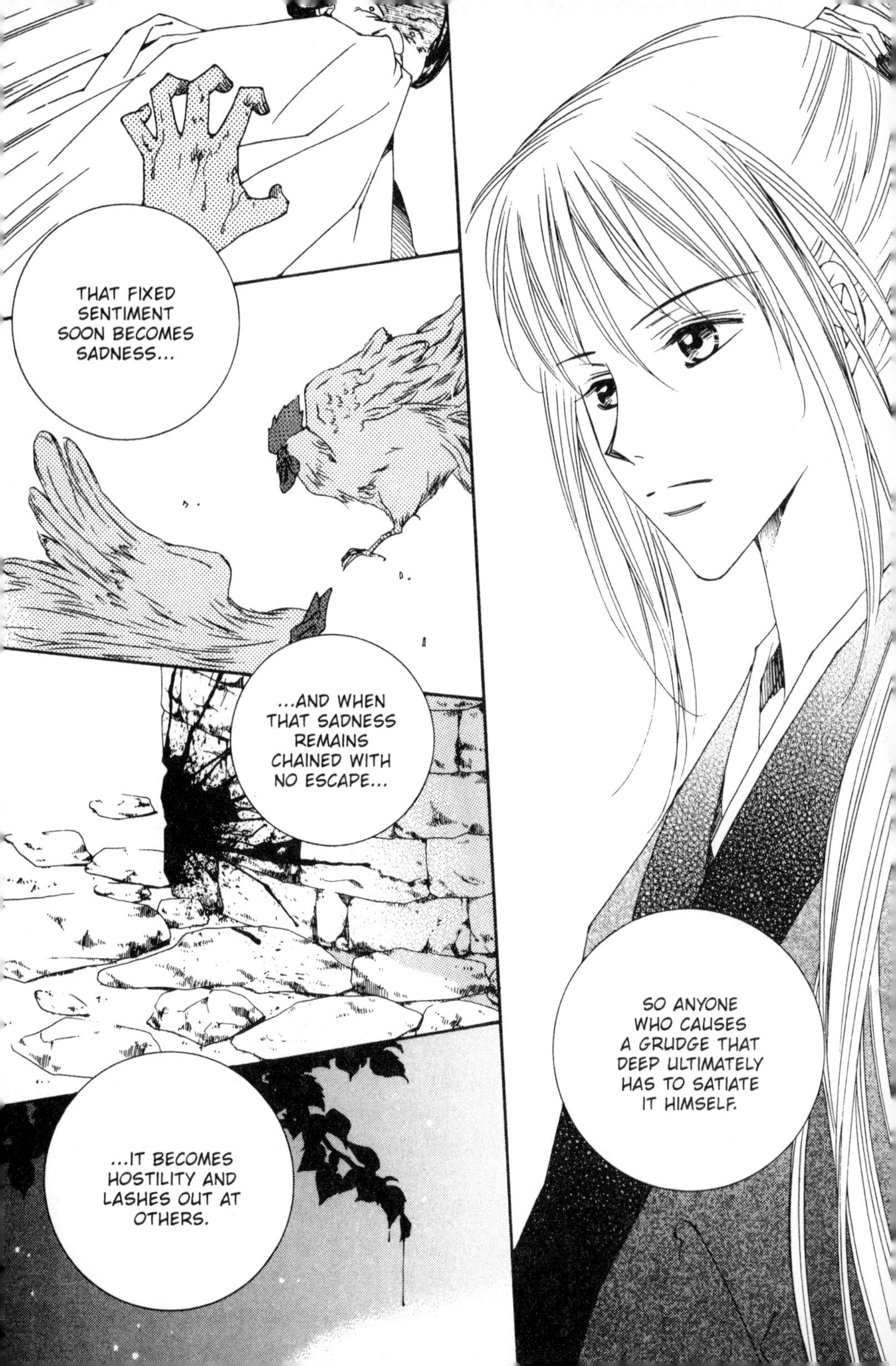
THAT FIXED SENTIMENT SOON BECOMES SADNESS...
...AND WHEN THAT SADNESS REMAINS CHAINED WITH NO ESCAPE...
...IT BECOMES HOSTILITY AND LASHES OUT AT OTHERS.
SO ANYONE WHO CAUSES A GRUDGE THAT DEEP ULTIMATELY HAS TO SATIATE IT HIMSELF.

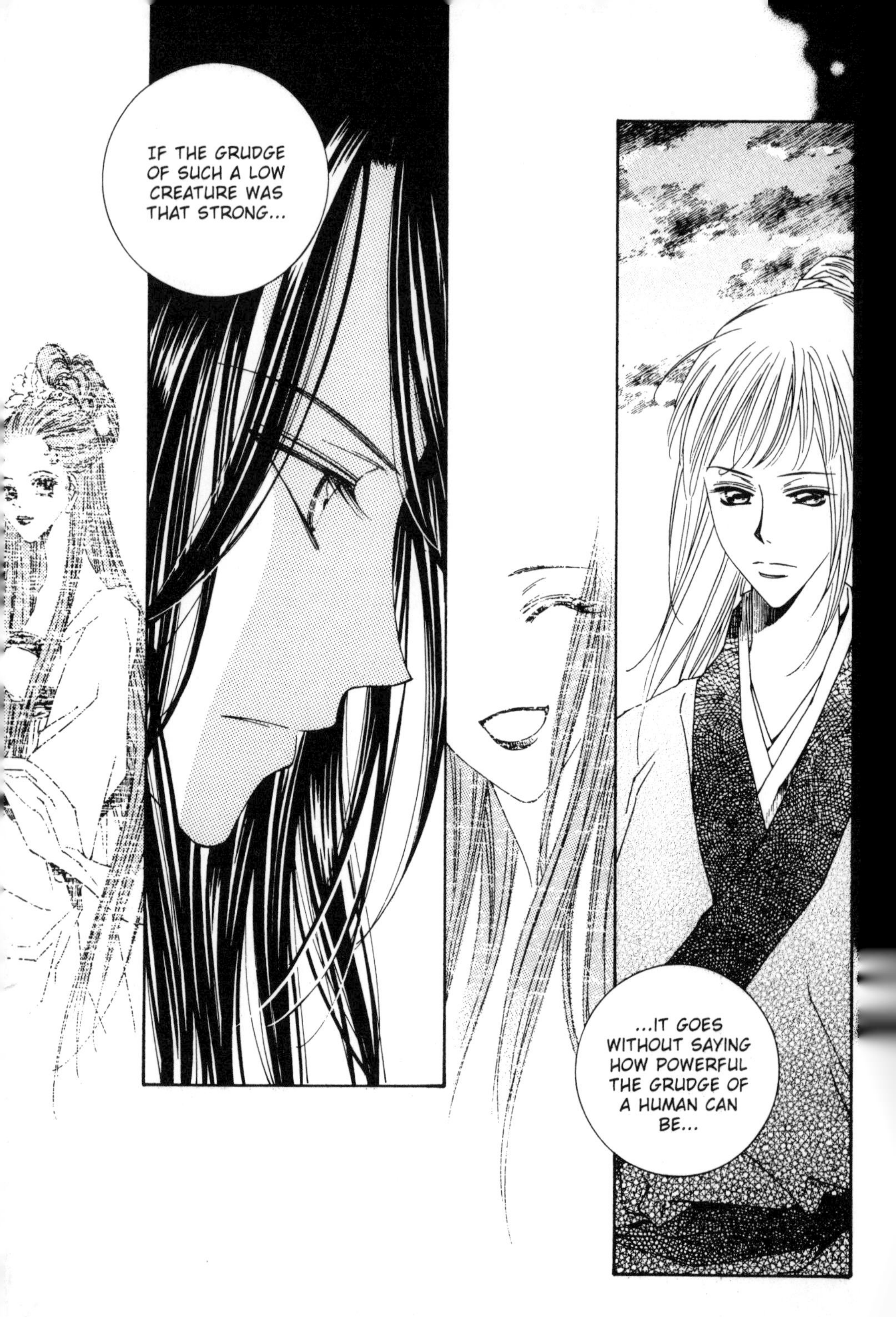
IF THE GRUDGE OF SUCH A LOW CREATURE WAS THAT STRONG...
...IT GOES WITHOUT SAYING HOW POWERFUL THE GRUDGE OF A HUMAN CAN BE...

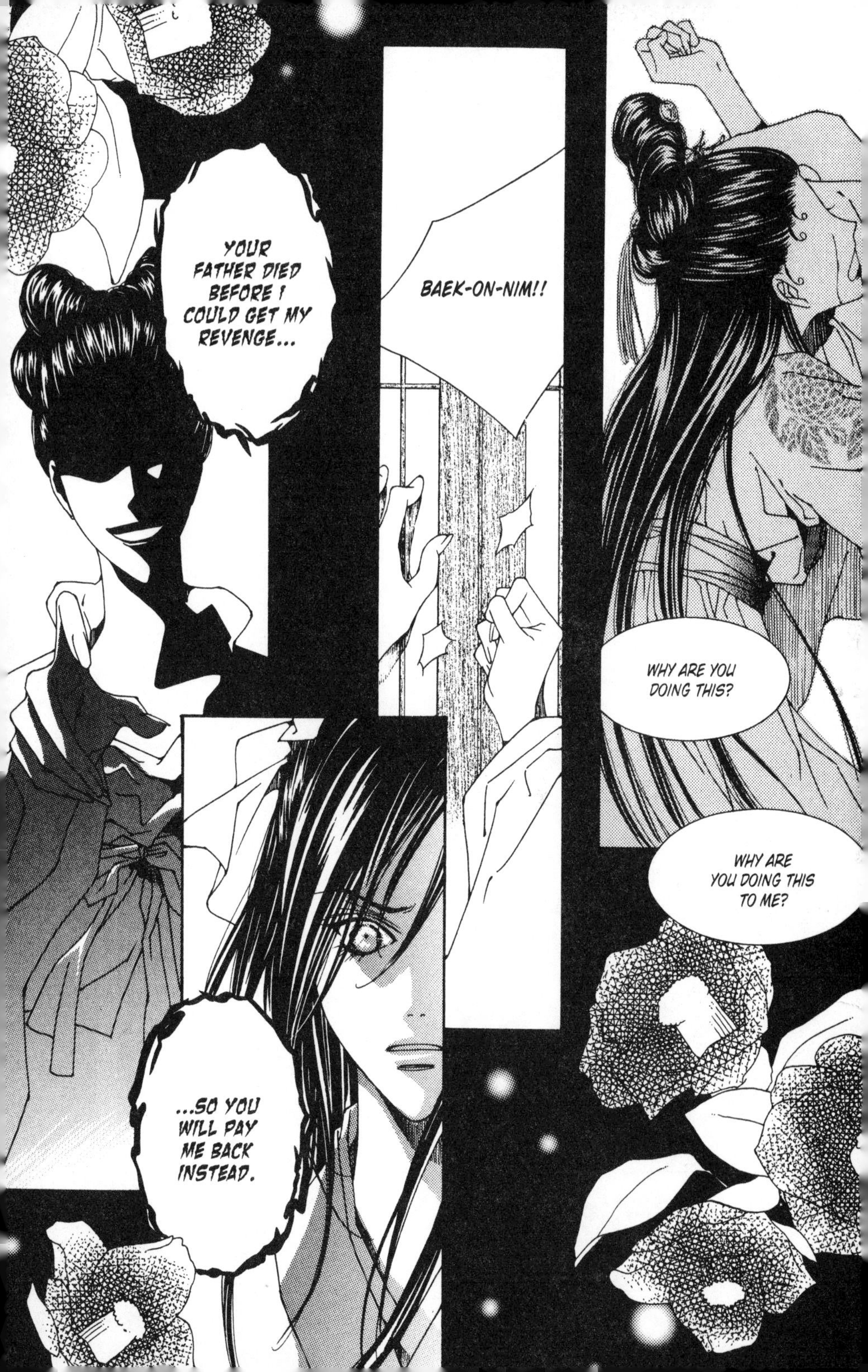
YOUR FATHER DIED BEFORE I COULD GET MY REVENGE...
...SO YOU WILL PAY ME BACK INSTEAD.
BAEK-ON-NIM!!
WHY ARE YOU DOING THIS?
WHY ARE YOU DOING THIS TO ME?

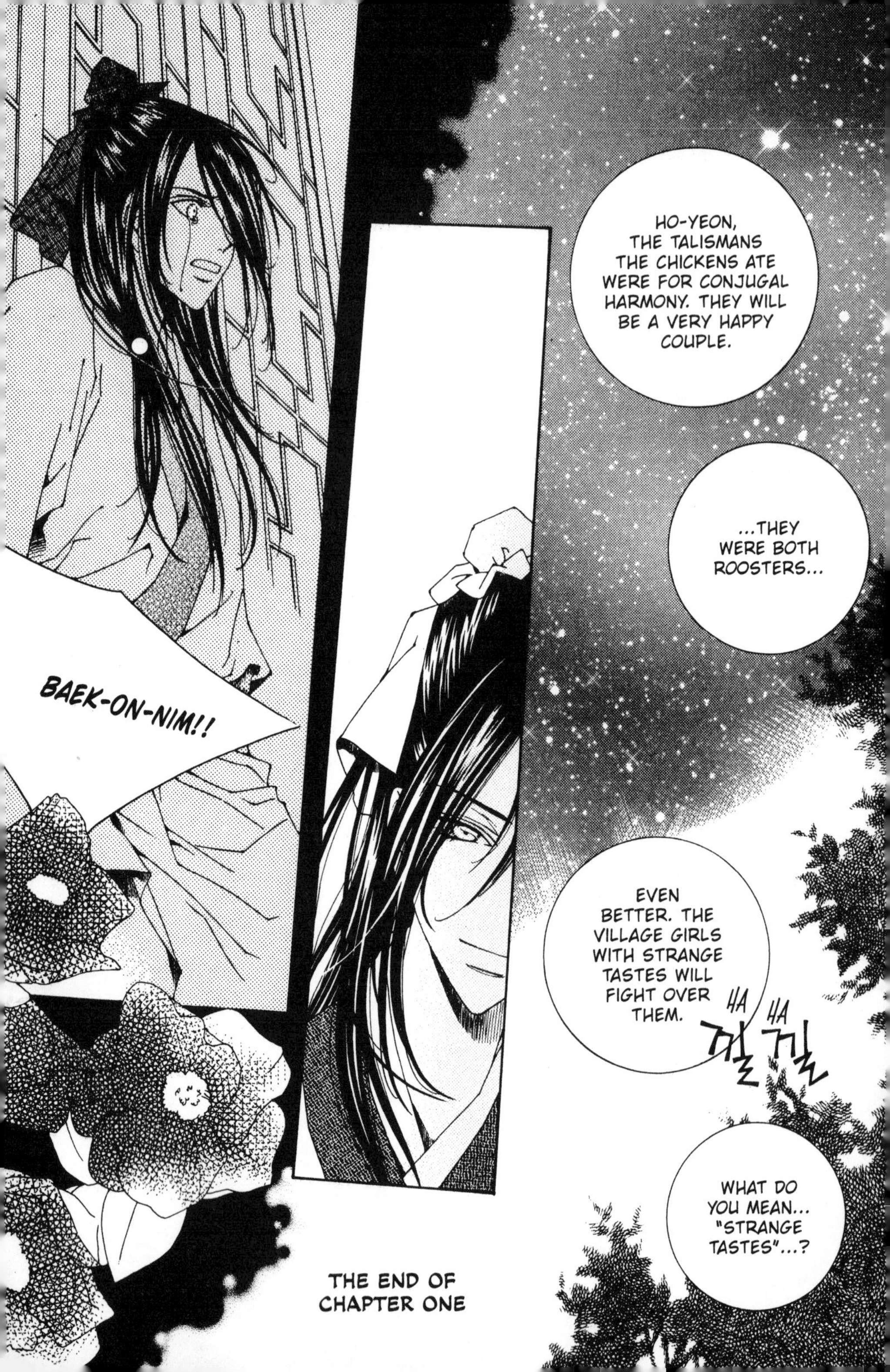
BAEK-ON-NIM!!
HO-YEON, THE TALISMANS THE CHICKENS ATE WERE FOR CONJUGAL HARMONY. THEY WILL BE A VERY HAPPY COUPLE.
...THEY WERE BOTH ROOSTERS...
EVEN BETTER. THE VILLAGE GIRLS WITH STRANGE TASTES WILL FIGHT OVER THEM.
HA HA
WHAT DO YOU MEAN... "STRANGE TASTES"...?
THE END OF CHAPTER ONE

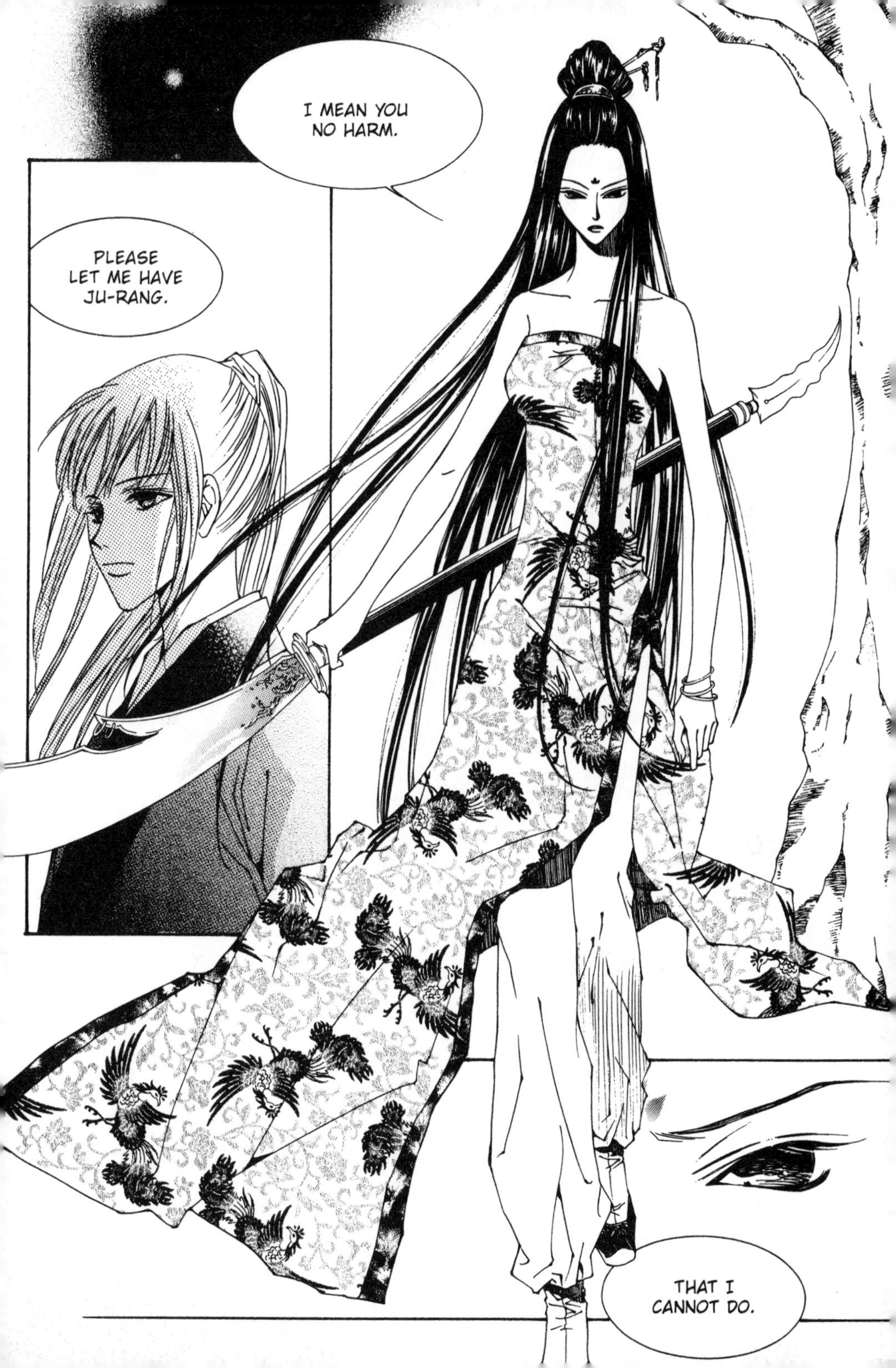
I MEAN YOU NO HARM.
PLEASE LET ME HAVE JU-RANG.
THAT I CANNOT DO.

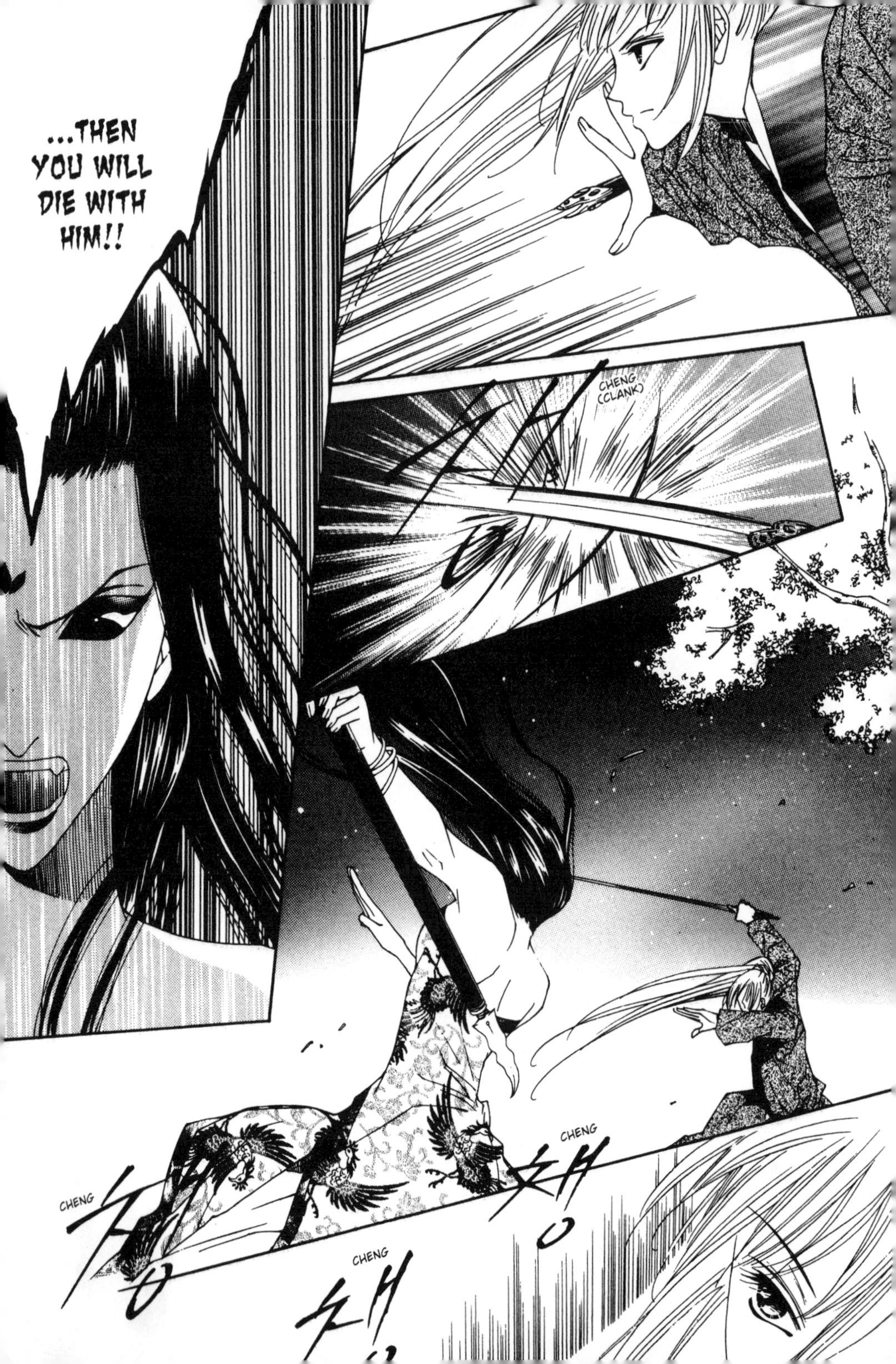
...THEN YOU WILL DIE WITH HIM!!
CHENG (CLANK)
CHENG
CHENG
CHENG

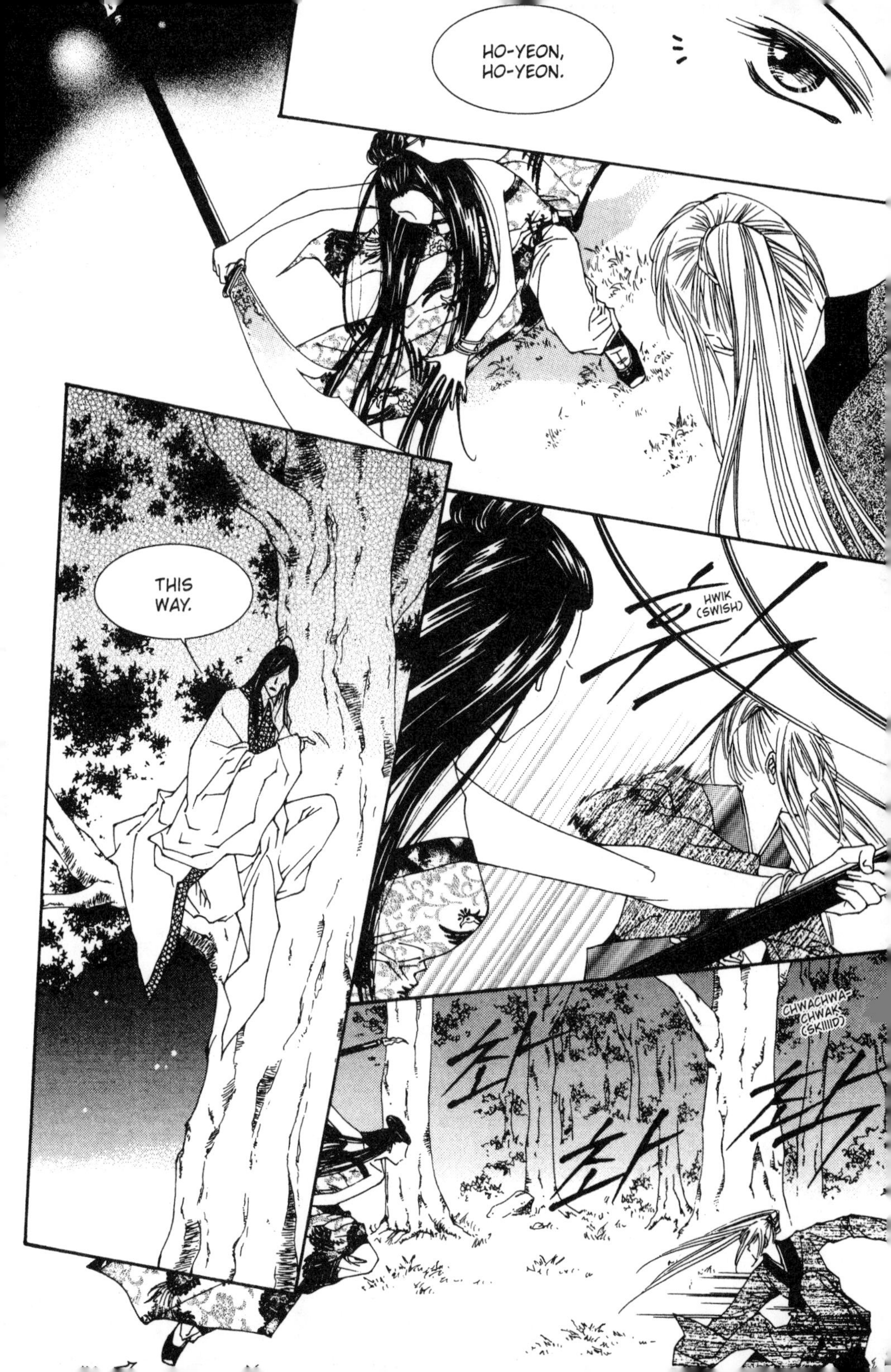
HO-YEON,
HO-YEON.
THIS WAY.
HWIK (SWISH)
CHWACHWA-CHWAK (SKIIIID)

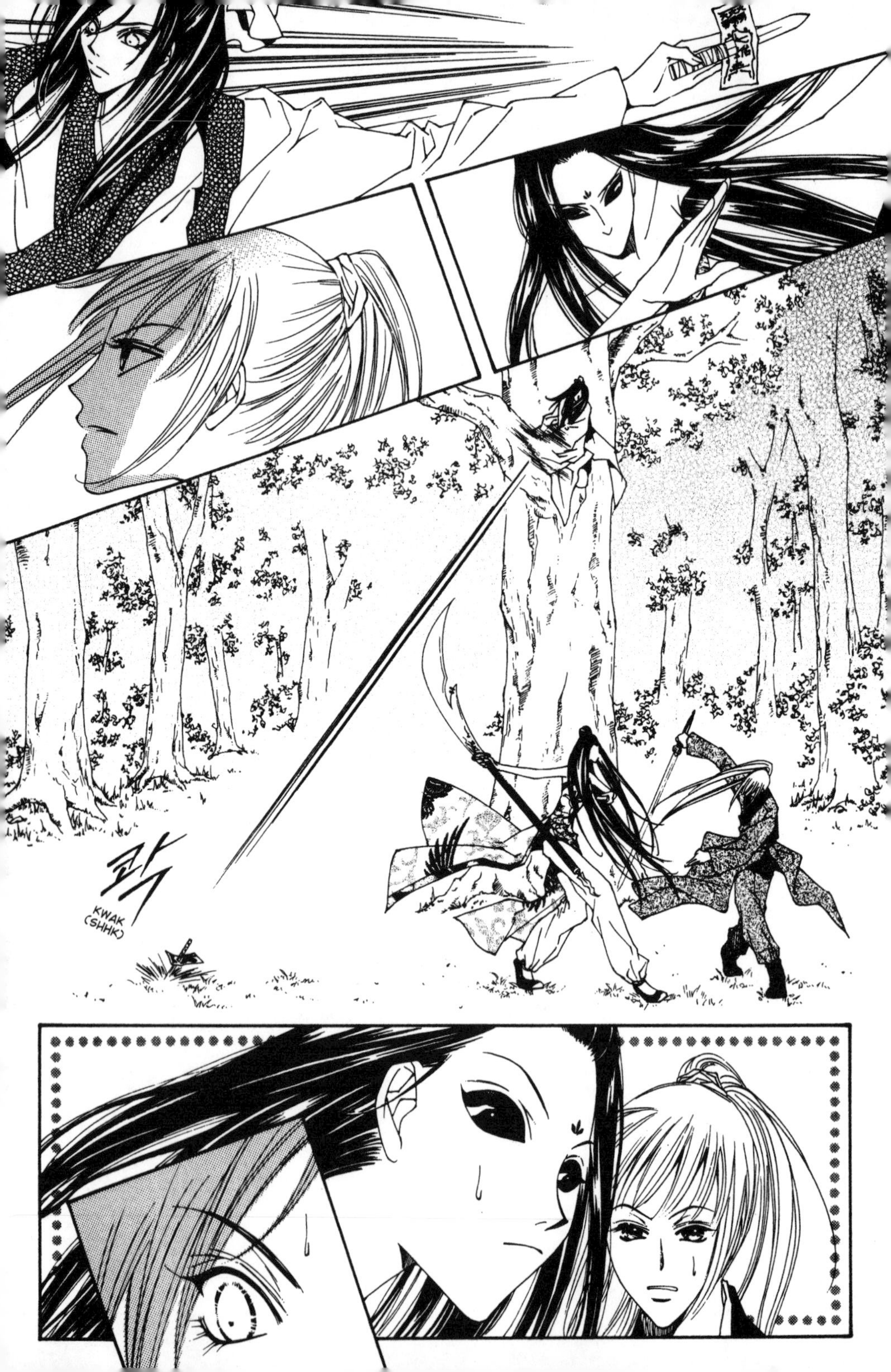
콱
KWAK
(SHHK)

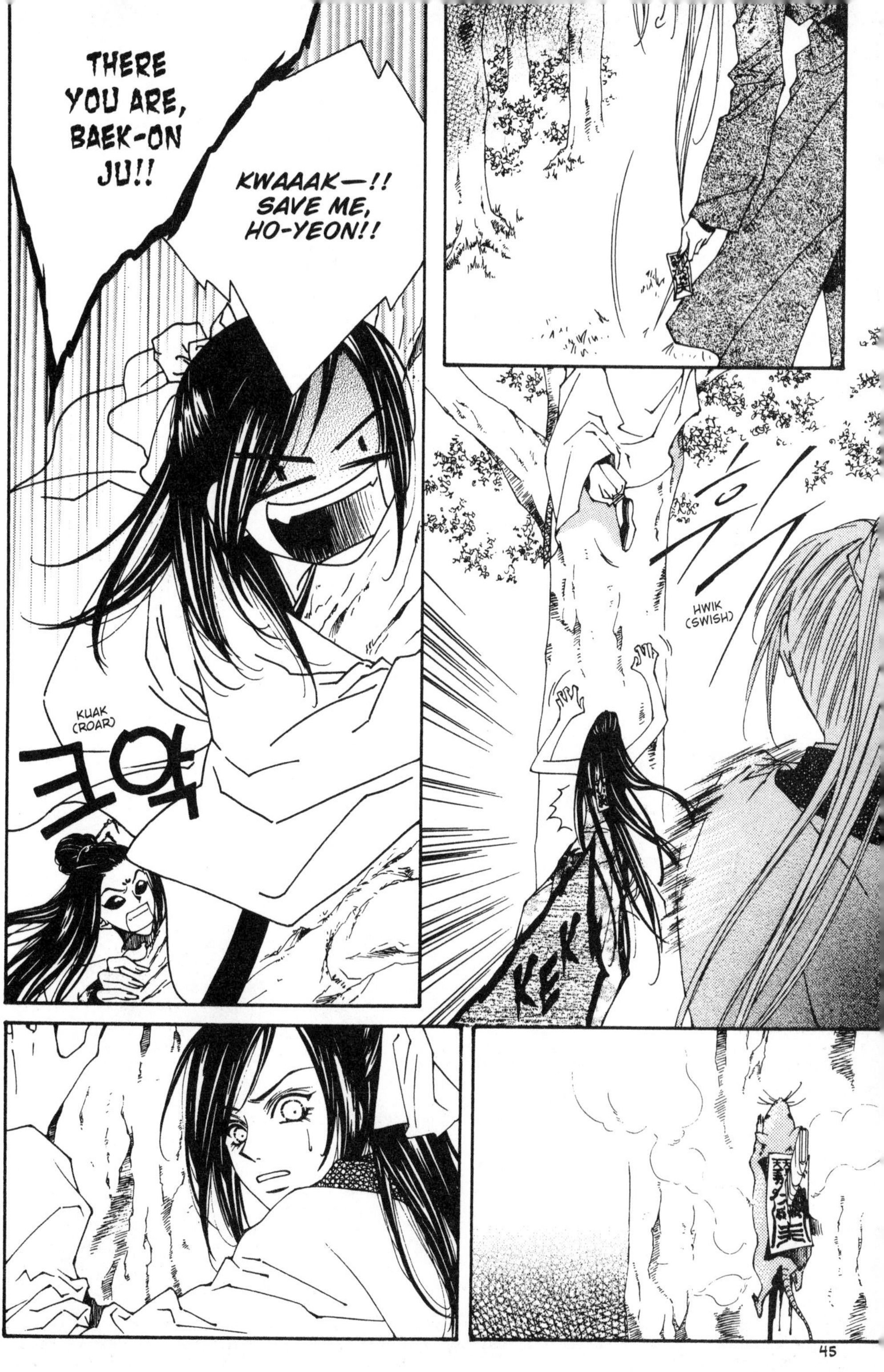
THERE YOU ARE, BAEK-ON JU!!
KWAAAK—!! SAVE ME, HO-YEON!!
KUAK (ROAR)
HWIK (SWISH)
KEK

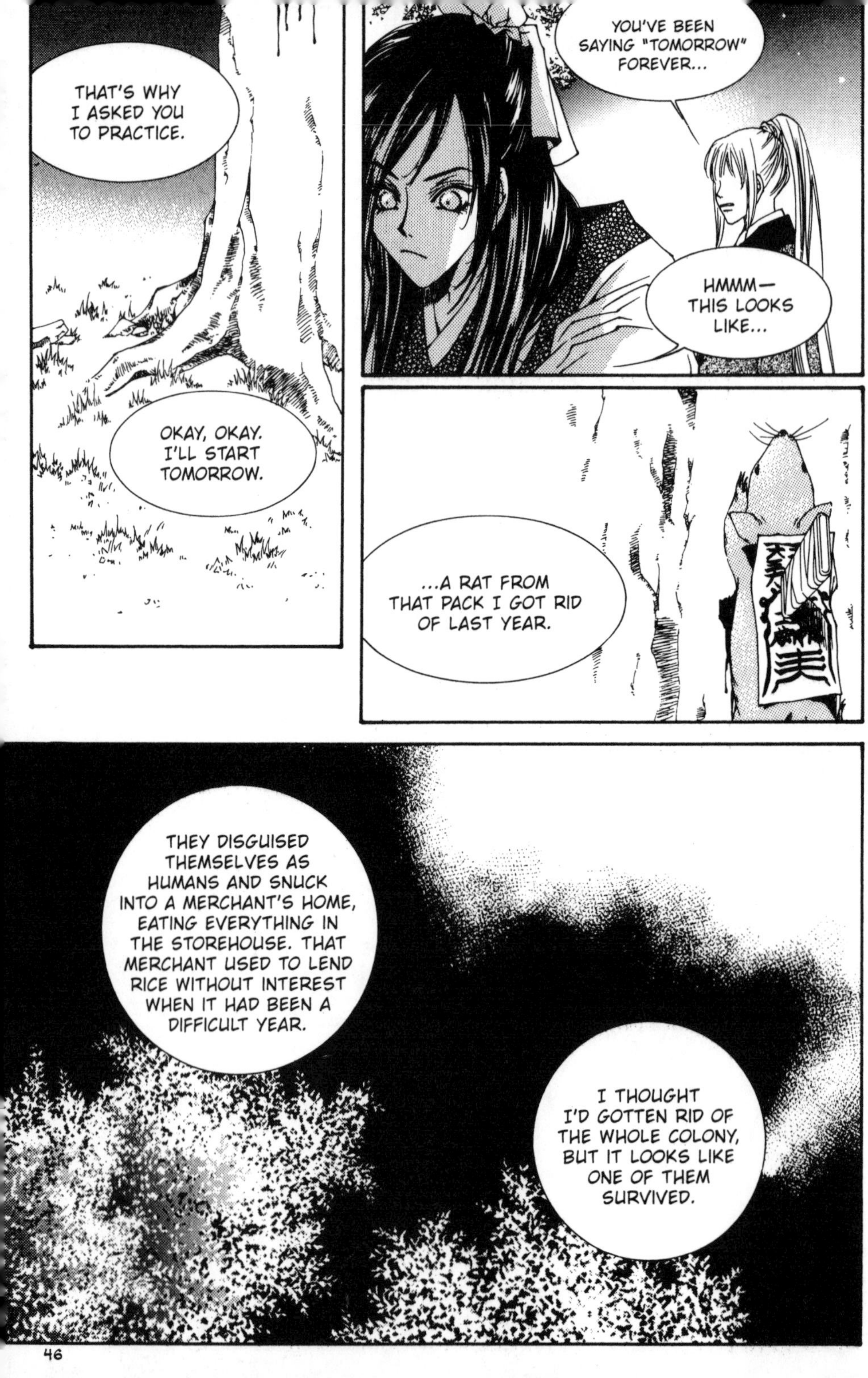
THAT'S WHY I ASKED YOU TO PRACTICE.
OKAY, OKAY. I'LL START TOMORROW.
YOU'VE BEEN SAYING "TOMORROW" FOREVER...
HMMM— THIS LOOKS LIKE...
...A RAT FROM THAT PACK I GOT RID OF LAST YEAR.
THEY DISGUISED THEMSELVES AS HUMANS AND SNUCK INTO A MERCHANT'S HOME, EATING EVERYTHING IN THE STOREHOUSE. THAT MERCHANT USED TO LEND RICE WITHOUT INTEREST WHEN IT HAD BEEN A DIFFICULT YEAR.
I THOUGHT I'D GOTTEN RID OF THE WHOLE COLONY, BUT IT LOOKS LIKE ONE OF THEM SURVIVED.

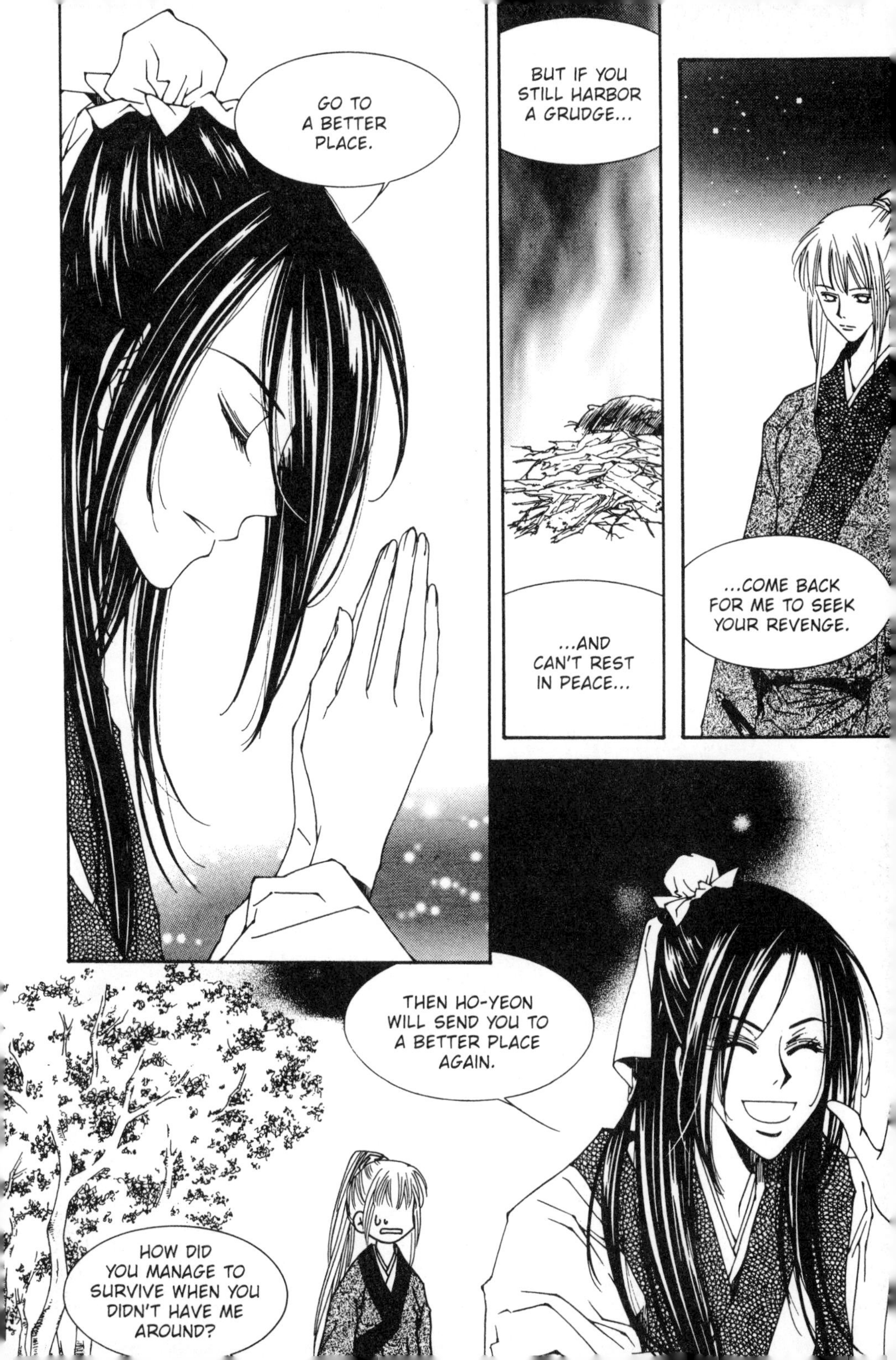
GO TO A BETTER PLACE.
BUT IF YOU STILL HARBOR A GRUDGE...
...AND CAN'T REST IN PEACE...
...COME BACK FOR ME TO SEEK YOUR REVENGE.
THEN HO-YEON WILL SEND YOU TO A BETTER PLACE AGAIN.
HOW DID YOU MANAGE TO SURVIVE WHEN YOU DIDN'T HAVE ME AROUND?

CHAPTER TWO
LIFE

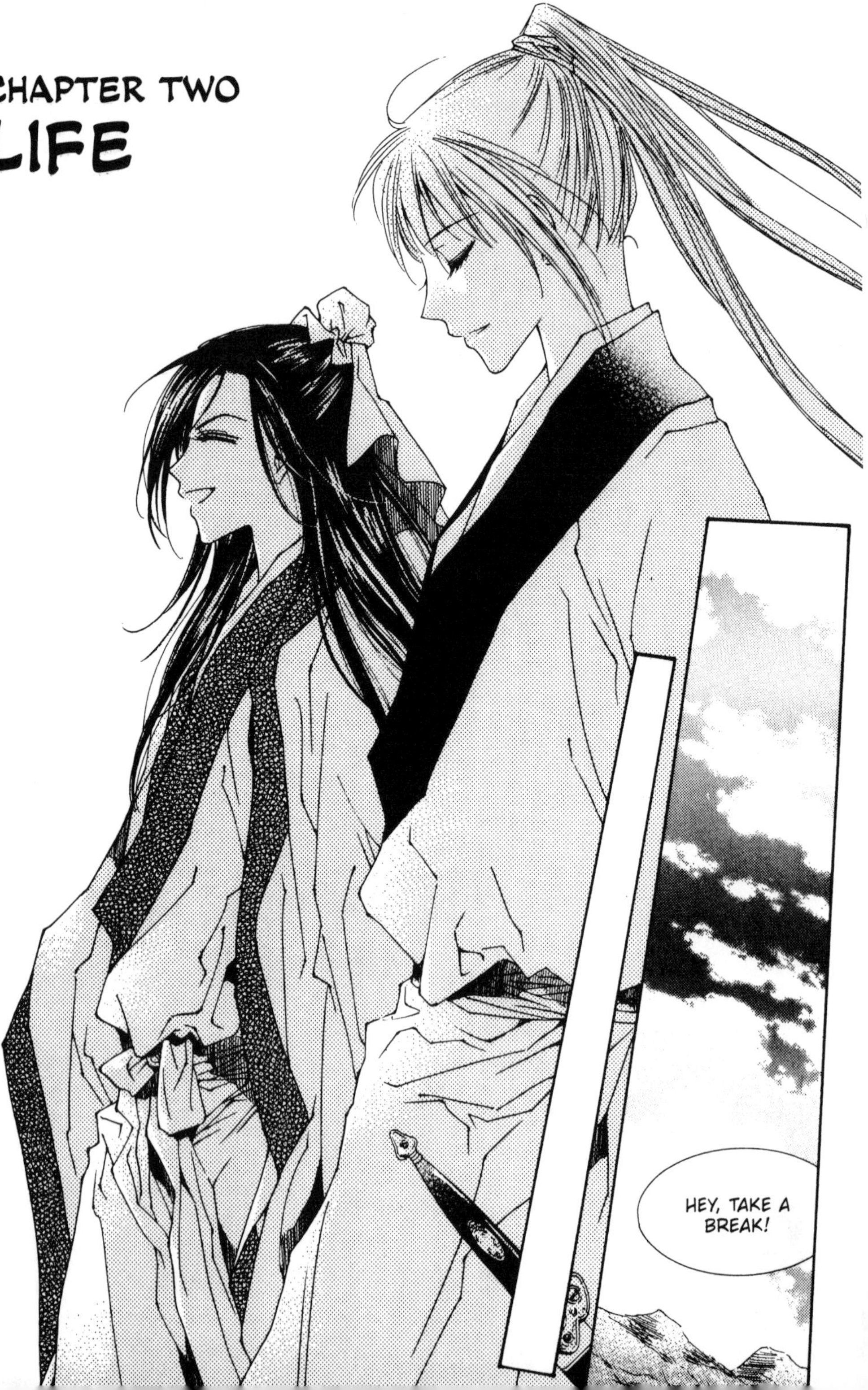
HEY, TAKE A BREAK!

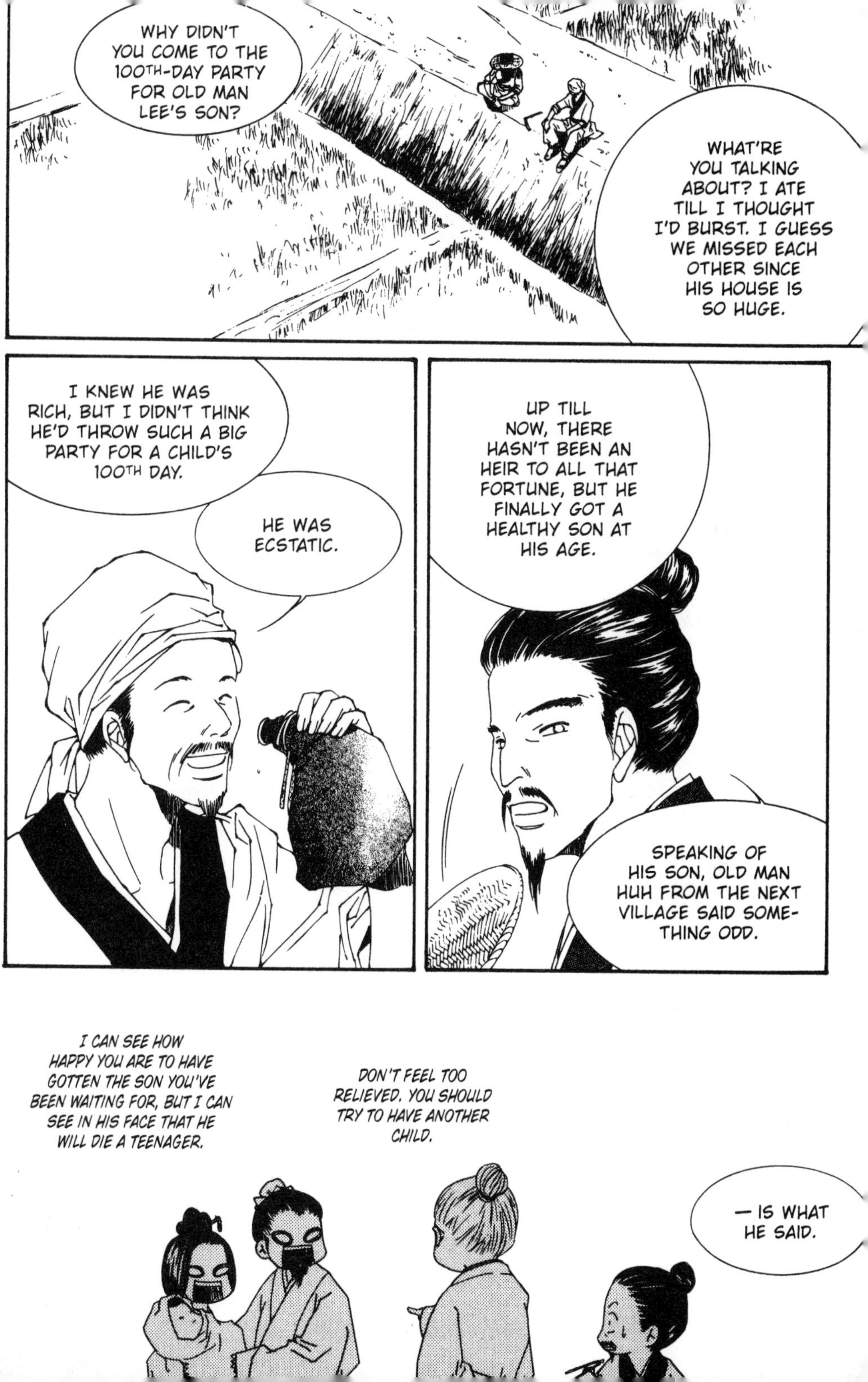
WHY DIDN'T YOU COME TO THE 100TH-DAY PARTY FOR OLD MAN LEE'S SON?
WHAT'RE YOU TALKING ABOUT? I ATE TILL I THOUGHT I'D BURST. I GUESS WE MISSED EACH OTHER SINCE HIS HOUSE IS SO HUGE.
I KNEW HE WAS RICH, BUT I DIDN'T THINK HE'D THROW SUCH A BIG PARTY FOR A CHILD'S 100TH DAY.
HE WAS ECSTATIC.
UP TILL NOW, THERE HASN'T BEEN AN HEIR TO ALL THAT FORTUNE, BUT HE FINALLY GOT A HEALTHY SON AT HIS AGE.
SPEAKING OF HIS SON, OLD MAN HUH FROM THE NEXT VILLAGE SAID SOMETHING ODD.
I CAN SEE HOW HAPPY YOU ARE TO HAVE GOTTEN THE SON YOU'VE BEEN WAITING FOR, BUT I CAN SEE IN HIS FACE THAT HE WILL DIE A TEENAGER.
DON'T FEEL TOO RELIEVED. YOU SHOULD TRY TO HAVE ANOTHER CHILD.
—IS WHAT HE SAID.

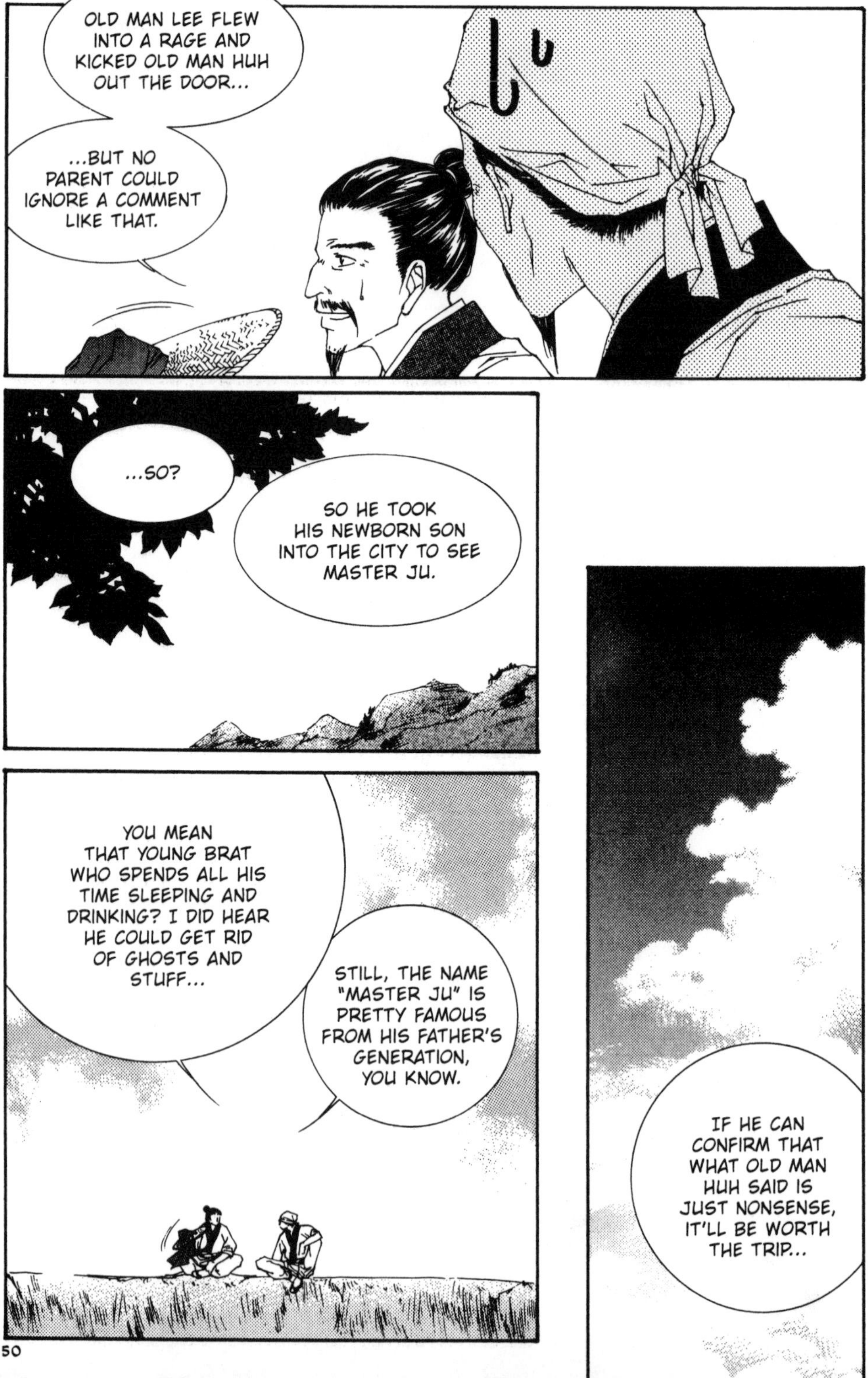
OLD MAN LEE FLEW INTO A RAGE AND KICKED OLD MAN HUH OUT THE DOOR...
...BUT NO PARENT COULD IGNORE A COMMENT LIKE THAT.
...SO?
SO HE TOOK HIS NEWBORN SON INTO THE CITY TO SEE MASTER JU.
YOU MEAN THAT YOUNG BRAT WHO SPENDS ALL HIS TIME SLEEPING AND DRINKING? I DID HEAR HE COULD GET RID OF GHOSTS AND STUFF...
STILL, THE NAME "MASTER JU" IS PRETTY FAMOUS FROM HIS FATHER'S GENERATION, YOU KNOW.
IF HE CAN CONFIRM THAT WHAT OLD MAN HUH SAID IS JUST NONSENSE, IT'LL BE WORTH THE TRIP...

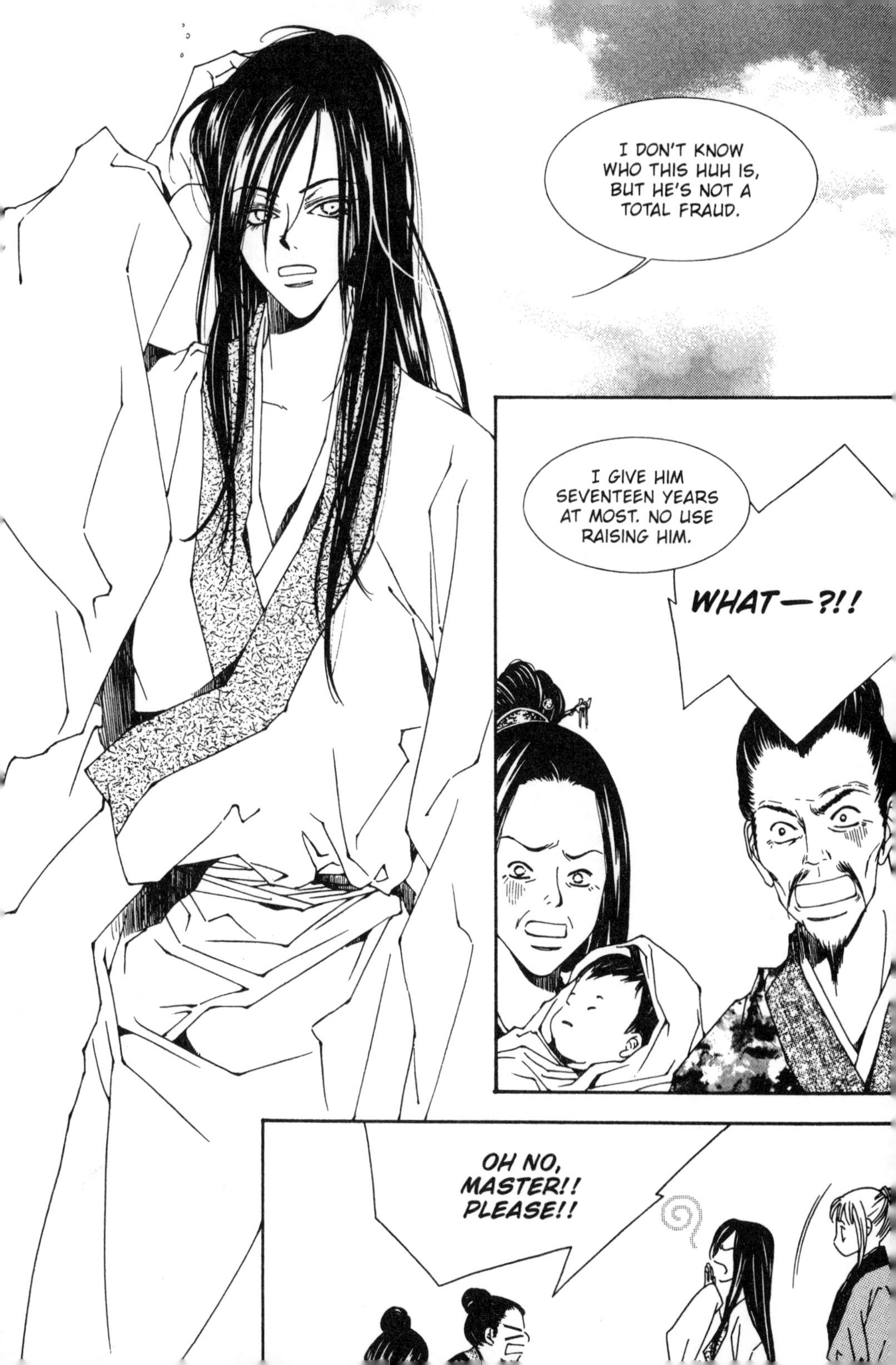
I DON'T KNOW WHO THIS HUH IS, BUT HE'S NOT A TOTAL FRAUD.
I GIVE HIM SEVENTEEN YEARS AT MOST. NO USE RAISING HIM.
WHAT—?!!
OH NO, MASTER!! PLEASE!!

I PRAYED AND PRAYED AND FINALLY GOT A CHILD OF MY OWN! HOW CAN THIS BE?

IT'S TOO EARLY IN THE MORNING...

IF YOU HAD A CHILD AT YOUR AGE, IT MEANS YOU'RE STILL FERTILE. WHY DON'T YOU JUST GET A CONCUBINE?

AH, THAT SOUNDS—

HOW CAN YOU SAY SUCH A THING WHEN MY WIFE IS STANDING RIGHT NEXT TO ME?!! OF COURSE I CAN'T!!

MAYBE THE FUNDAMENTAL PROBLEM LIES ELSEWHERE.

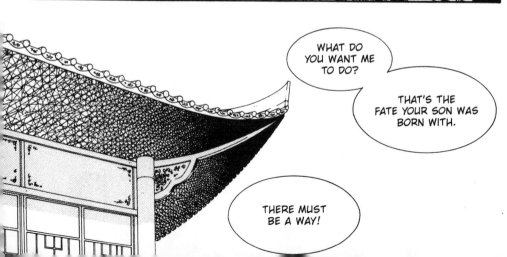

WHAT DO YOU WANT ME TO DO?

THAT'S THE FATE YOUR SON WAS BORN WITH.

THERE MUST BE A WAY!

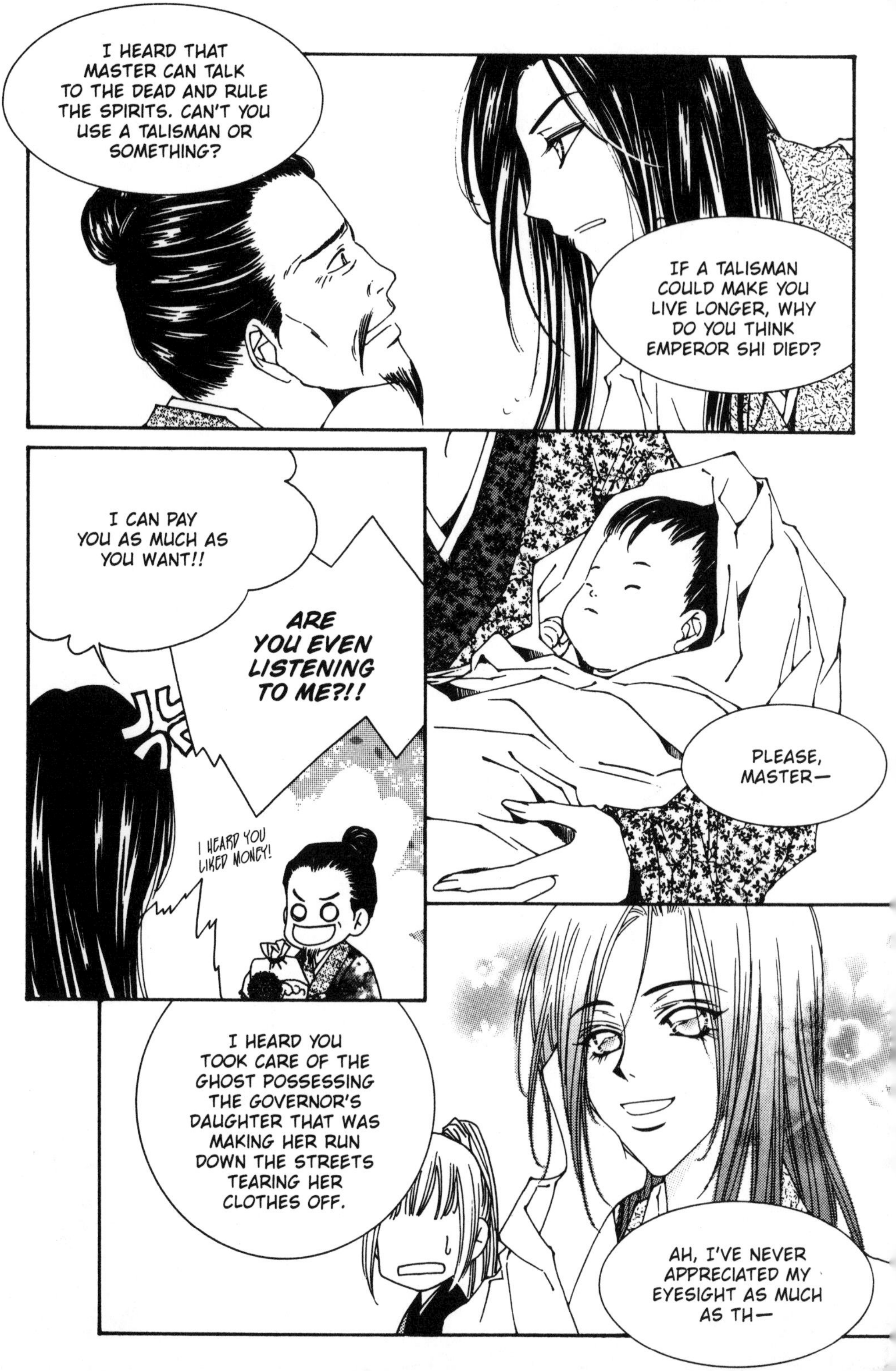
I HEARD THAT MASTER CAN TALK TO THE DEAD AND RULE THE SPIRITS. CAN'T YOU USE A TALISMAN OR SOMETHING?
IF A TALISMAN COULD MAKE YOU LIVE LONGER, WHY DO YOU THINK EMPEROR SHI DIED?
I CAN PAY YOU AS MUCH AS YOU WANT!!
ARE YOU EVEN LISTENING TO ME?!!
I HEARD YOU LIKED MONEY!
PLEASE, MASTER—
I HEARD YOU TOOK CARE OF THE GHOST POSSESSING THE GOVERNOR'S DAUGHTER THAT WAS MAKING HER RUN DOWN THE STREETS TEARING HER CLOTHES OFF.
AH, I'VE NEVER APPRECIATED MY EYESIGHT AS MUCH AS TH—

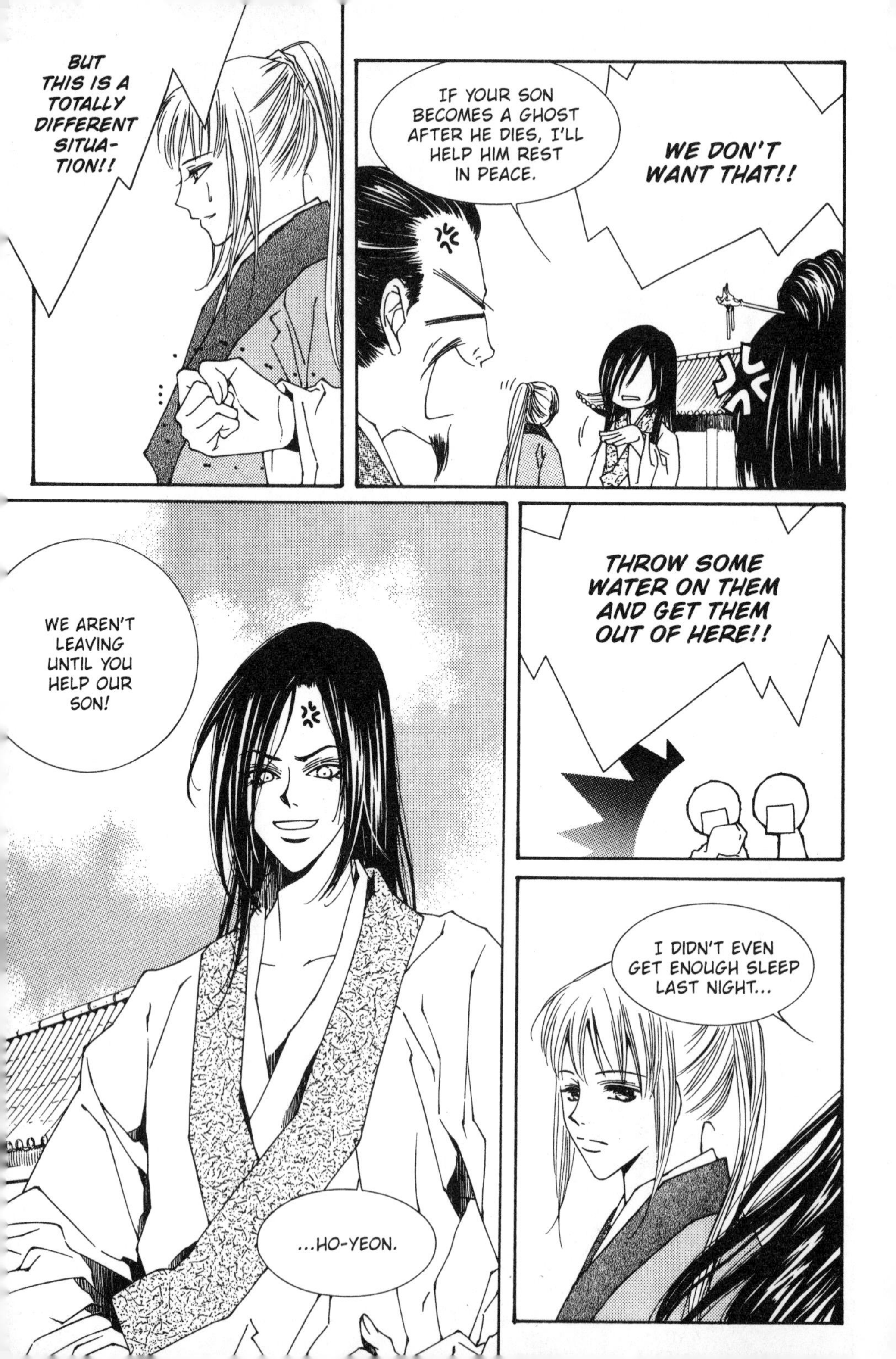
BUT THIS IS A TOTALLY DIFFERENT SITUA-TION!!
...
IF YOUR SON BECOMES A GHOST AFTER HE DIES, I'LL HELP HIM REST IN PEACE.
WE DON'T WANT THAT!!
WE AREN'T LEAVING UNTIL YOU HELP OUR SON!
...HO-YEON.
THROW SOME WATER ON THEM AND GET THEM OUT OF HERE!!
I DIDN'T EVEN GET ENOUGH SLEEP LAST NIGHT...

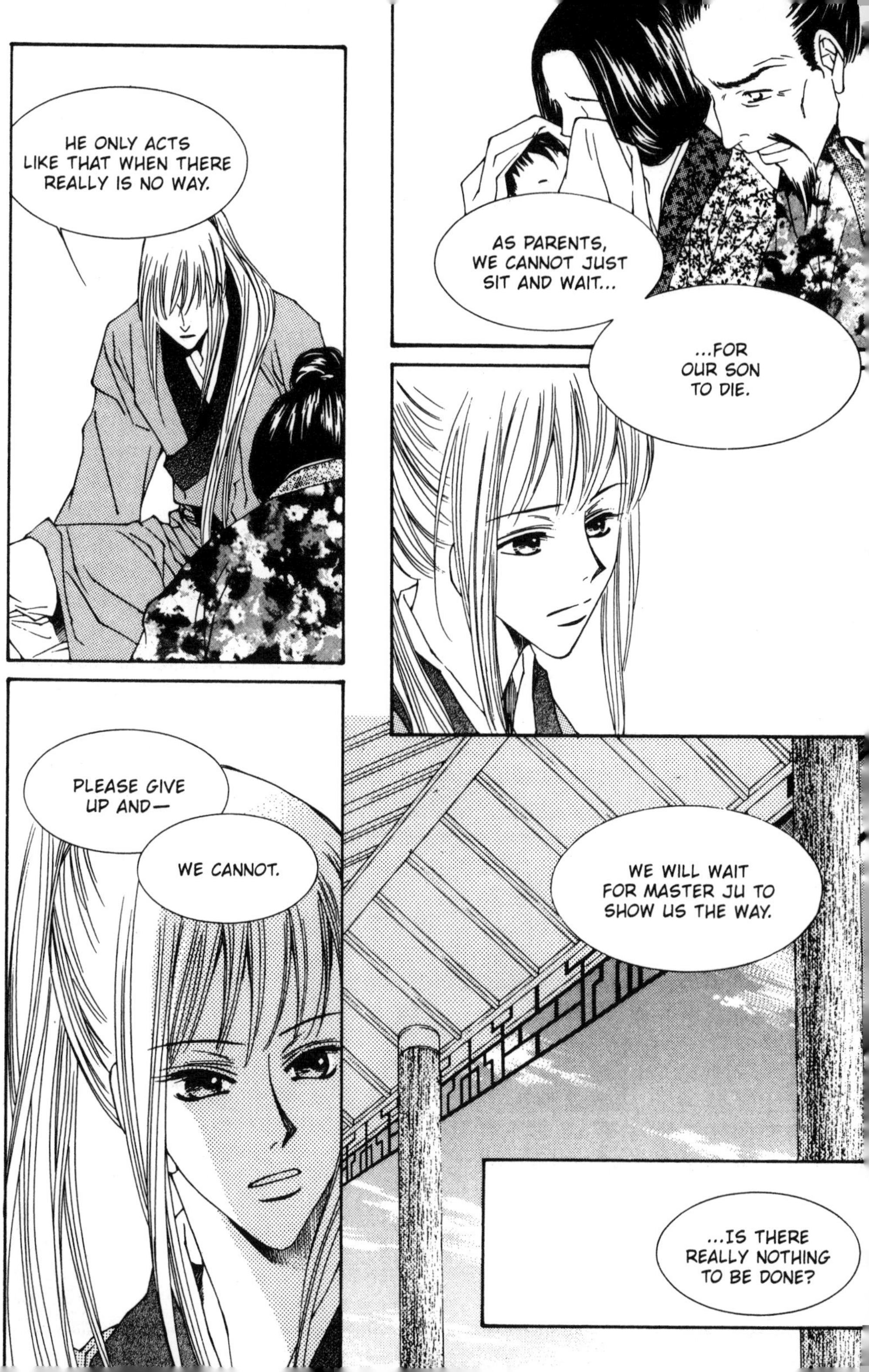
HE ONLY ACTS LIKE THAT WHEN THERE REALLY IS NO WAY.
AS PARENTS, WE CANNOT JUST SIT AND WAIT...
...FOR OUR SON TO DIE.
PLEASE GIVE UP AND—
WE CANNOT.
WE WILL WAIT FOR MASTER JU TO SHOW US THE WAY.
...IS THERE REALLY NOTHING TO BE DONE?

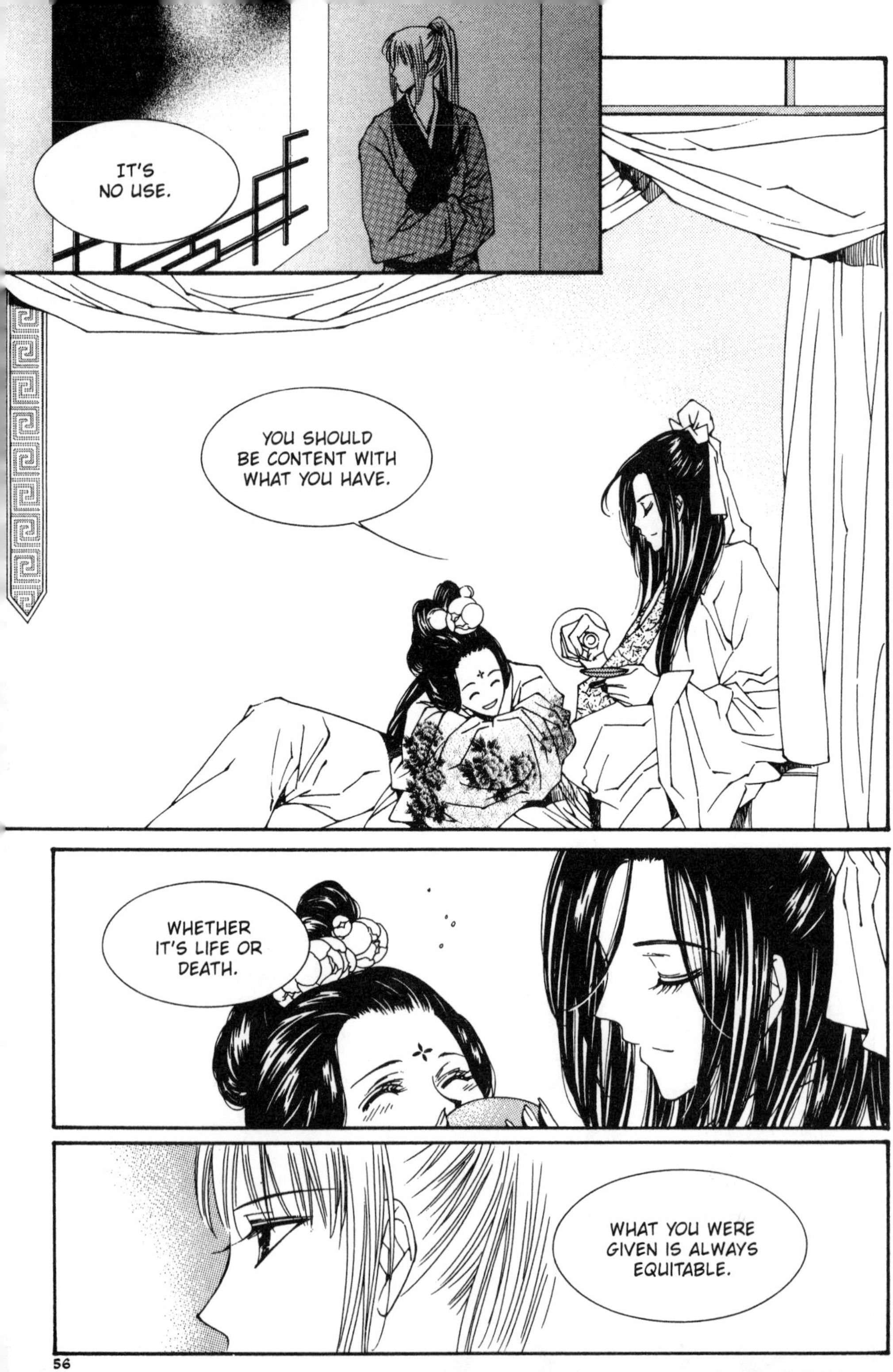
IT'S NO USE.
YOU SHOULD BE CONTENT WITH WHAT YOU HAVE.
WHETHER IT'S LIFE OR DEATH.
WHAT YOU WERE GIVEN IS ALWAYS EQUITABLE.

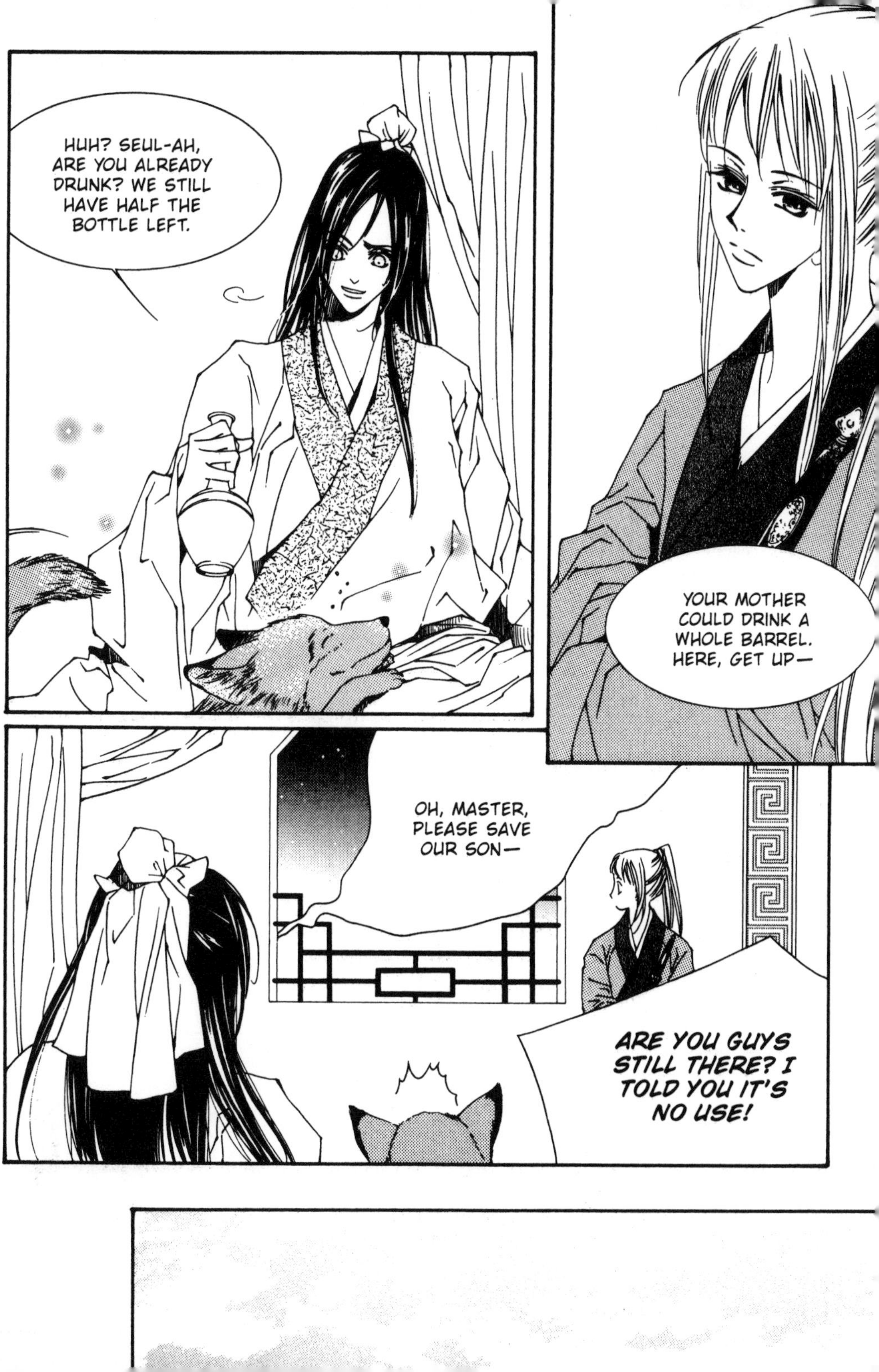
HUH? SEUL-AH, ARE YOU ALREADY DRUNK? WE STILL HAVE HALF THE BOTTLE LEFT.
YOUR MOTHER COULD DRINK A WHOLE BARREL. HERE, GET UP—
OH, MASTER, PLEASE SAVE OUR SON—
ARE YOU GUYS STILL THERE? I TOLD YOU IT'S NO USE!

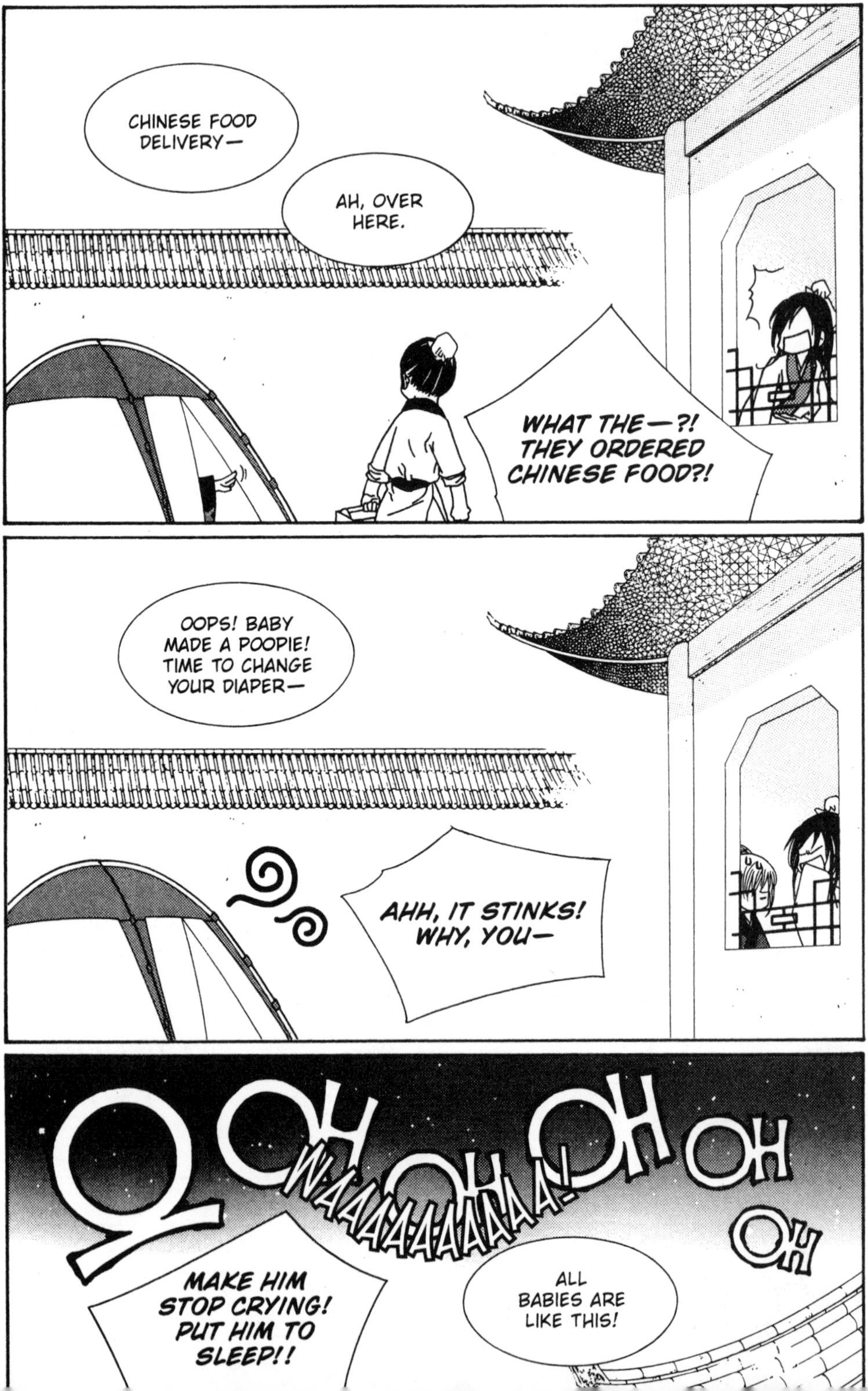
CHINESE FOOD DELIVERY—
AH, OVER HERE.
WHAT THE—?! THEY ORDERED CHINESE FOOD?!
OOPS! BABY MADE A POOPIE! TIME TO CHANGE YOUR DIAPER—
AHH, IT STINKS! WHY, YOU—
OOHOHOHOHOHOHOH
WAAAAAAAAAAAAA!
MAKE HIM STOP CRYING! PUT HIM TO SLEEP!!
ALL BABIES ARE LIKE THIS!

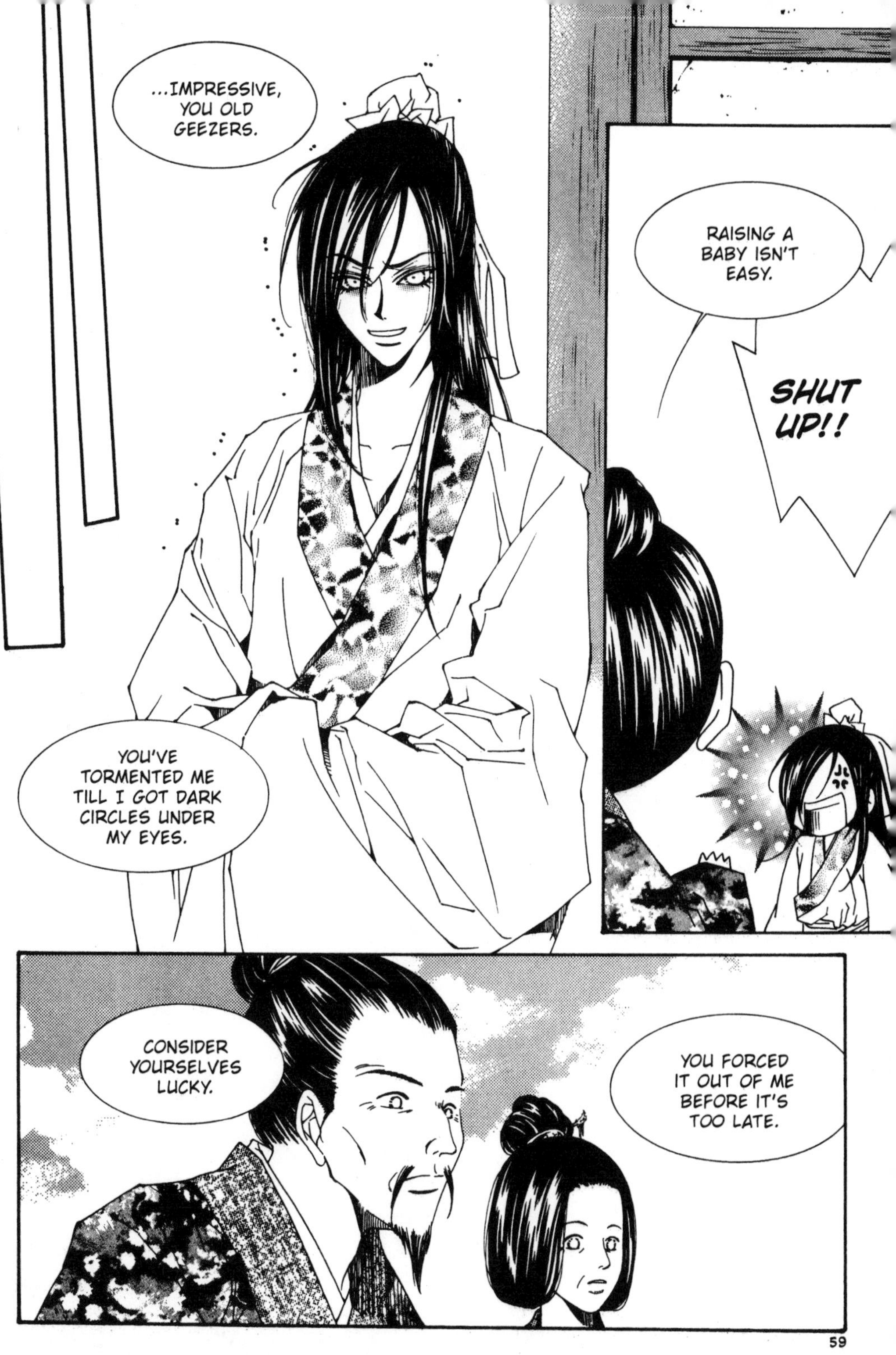
...IMPRESSIVE, YOU OLD GEEZERS.
YOU'VE TORMENTED ME TILL I GOT DARK CIRCLES UNDER MY EYES.
RAISING A BABY ISN'T EASY.
SHUT UP!!
CONSIDER YOURSELVES LUCKY.
YOU FORCED IT OUT OF ME BEFORE IT'S TOO LATE.

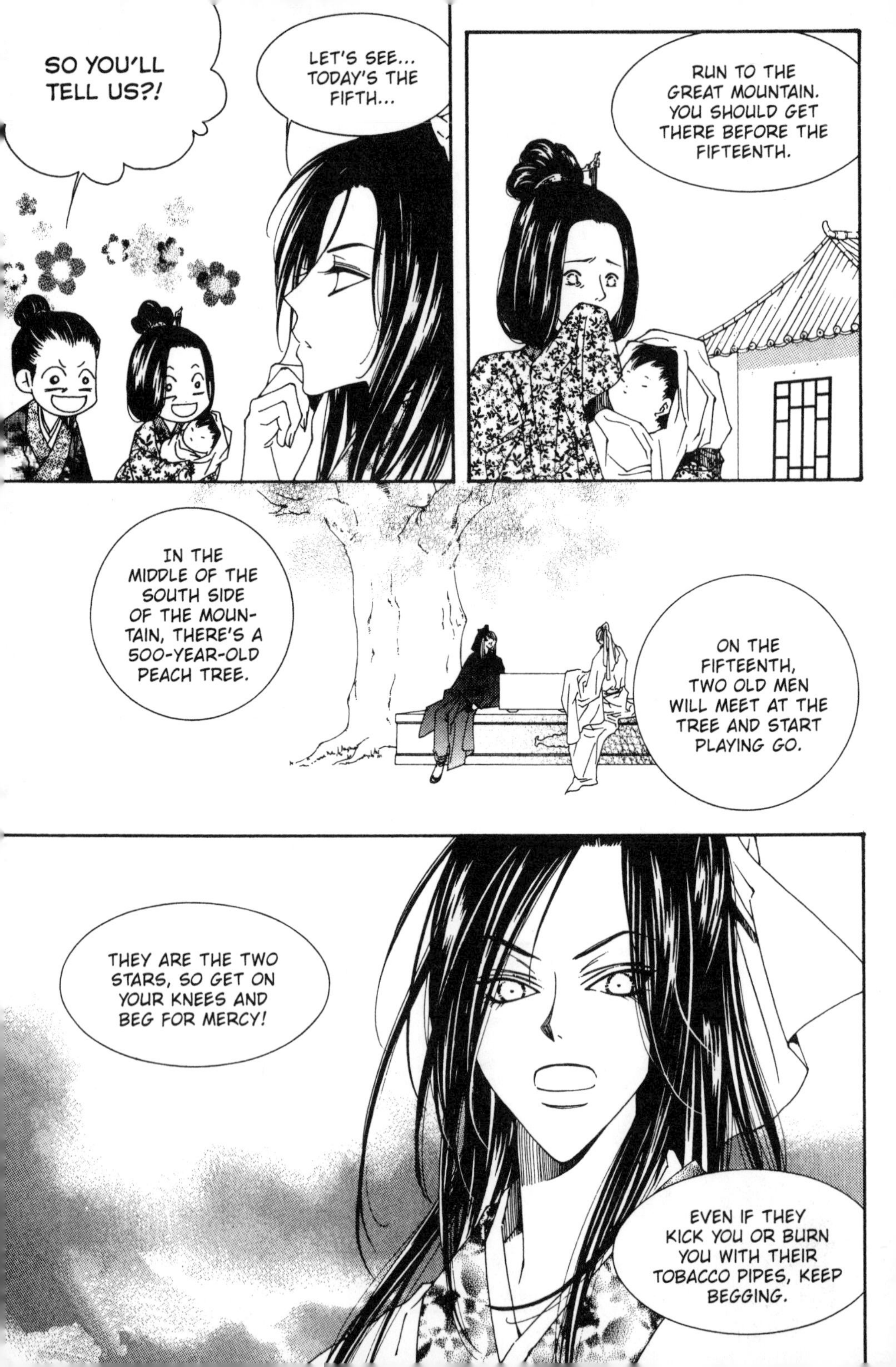
SO YOU'LL TELL US?!
LET'S SEE... TODAY'S THE FIFTH...
RUN TO THE GREAT MOUNTAIN. YOU SHOULD GET THERE BEFORE THE FIFTEENTH.
IN THE MIDDLE OF THE SOUTH SIDE OF THE MOUNTAIN, THERE'S A 500-YEAR-OLD PEACH TREE.
ON THE FIFTEENTH, TWO OLD MEN WILL MEET AT THE TREE AND START PLAYING GO.
THEY ARE THE TWO STARS, SO GET ON YOUR KNEES AND BEG FOR MERCY!
EVEN IF THEY KICK YOU OR BURN YOU WITH THEIR TOBACCO PIPES, KEEP BEGGING.

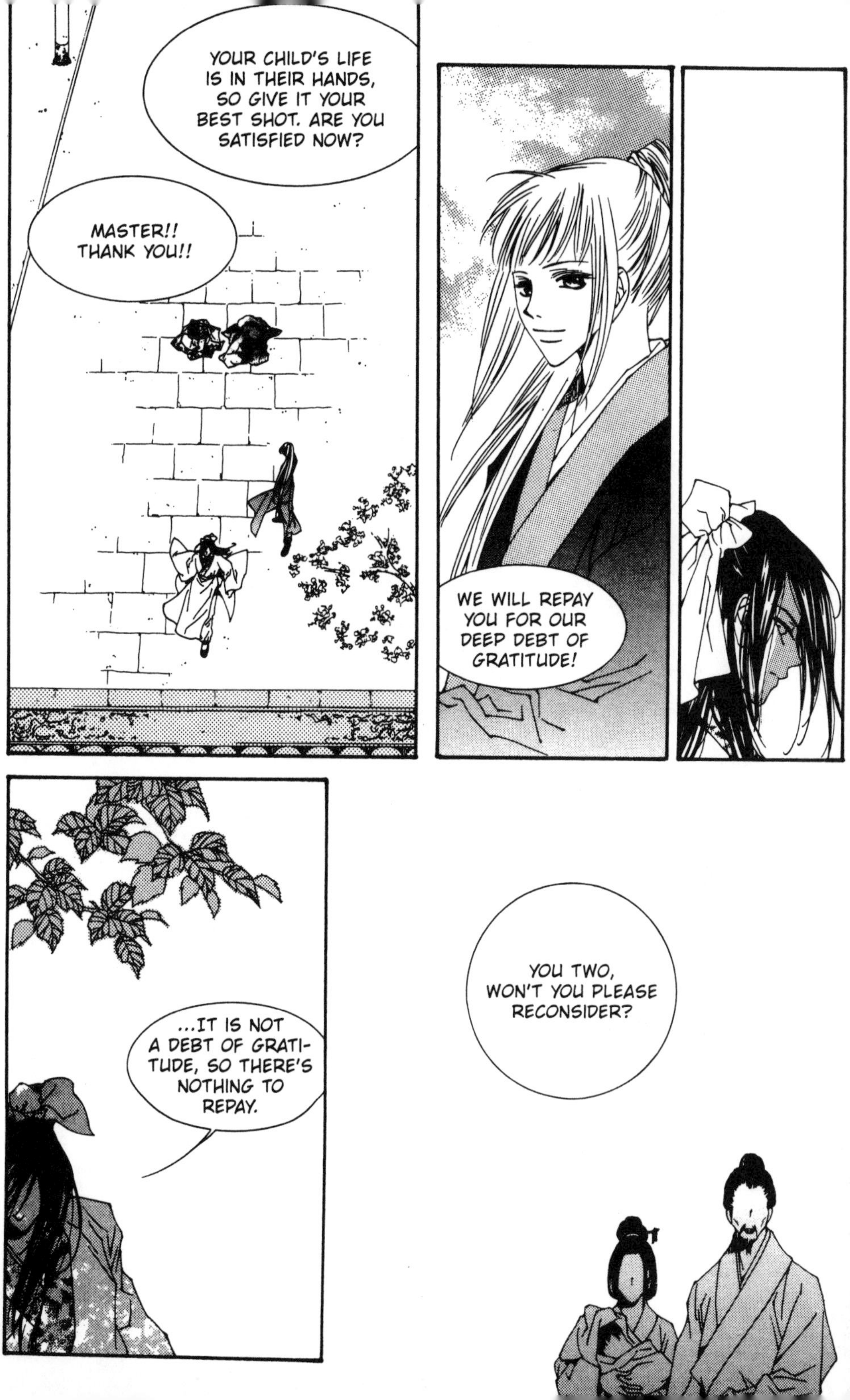
YOUR CHILD'S LIFE IS IN THEIR HANDS, SO GIVE IT YOUR BEST SHOT. ARE YOU SATISFIED NOW?
MASTER!! THANK YOU!!
WE WILL REPAY YOU FOR OUR DEEP DEBT OF GRATITUDE!
...IT IS NOT A DEBT OF GRATI-TUDE, SO THERE'S NOTHING TO REPAY.
YOU TWO, WON'T YOU PLEASE RECONSIDER?

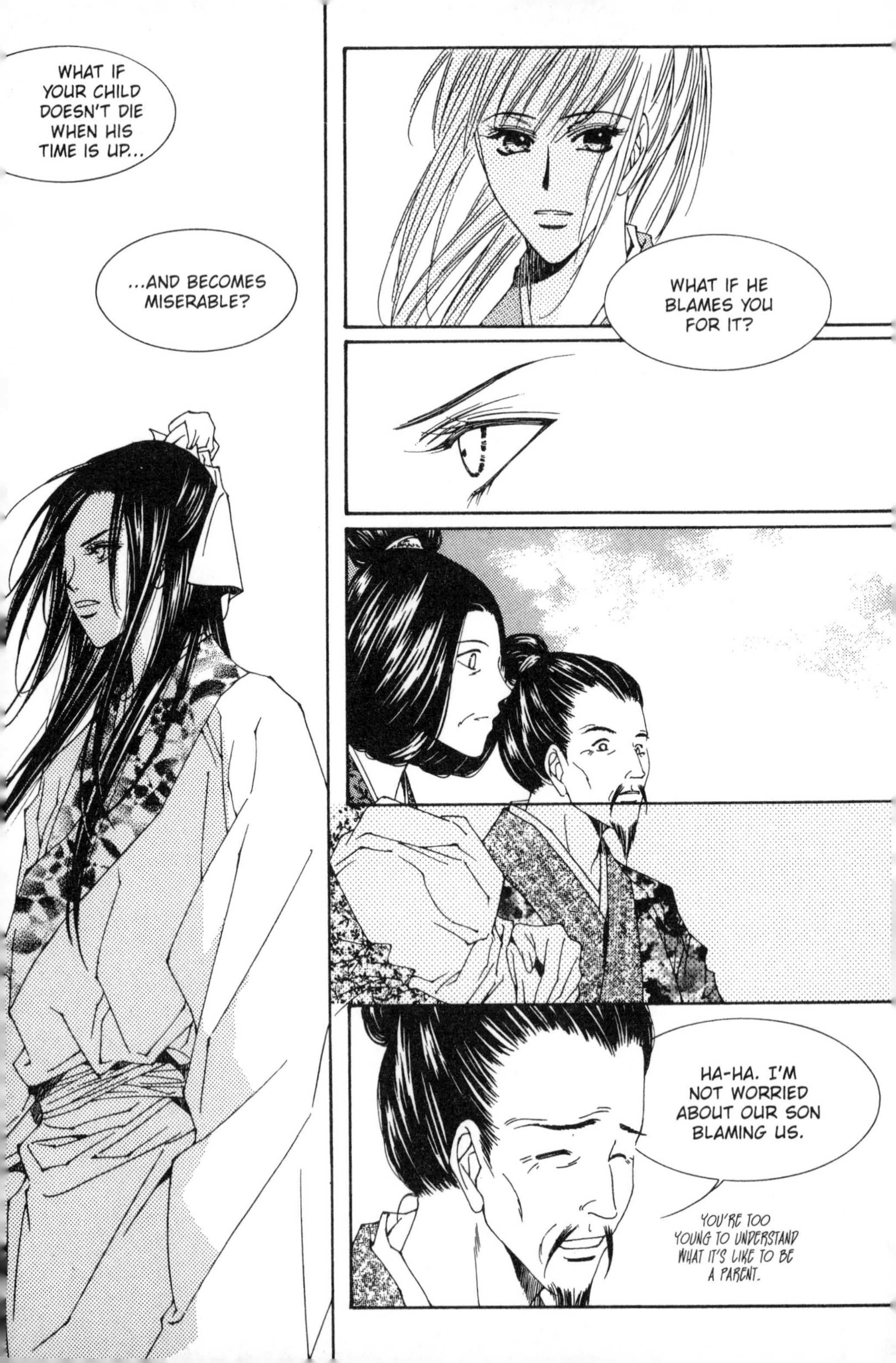
WHAT IF YOUR CHILD DOESN'T DIE WHEN HIS TIME IS UP...
...AND BECOMES MISERABLE?
WHAT IF HE BLAMES YOU FOR IT?
HA-HA. I'M NOT WORRIED ABOUT OUR SON BLAMING US.
YOU'RE TOO YOUNG TO UNDERSTAND WHAT IT'S LIKE TO BE A PARENT.

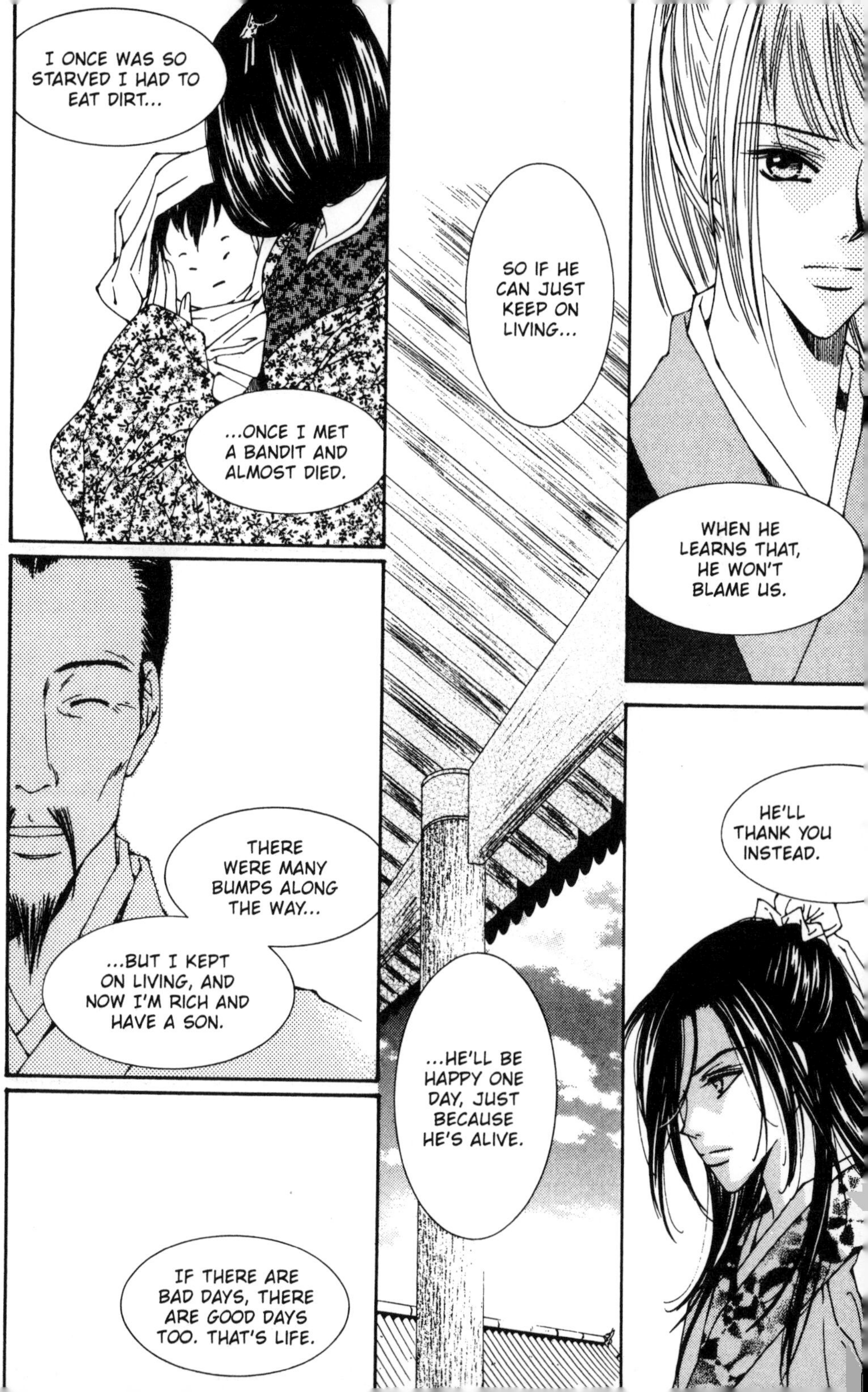
I ONCE WAS SO STARVED I HAD TO EAT DIRT...
...ONCE I MET A BANDIT AND ALMOST DIED.
THERE WERE MANY BUMPS ALONG THE WAY...
...BUT I KEPT ON LIVING, AND NOW I'M RICH AND HAVE A SON.
IF THERE ARE BAD DAYS, THERE ARE GOOD DAYS TOO. THAT'S LIFE.
SO IF HE CAN JUST KEEP ON LIVING...
...HE'LL BE HAPPY ONE DAY, JUST BECAUSE HE'S ALIVE.
WHEN HE LEARNS THAT, HE WON'T BLAME US.
HE'LL THANK YOU INSTEAD.

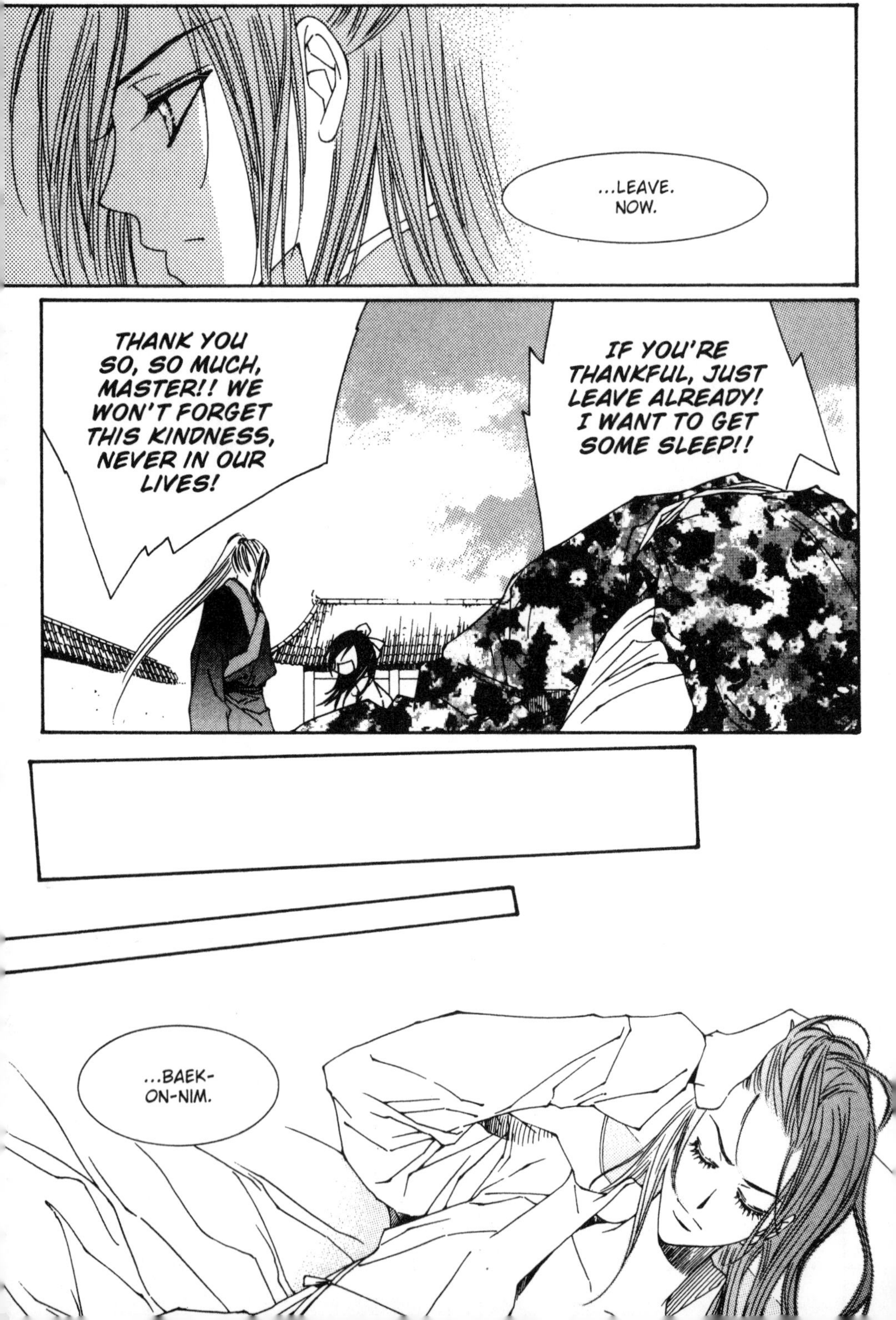
...LEAVE. NOW.
THANK YOU SO, SO MUCH, MASTER!! WE WON'T FORGET THIS KINDNESS, NEVER IN OUR LIVES!
IF YOU'RE THANKFUL, JUST LEAVE ALREADY! I WANT TO GET SOME SLEEP!!
...BAEK-ON-NIM.

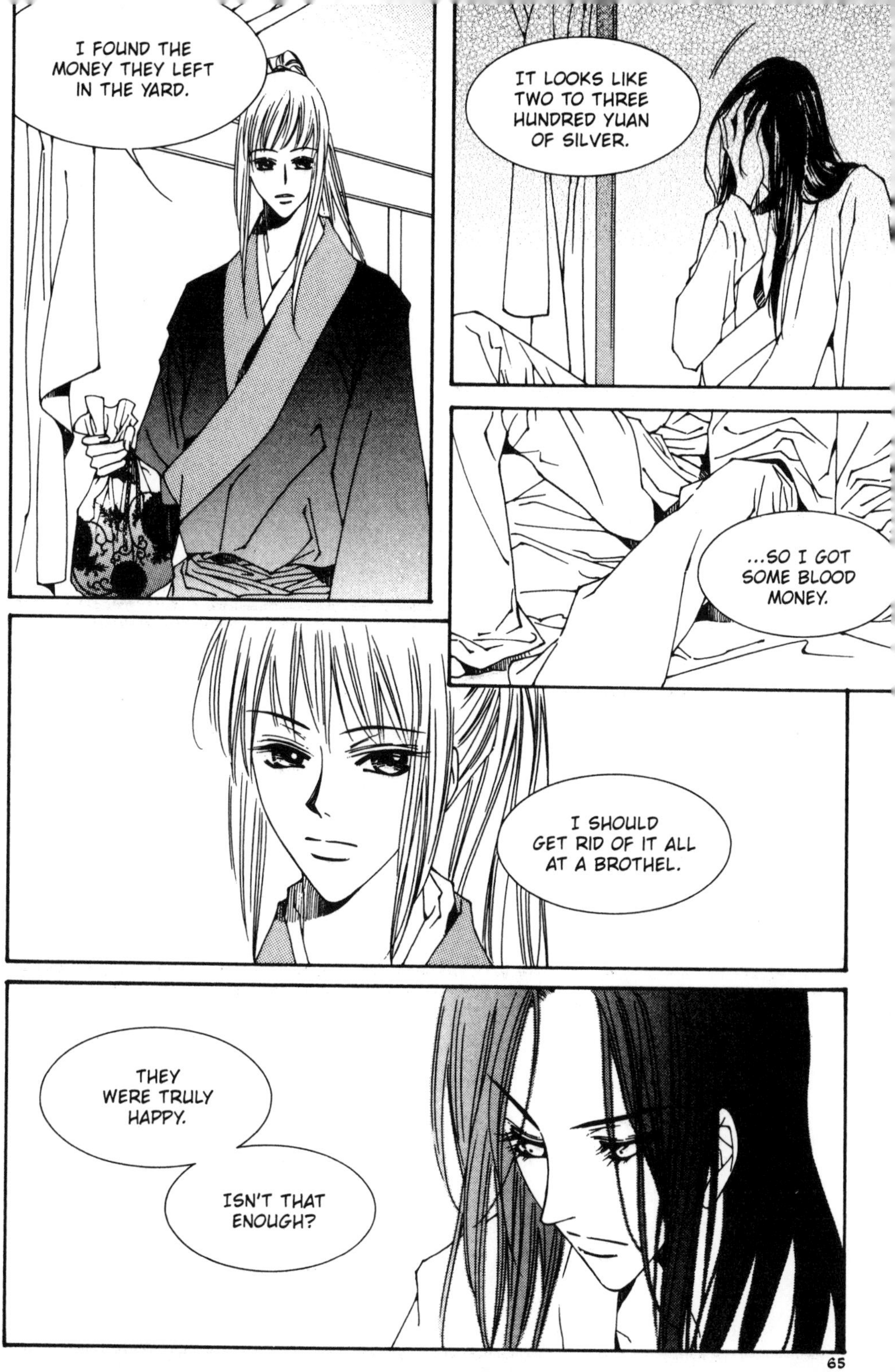
I FOUND THE MONEY THEY LEFT IN THE YARD.
IT LOOKS LIKE TWO TO THREE HUNDRED YUAN OF SILVER.
...SO I GOT SOME BLOOD MONEY.
I SHOULD GET RID OF IT ALL AT A BROTHEL.
THEY WERE TRULY HAPPY.
ISN'T THAT ENOUGH?

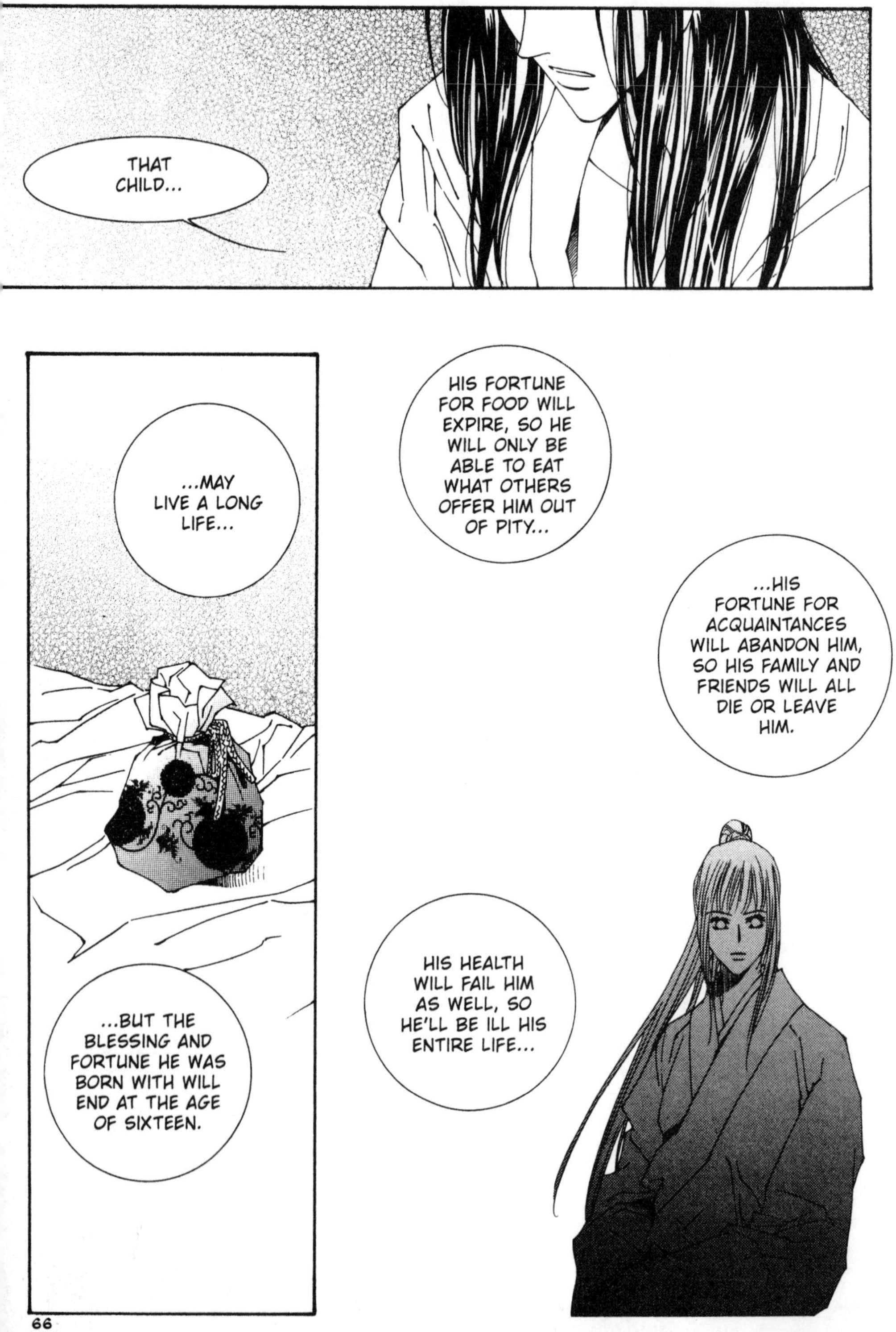
THAT CHILD...
...MAY LIVE A LONG LIFE...
...BUT THE BLESSING AND FORTUNE HE WAS BORN WITH WILL END AT THE AGE OF SIXTEEN.
HIS FORTUNE FOR FOOD WILL EXPIRE, SO HE WILL ONLY BE ABLE TO EAT WHAT OTHERS OFFER HIM OUT OF PITY...
...HIS FORTUNE FOR ACQUAINTANCES WILL ABANDON HIM, SO HIS FAMILY AND FRIENDS WILL ALL DIE OR LEAVE HIM.
HIS HEALTH WILL FAIL HIM AS WELL, SO HE'LL BE ILL HIS ENTIRE LIFE...

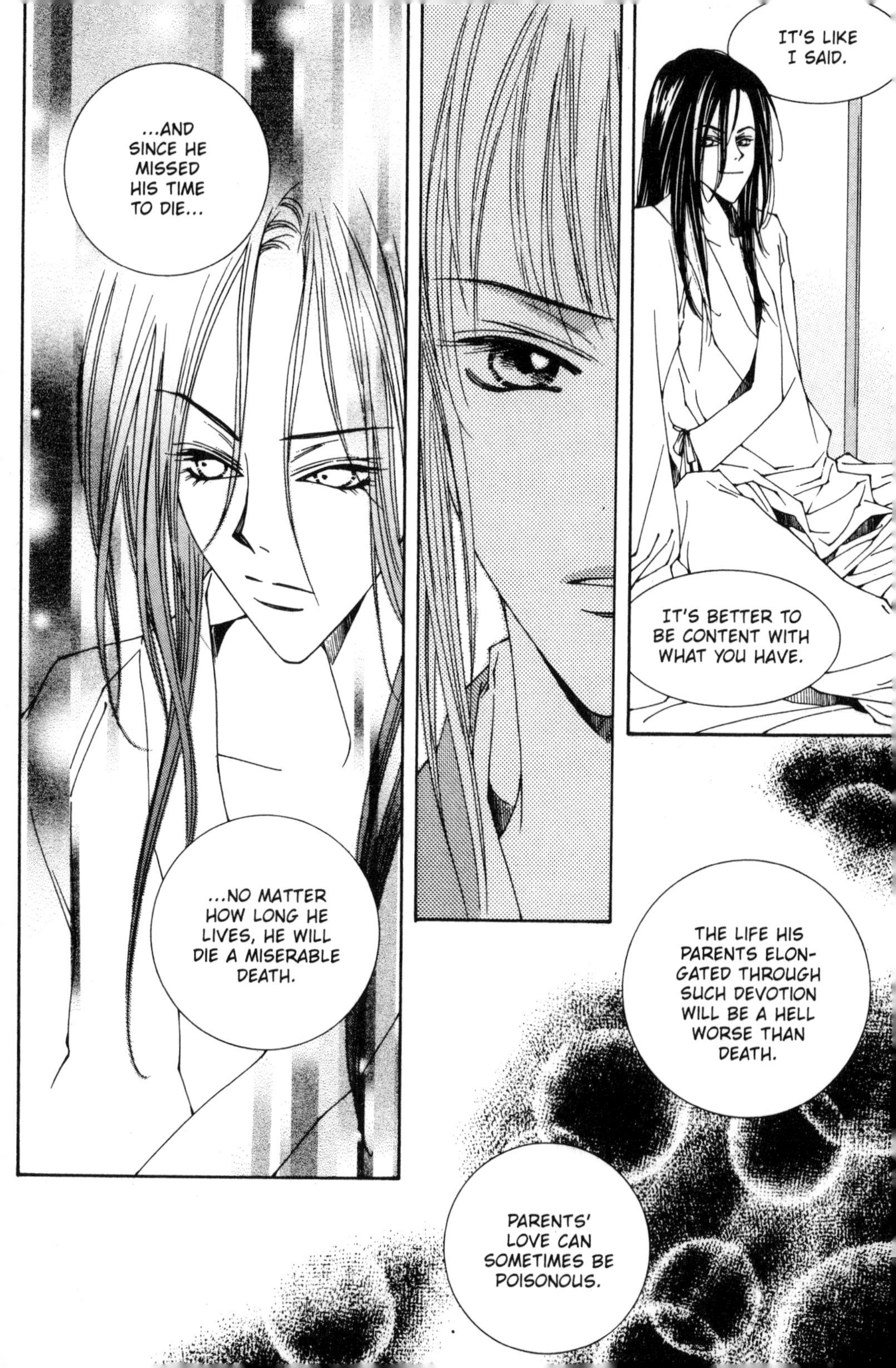
...AND SINCE HE MISSED HIS TIME TO DIE...
...NO MATTER HOW LONG HE LIVES, HE WILL DIE A MISERABLE DEATH.
IT'S LIKE I SAID.
IT'S BETTER TO BE CONTENT WITH WHAT YOU HAVE.
THE LIFE HIS PARENTS ELON-GATED THROUGH SUCH DEVOTION WILL BE A HELL WORSE THAN DEATH.
PARENTS' LOVE CAN SOMETIMES BE POISONOUS.

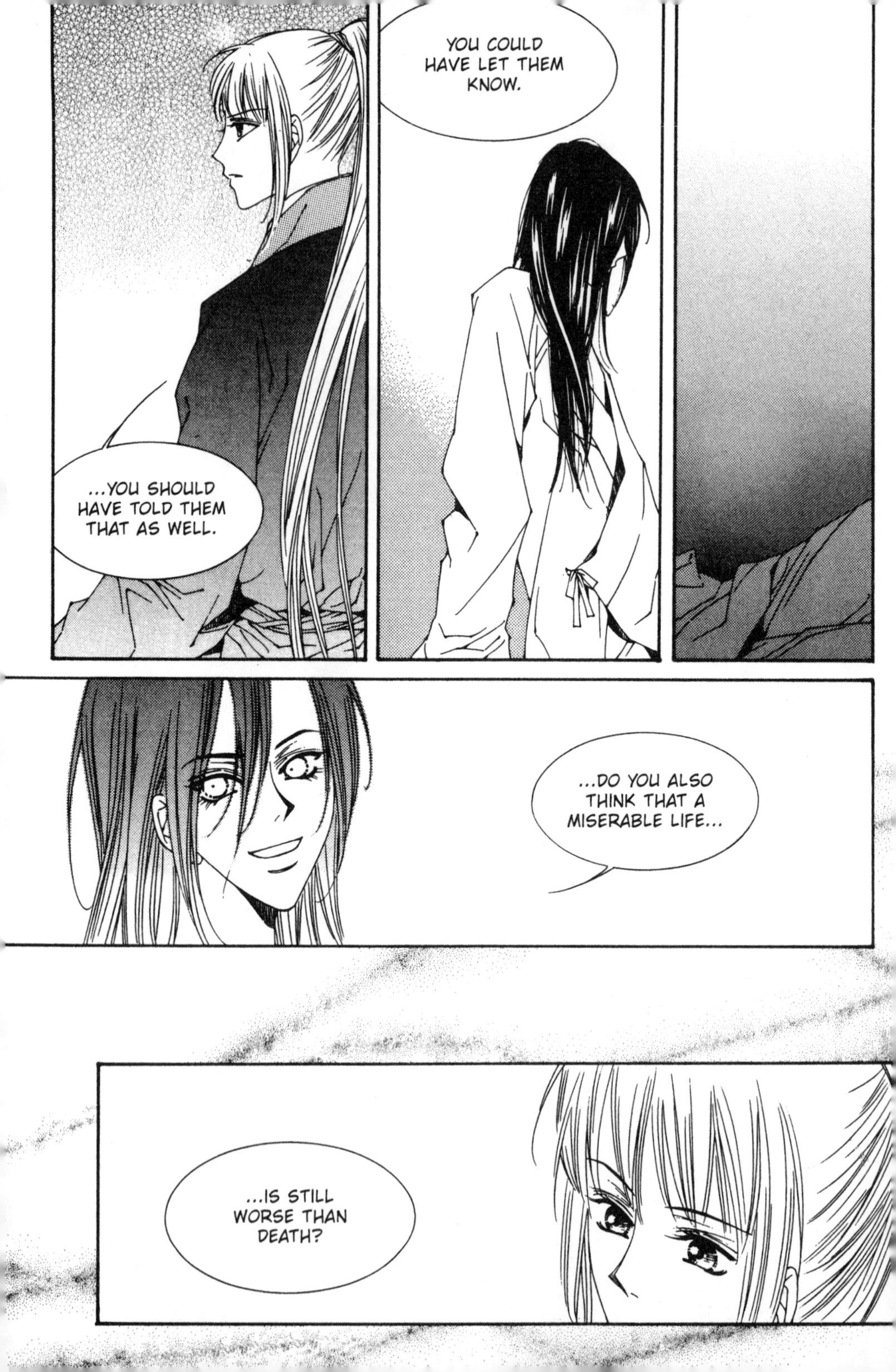
...YOU SHOULD HAVE TOLD THEM THAT AS WELL.
YOU COULD HAVE LET THEM KNOW.
...DO YOU ALSO THINK THAT A MISERABLE LIFE...
...IS STILL WORSE THAN DEATH?

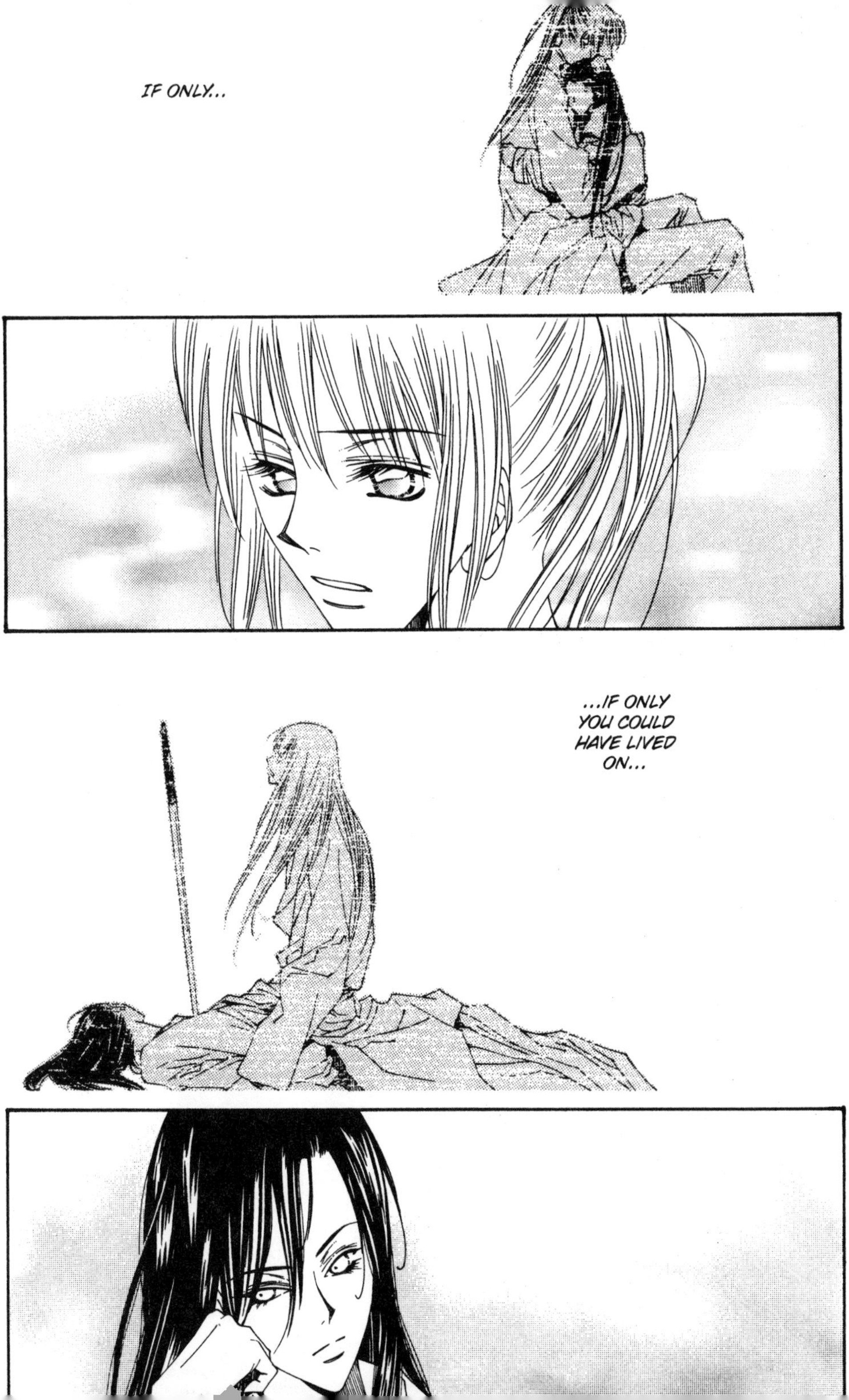
IF ONLY...
...IF ONLY YOU COULD HAVE LIVED ON...

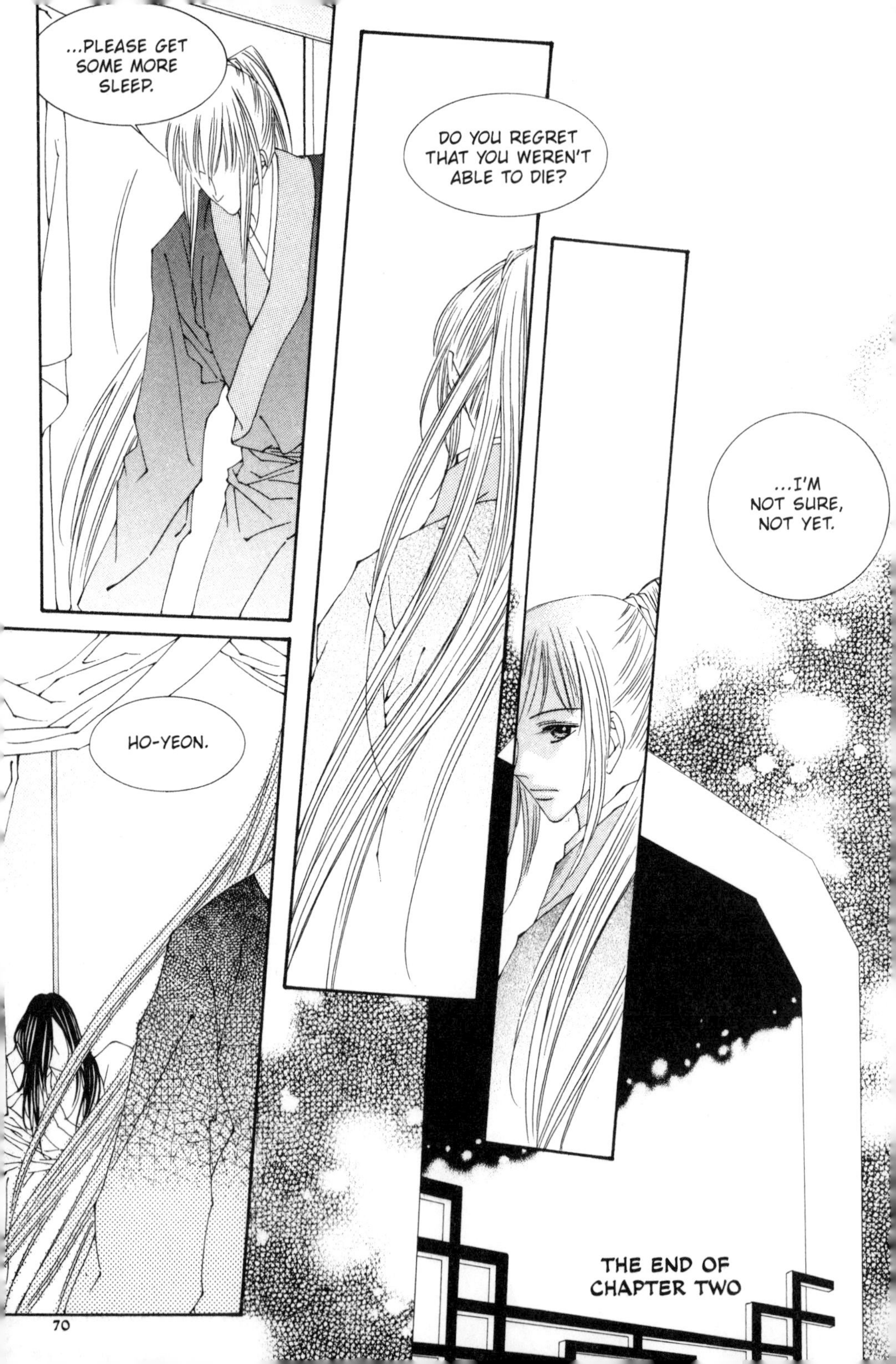
...PLEASE GET SOME MORE SLEEP.
HO-YEON.
DO YOU REGRET THAT YOU WEREN'T ABLE TO DIE?
...I'M NOT SURE, NOT YET.
THE END OF CHAPTER TWO

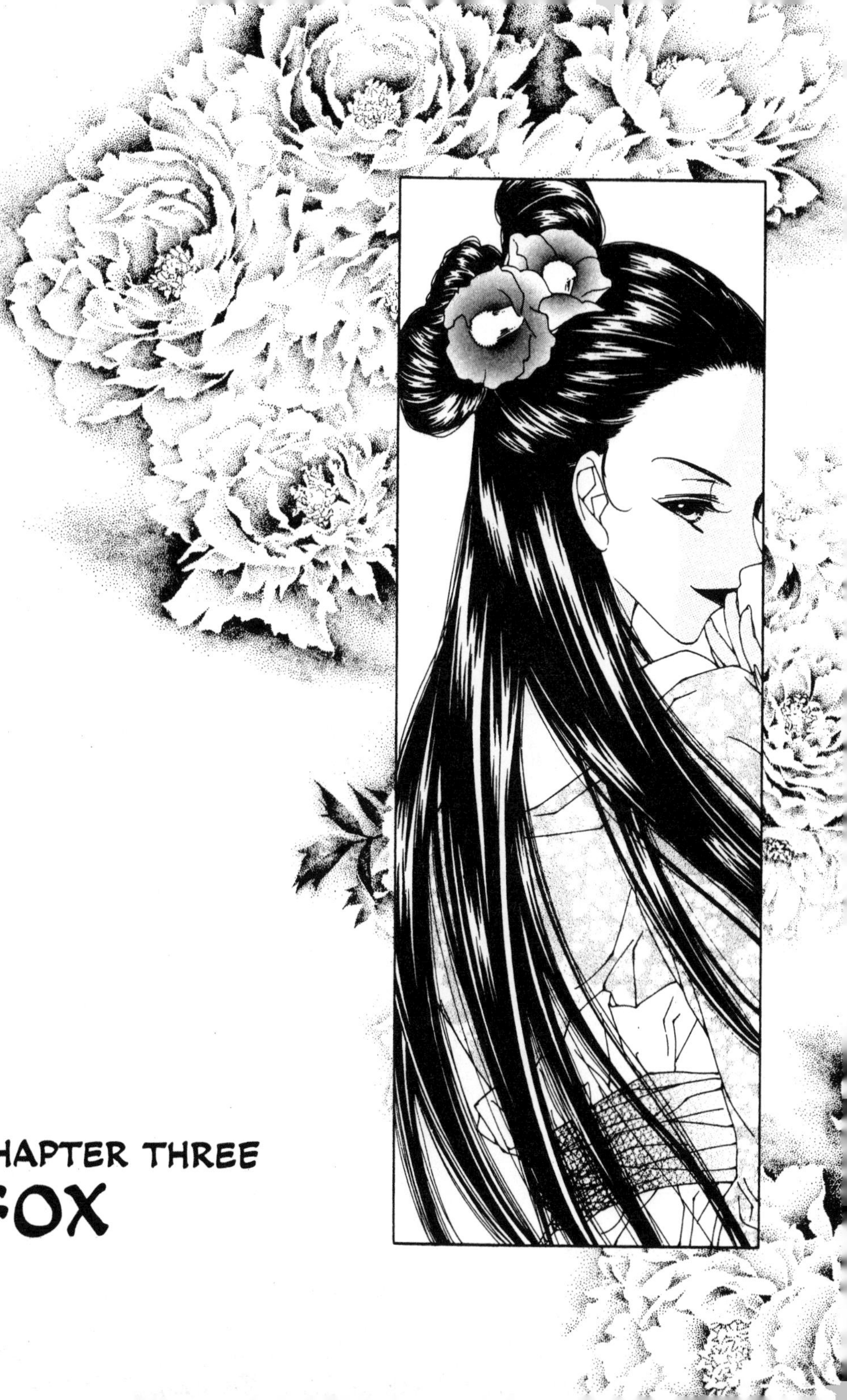

CHAPTER THREE
FOX

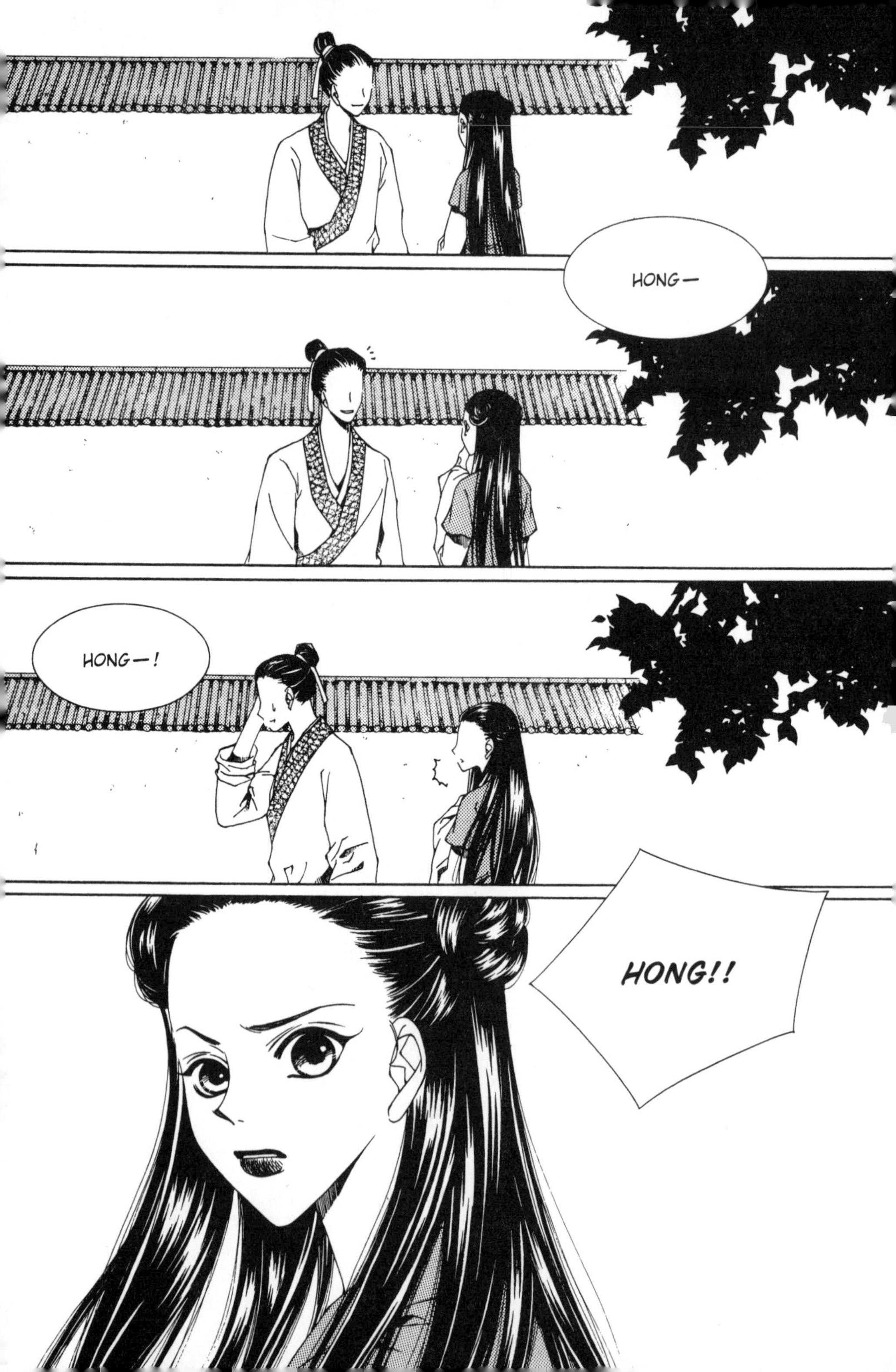
HONG—
HONG—!
HONG!!

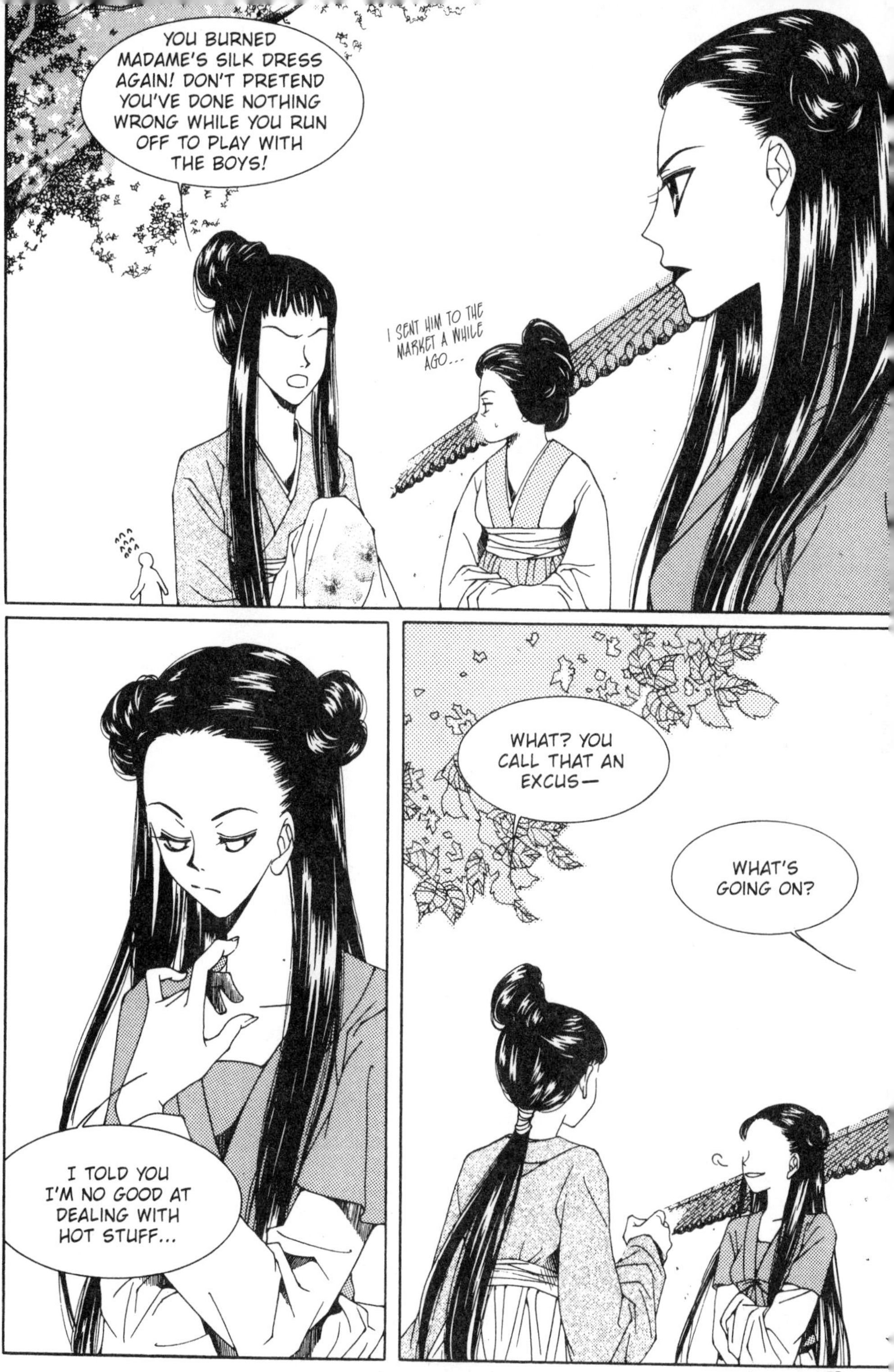
YOU BURNED MADAME'S SILK DRESS AGAIN! DON'T PRETEND YOU'VE DONE NOTHING WRONG WHILE YOU RUN OFF TO PLAY WITH THE BOYS!
I SENT HIM TO THE MARKET A WHILE AGO...
I TOLD YOU I'M NO GOOD AT DEALING WITH HOT STUFF...
WHAT? YOU CALL THAT AN EXCUS—
WHAT'S GOING ON?

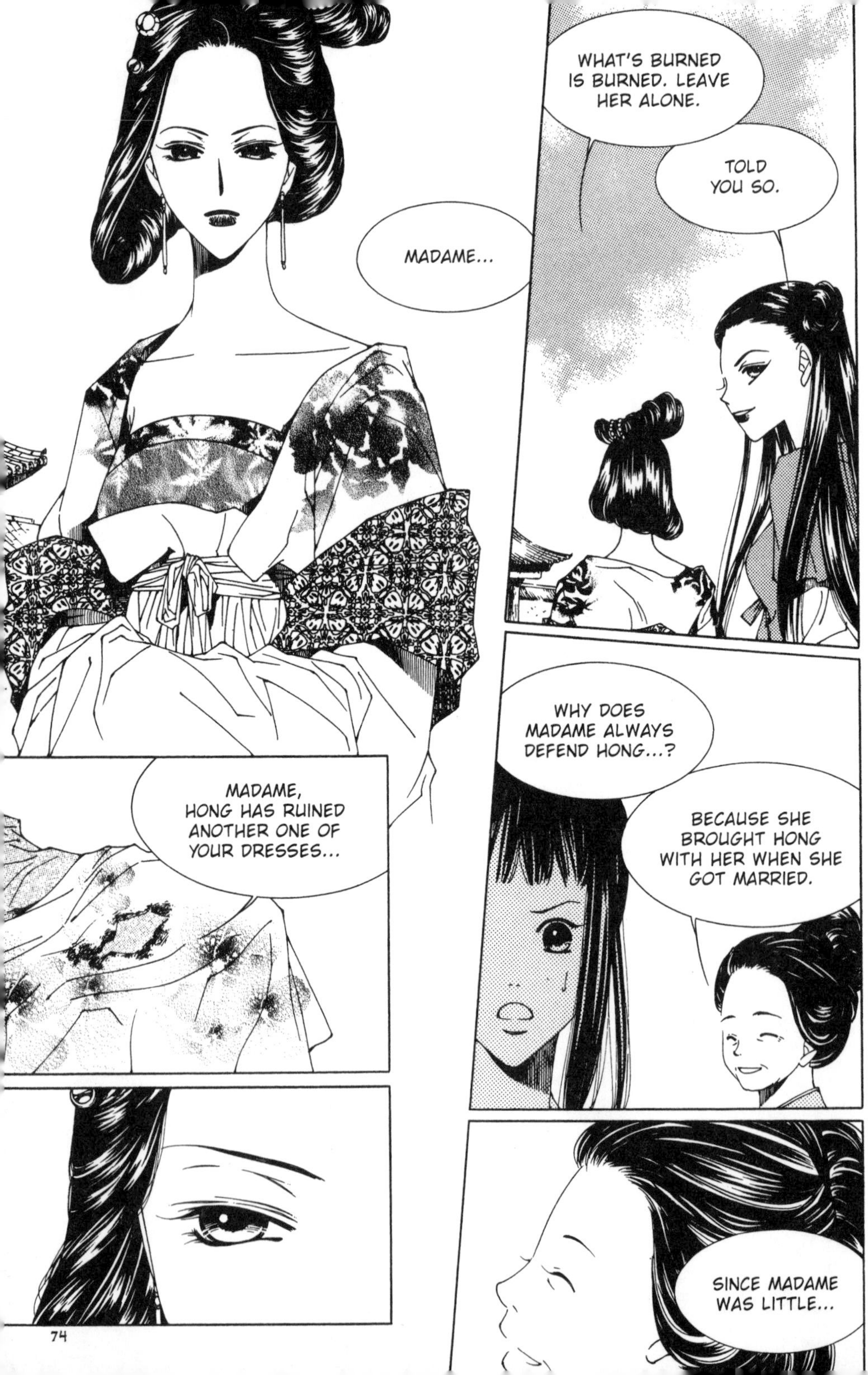
MADAME...
MADAME, HONG HAS RUINED ANOTHER ONE OF YOUR DRESSES...
WHAT'S BURNED IS BURNED. LEAVE HER ALONE.
TOLD YOU SO.
WHY DOES MADAME ALWAYS DEFEND HONG...?
BECAUSE SHE BROUGHT HONG WITH HER WHEN SHE GOT MARRIED.
SINCE MADAME WAS LITTLE...

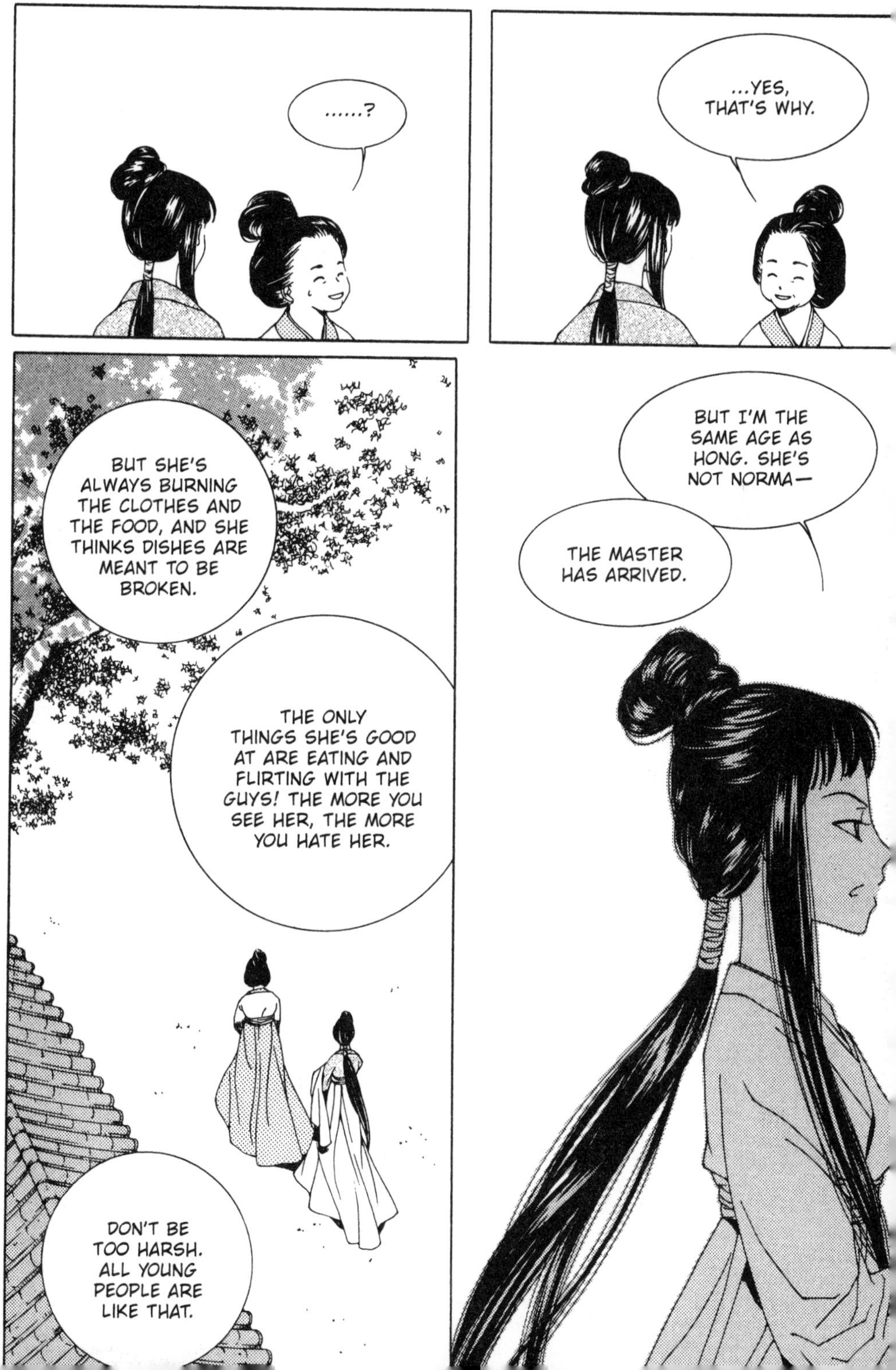
......?
...YES, THAT'S WHY.
BUT SHE'S ALWAYS BURNING THE CLOTHES AND THE FOOD, AND SHE THINKS DISHES ARE MEANT TO BE BROKEN.
THE ONLY THINGS SHE'S GOOD AT ARE EATING AND FLIRTING WITH THE GUYS! THE MORE YOU SEE HER, THE MORE YOU HATE HER.
DON'T BE TOO HARSH. ALL YOUNG PEOPLE ARE LIKE THAT.
BUT I'M THE SAME AGE AS HONG. SHE'S NOT NORMA—
THE MASTER HAS ARRIVED.

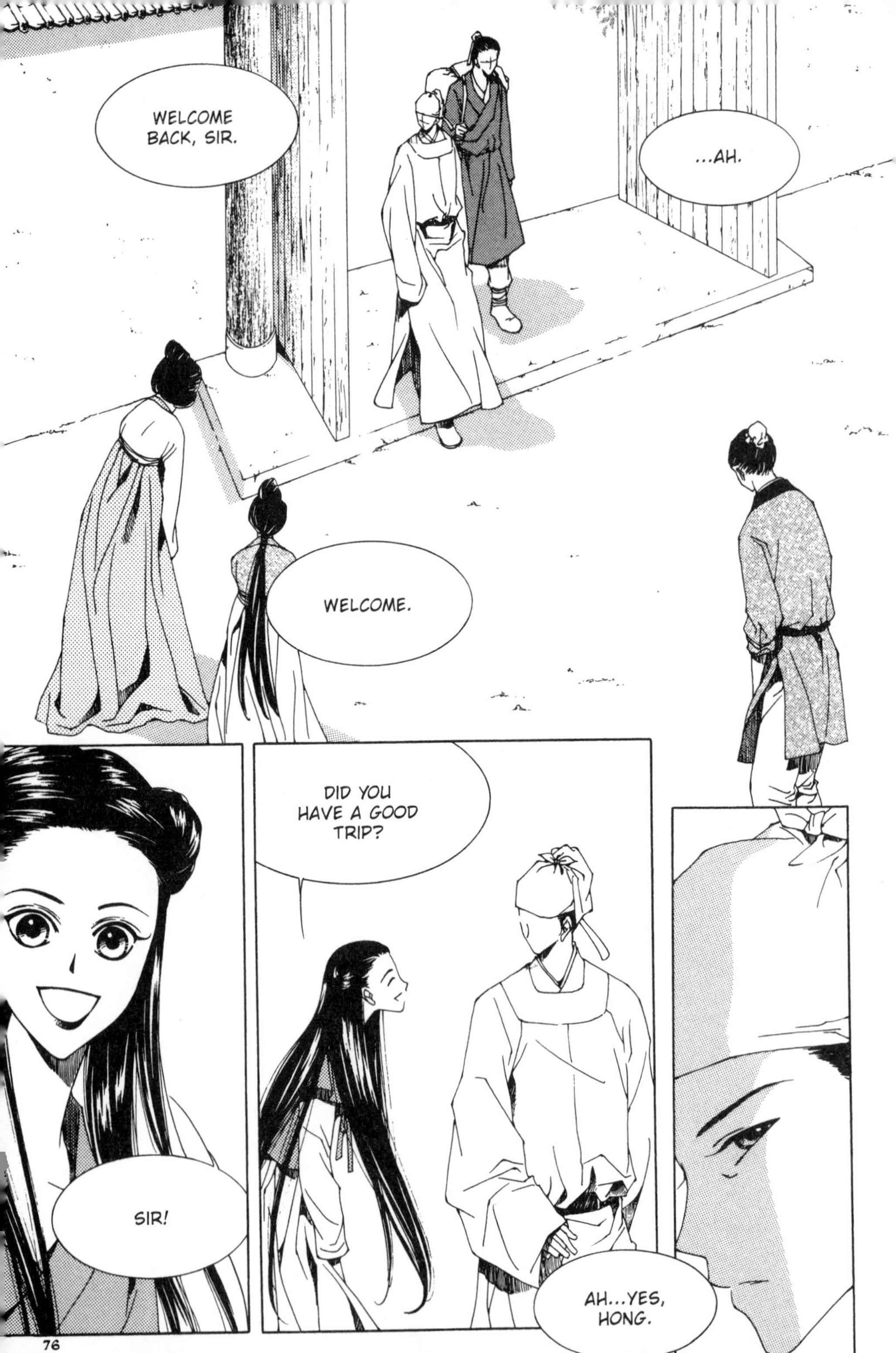
WELCOME BACK, SIR.
...AH.
WELCOME.
SIR!
DID YOU HAVE A GOOD TRIP?
AH...YES, HONG.

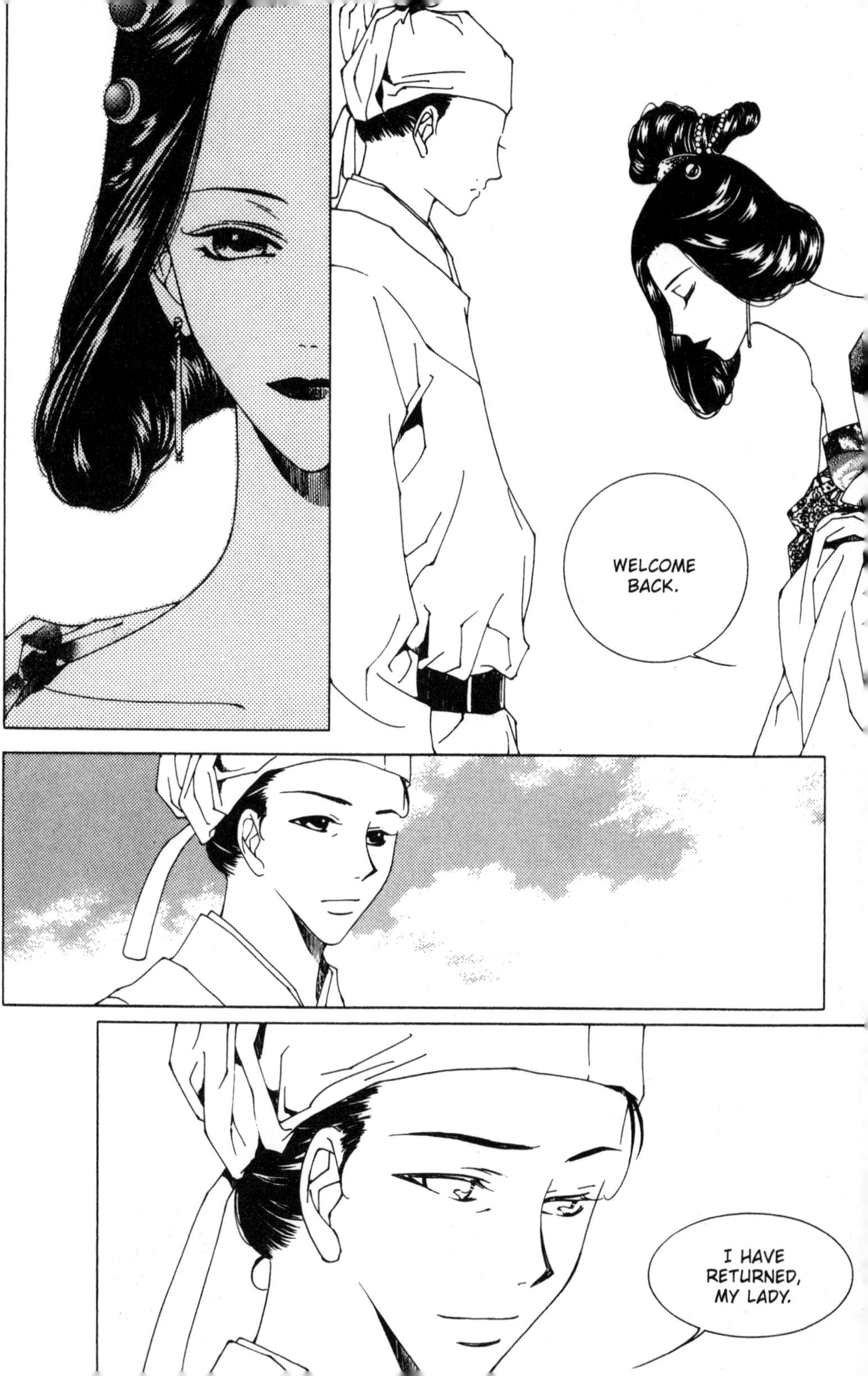
WELCOME BACK.
I HAVE RETURNED, MY LADY.

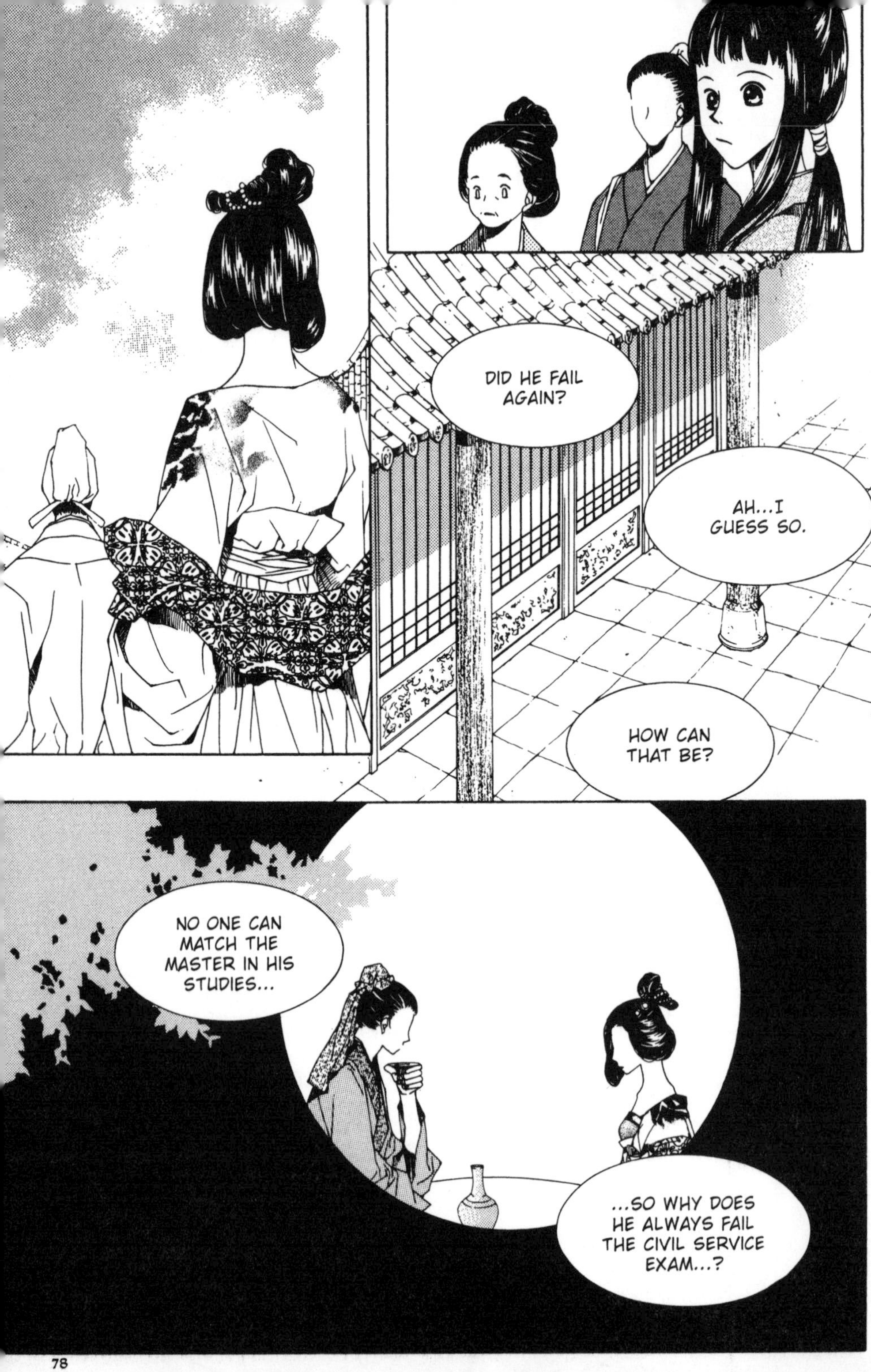
DID HE FAIL AGAIN?
AH...I GUESS SO.
HOW CAN THAT BE?
NO ONE CAN MATCH THE MASTER IN HIS STUDIES...
...SO WHY DOES HE ALWAYS FAIL THE CIVIL SERVICE EXAM...?

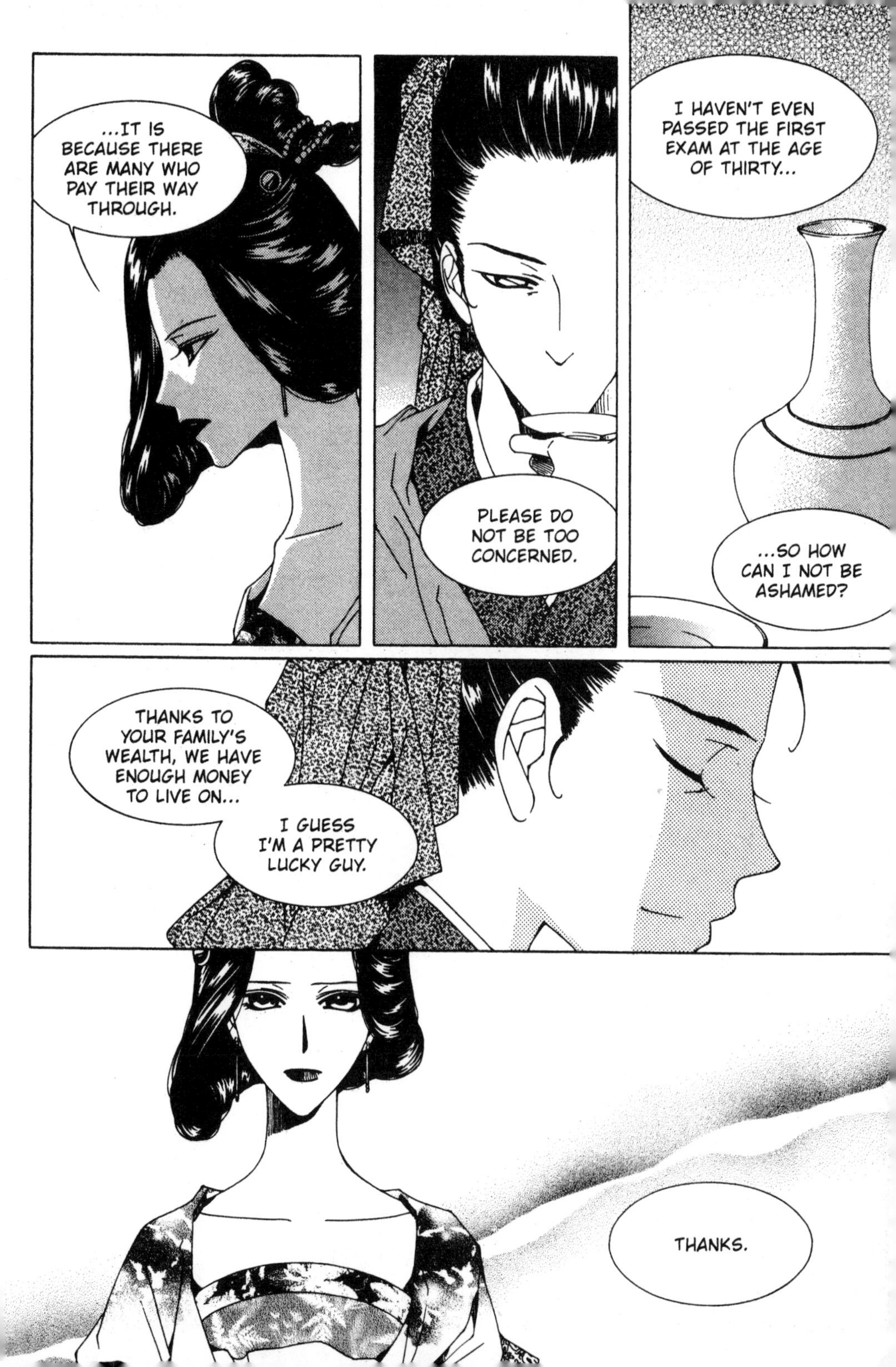
...IT IS BECAUSE THERE ARE MANY WHO PAY THEIR WAY THROUGH.
PLEASE DO NOT BE TOO CONCERNED.
I HAVEN'T EVEN PASSED THE FIRST EXAM AT THE AGE OF THIRTY...
...SO HOW CAN I NOT BE ASHAMED?
THANKS TO YOUR FAMILY'S WEALTH, WE HAVE ENOUGH MONEY TO LIVE ON...
I GUESS I'M A PRETTY LUCKY GUY.
THANKS.

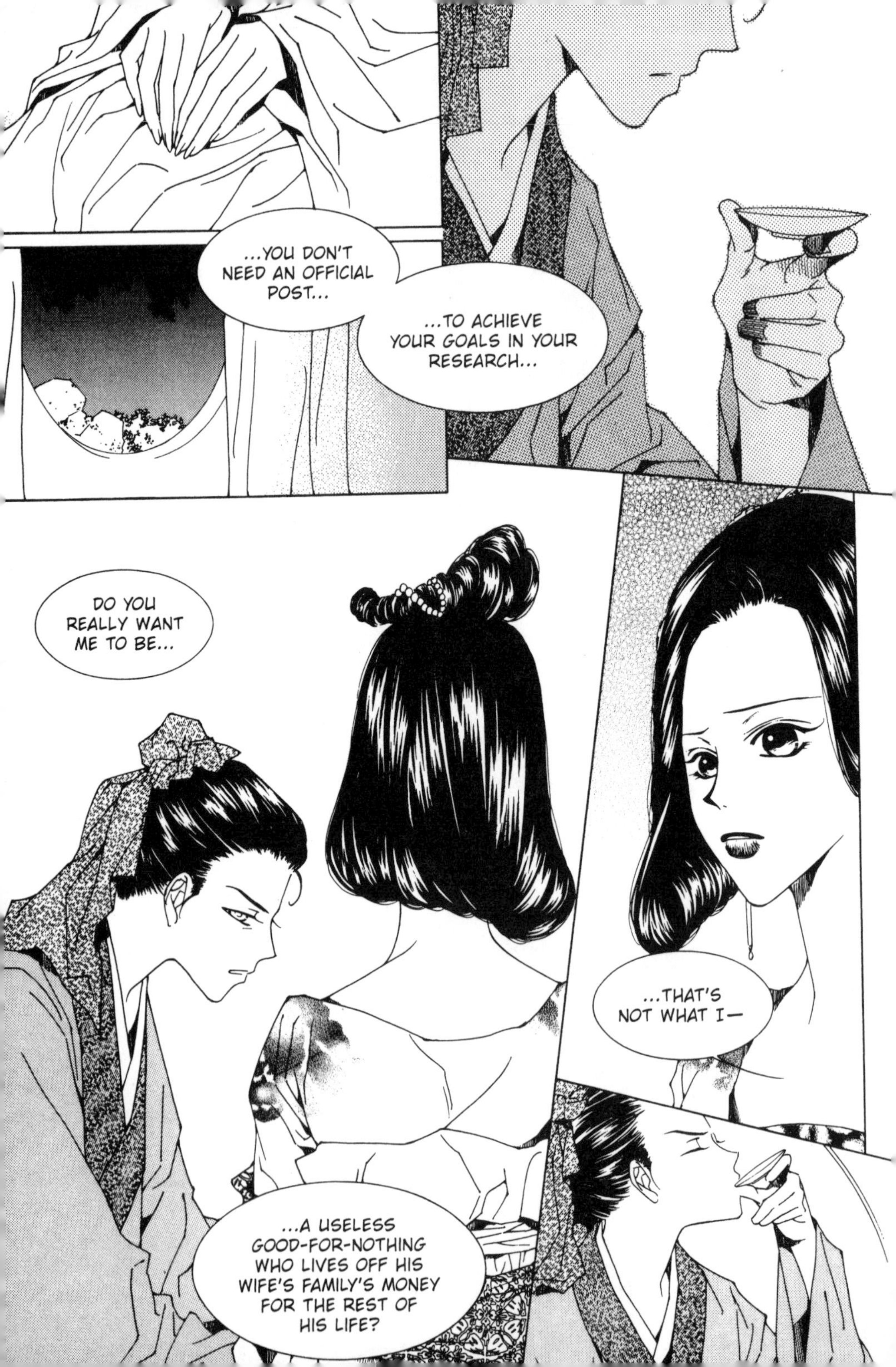
...YOU DON'T NEED AN OFFICIAL POST...
...TO ACHIEVE YOUR GOALS IN YOUR RESEARCH...
DO YOU REALLY WANT ME TO BE...
...A USELESS GOOD-FOR-NOTHING WHO LIVES OFF HIS WIFE'S FAMILY'S MONEY FOR THE REST OF HIS LIFE?
...THAT'S NOT WHAT I—

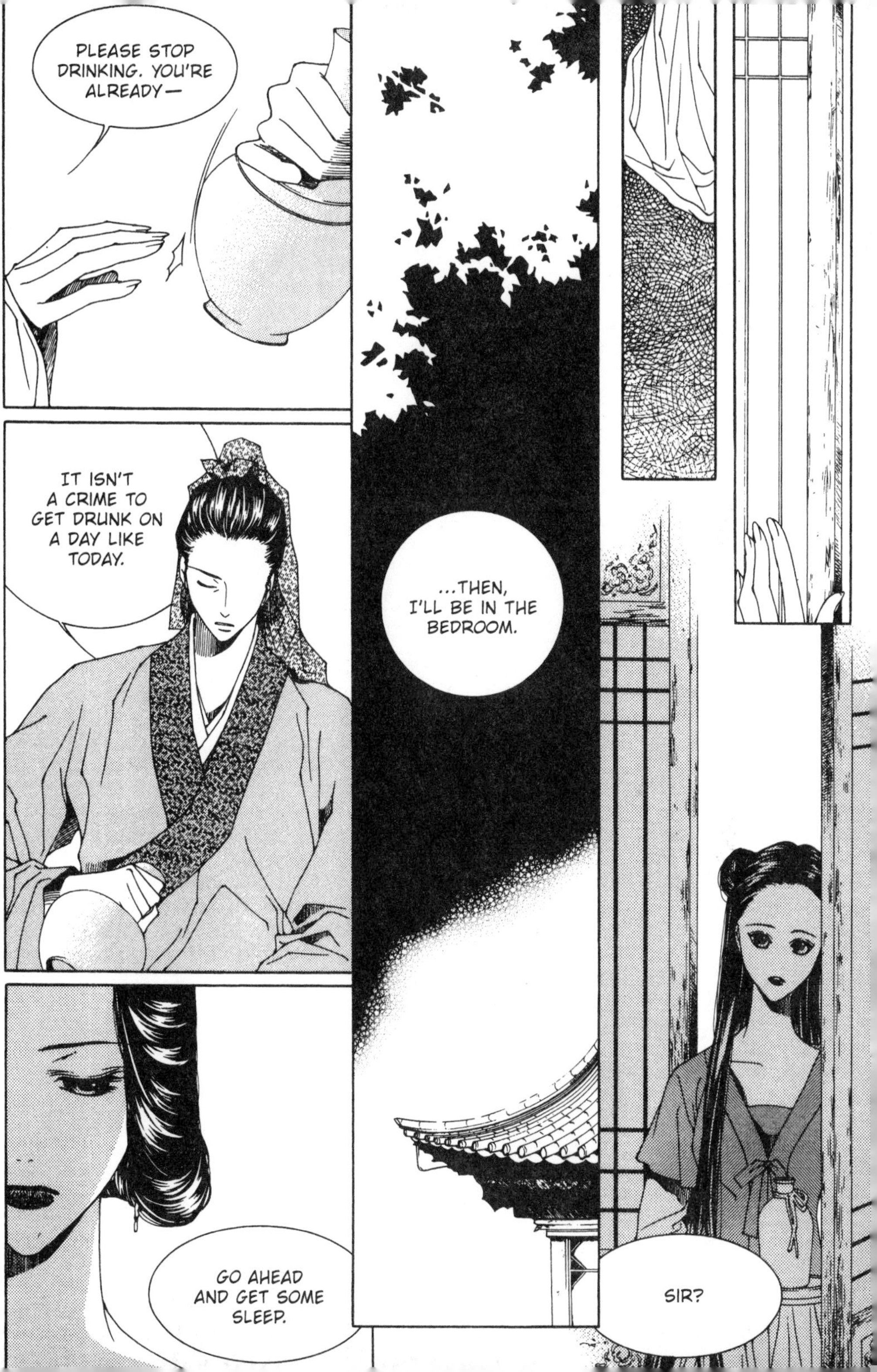
PLEASE STOP DRINKING. YOU'RE ALREADY—
IT ISN'T A CRIME TO GET DRUNK ON A DAY LIKE TODAY.
GO AHEAD AND GET SOME SLEEP.
...THEN, I'LL BE IN THE BEDROOM.
SIR?

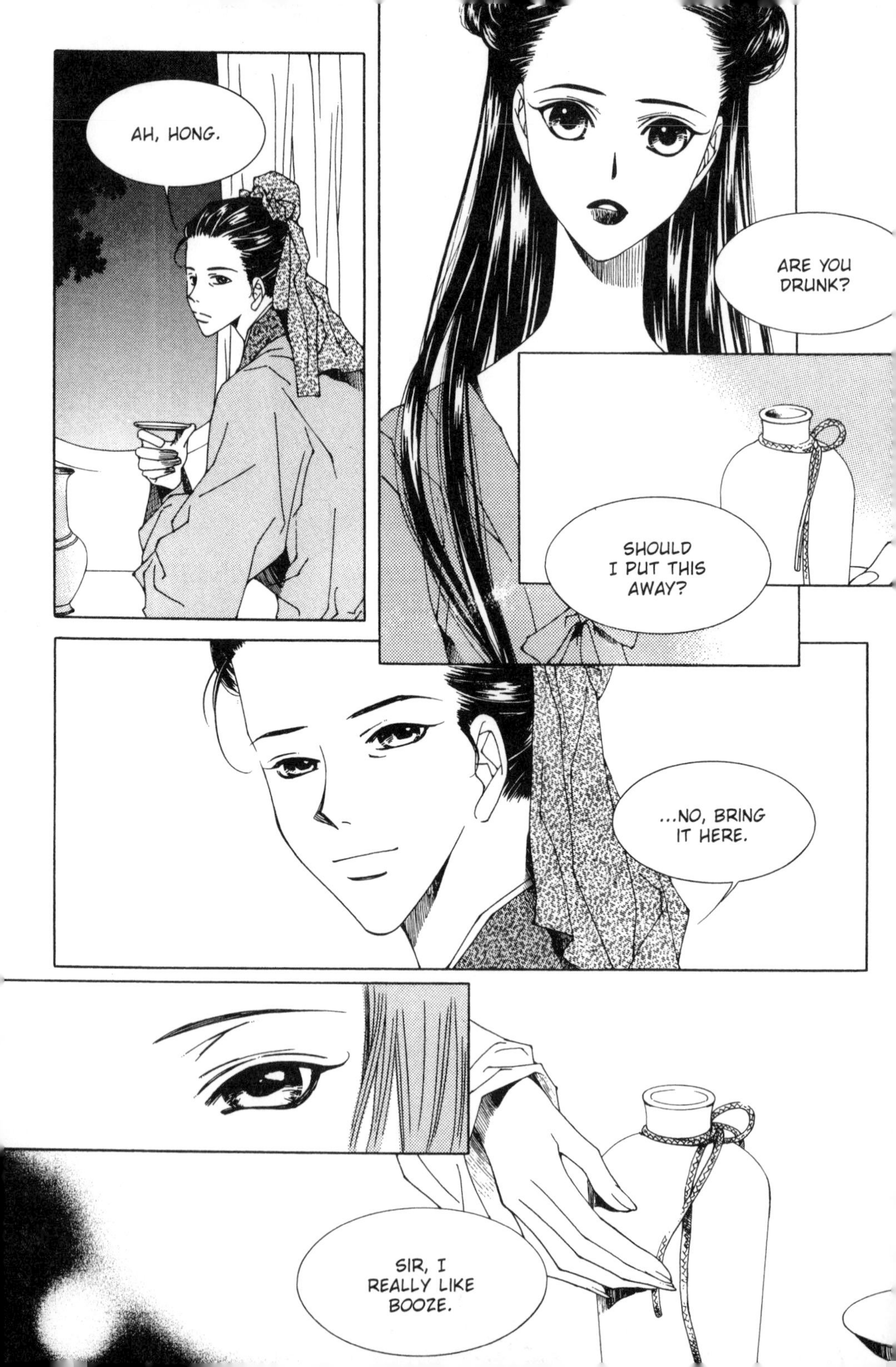
AH, HONG.
ARE YOU DRUNK?
SHOULD I PUT THIS AWAY?
...NO, BRING IT HERE.
SIR, I REALLY LIKE BOOZE.

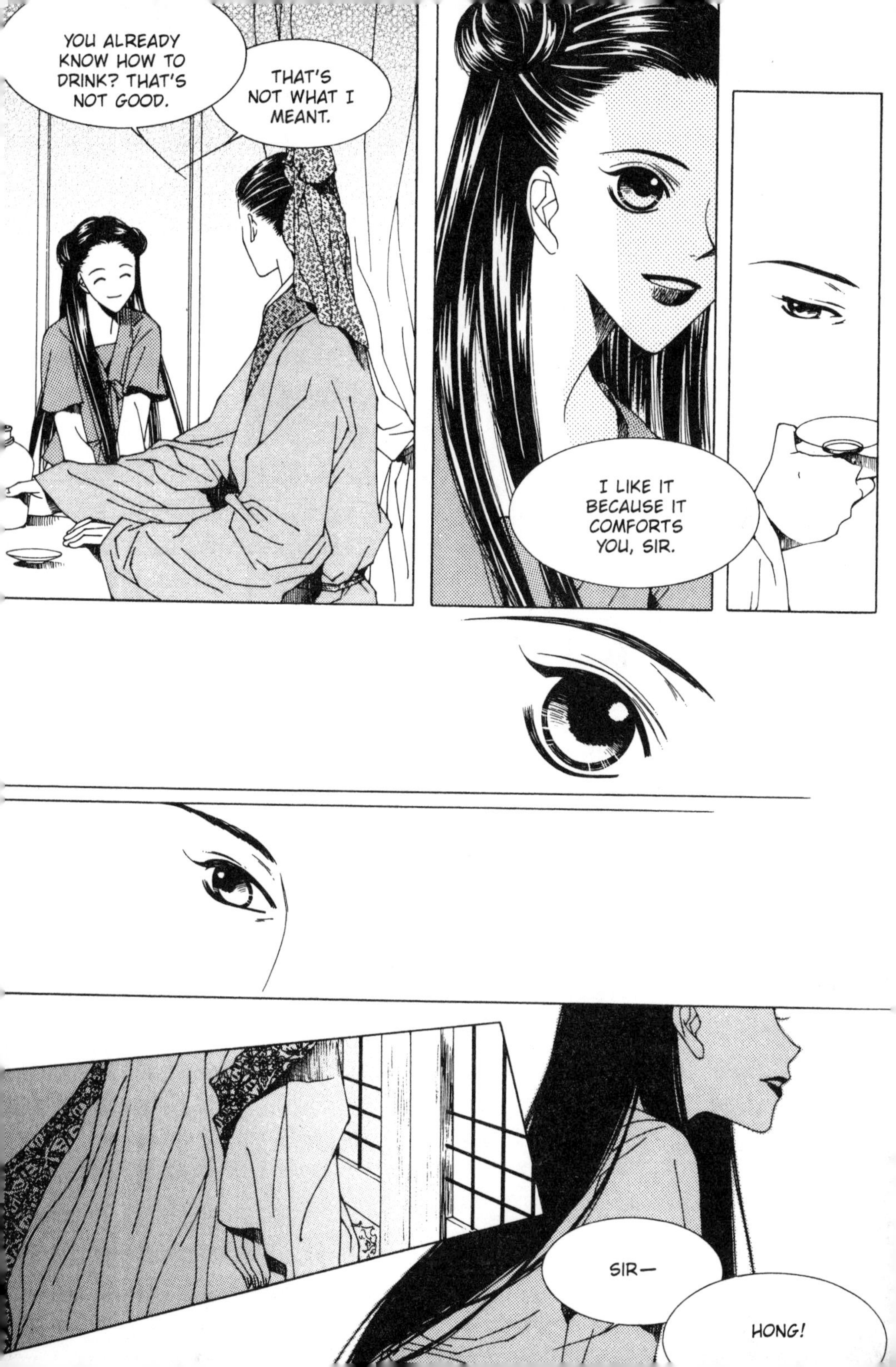
YOU ALREADY KNOW HOW TO DRINK? THAT'S NOT GOOD.
THAT'S NOT WHAT I MEANT.
I LIKE IT BECAUSE IT COMFORTS YOU, SIR.
SIR—
HONG!

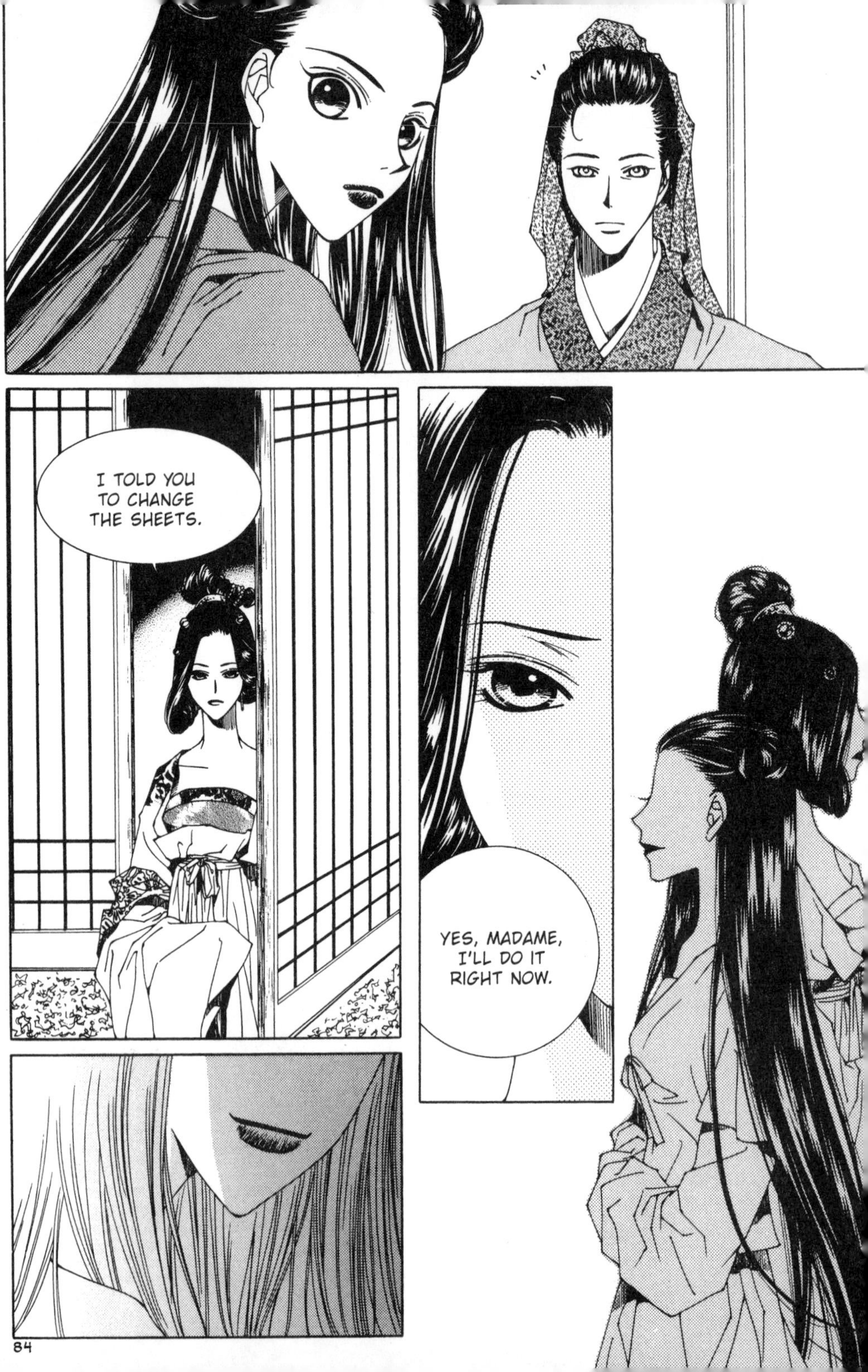
I TOLD YOU TO CHANGE THE SHEETS.
YES, MADAME, I'LL DO IT RIGHT NOW.

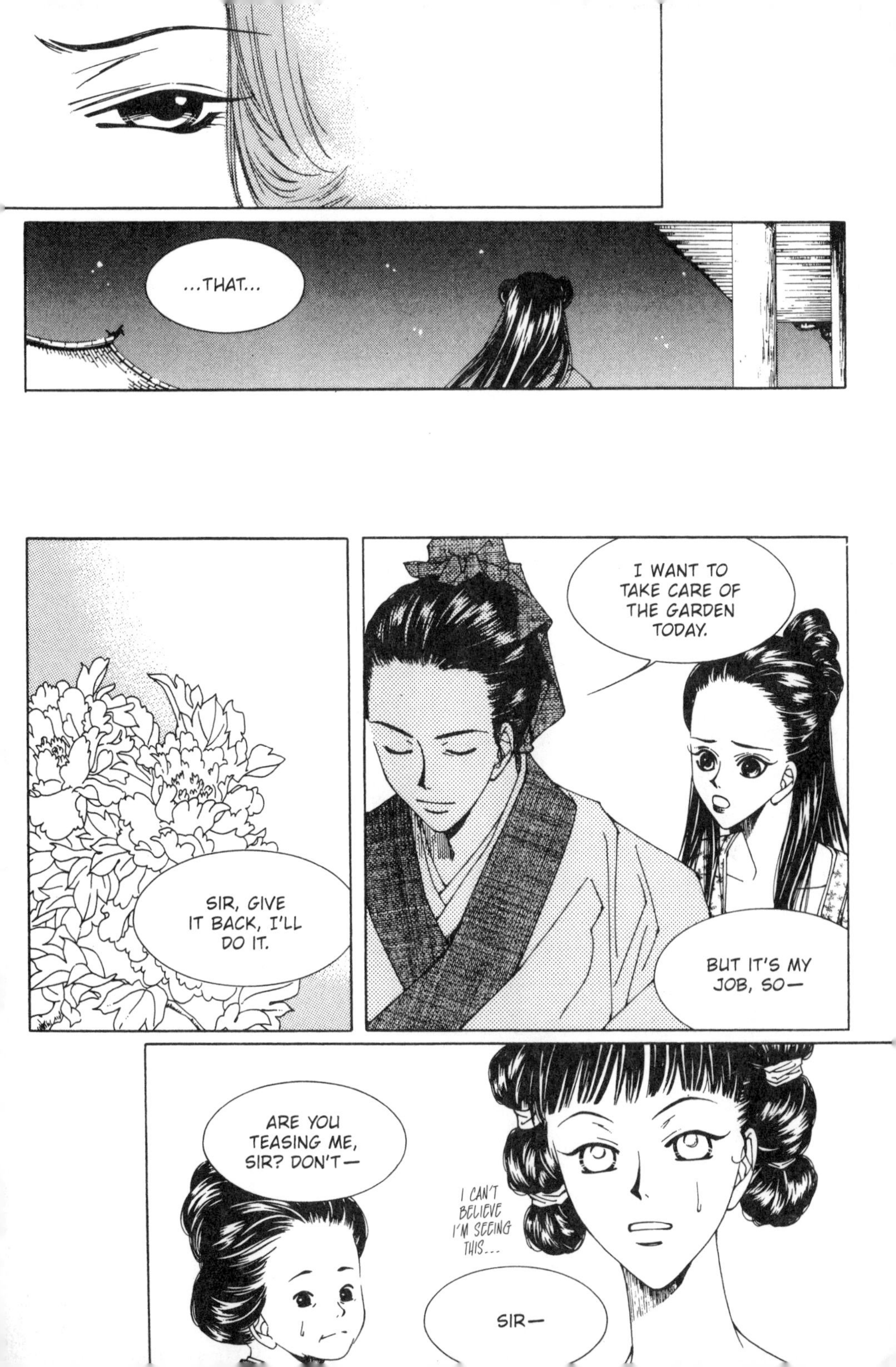
...THAT...
SIR, GIVE IT BACK, I'LL DO IT.
I WANT TO TAKE CARE OF THE GARDEN TODAY.
BUT IT'S MY JOB, SO—
ARE YOU TEASING ME, SIR? DON'T—
I CAN'T BELIEVE I'M SEEING THIS...
SIR—

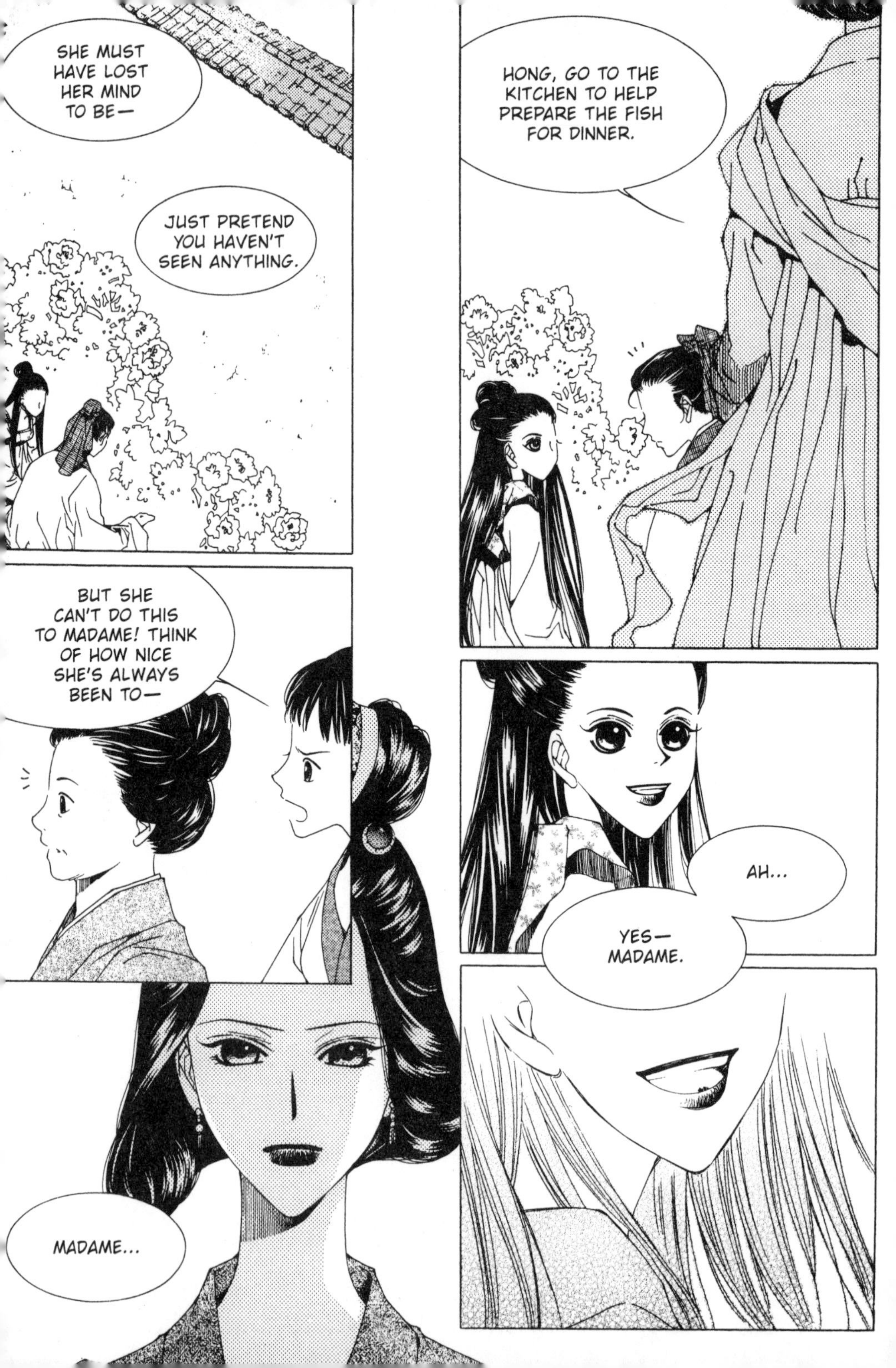

SHE MUST HAVE LOST HER MIND TO BE—
JUST PRETEND YOU HAVEN'T SEEN ANYTHING.
BUT SHE CAN'T DO THIS TO MADAME! THINK OF HOW NICE SHE'S ALWAYS BEEN TO—
MADAME...
HONG, GO TO THE KITCHEN TO HELP PREPARE THE FISH FOR DINNER.
AH...
YES— MADAME.

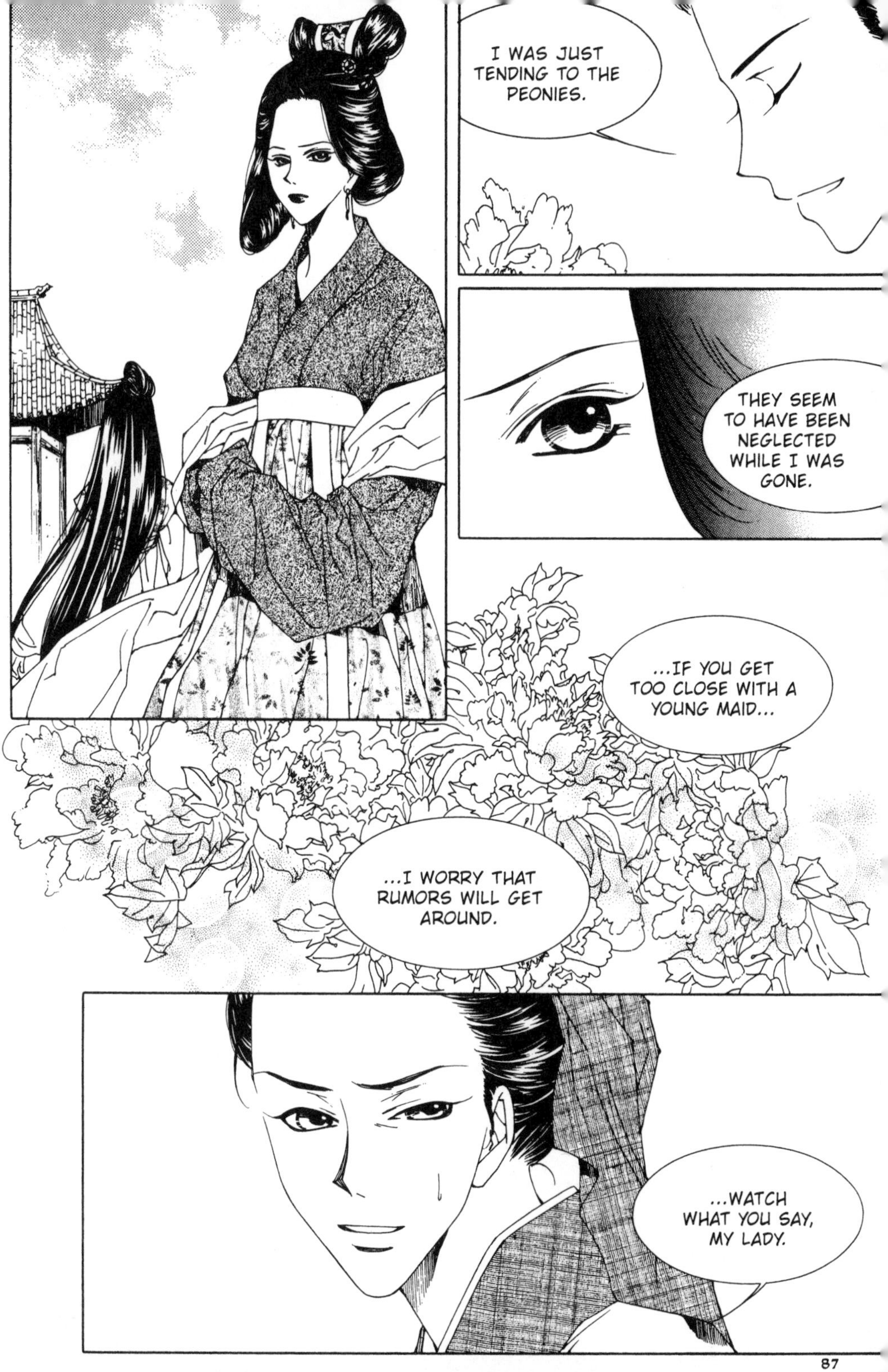
I WAS JUST TENDING TO THE PEONIES.
THEY SEEM TO HAVE BEEN NEGLECTED WHILE I WAS GONE.
...IF YOU GET TOO CLOSE WITH A YOUNG MAID...
...I WORRY THAT RUMORS WILL GET AROUND.
...WATCH WHAT YOU SAY, MY LADY.

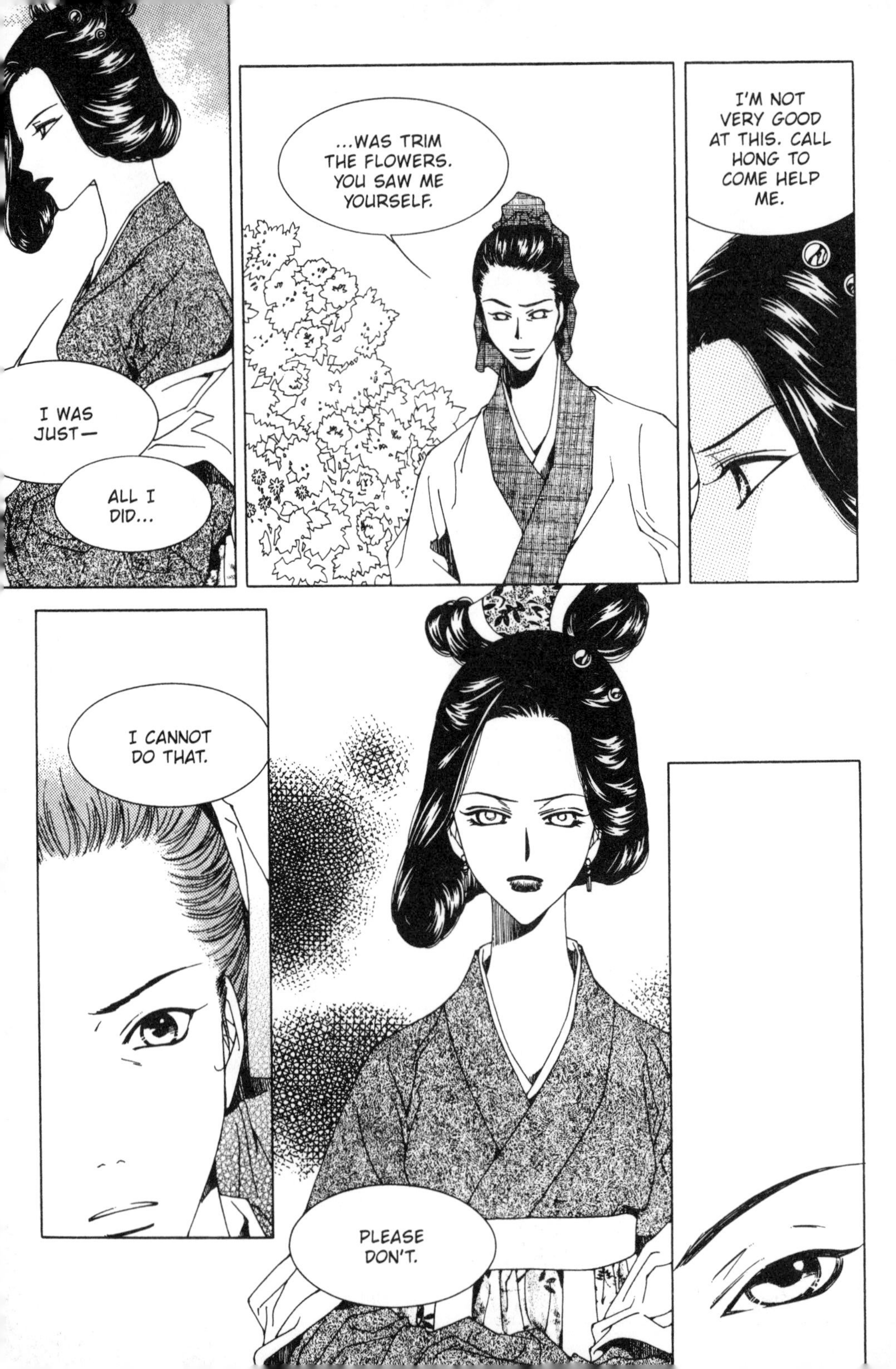
I WAS JUST—
ALL I DID...
...WAS TRIM THE FLOWERS. YOU SAW ME YOURSELF.
I'M NOT VERY GOOD AT THIS. CALL HONG TO COME HELP ME.
I CANNOT DO THAT.
PLEASE DON'T.

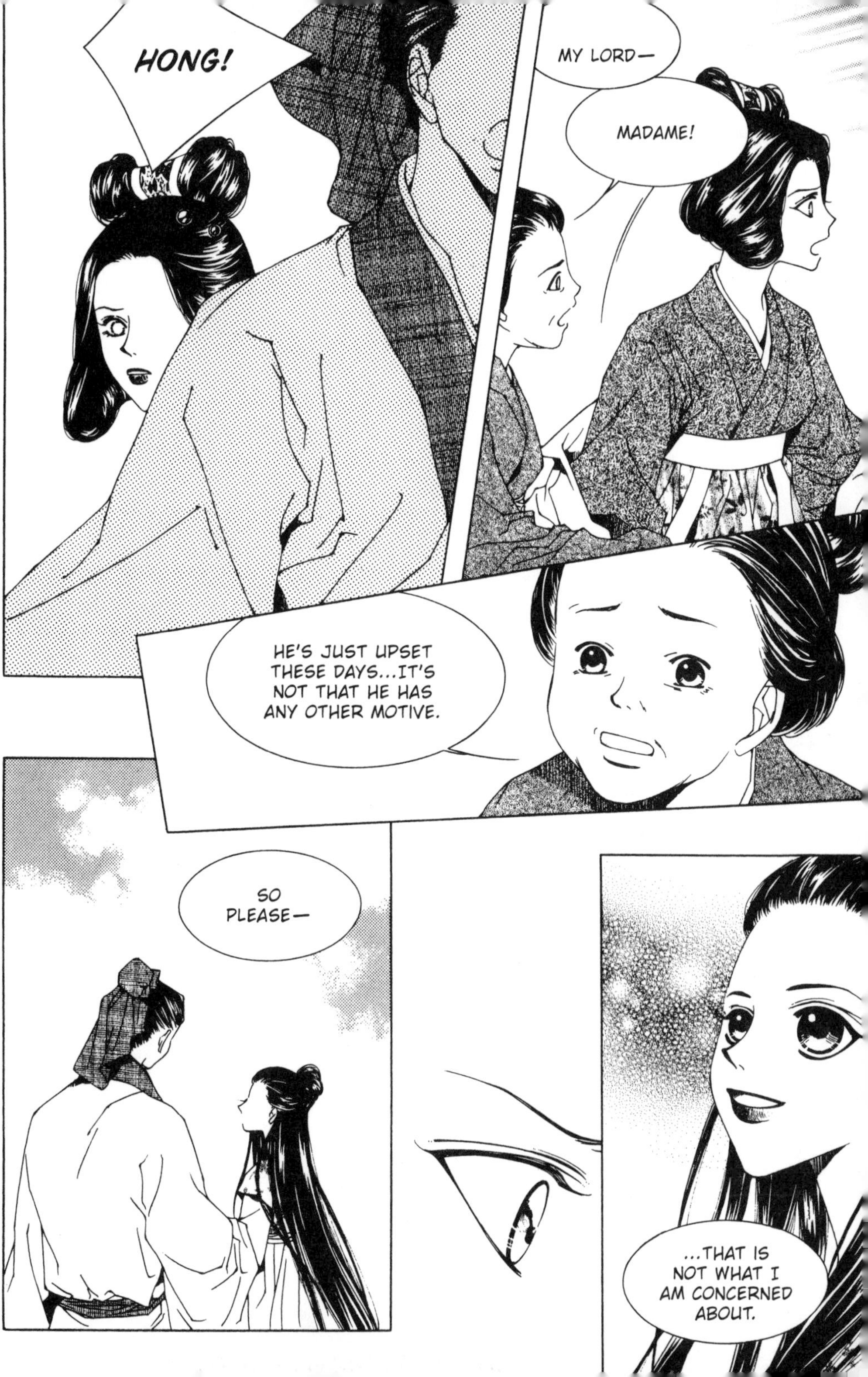
HONG!
MY LORD—
MADAME!
HE'S JUST UPSET THESE DAYS...IT'S NOT THAT HE HAS ANY OTHER MOTIVE.
SO PLEASE—
...THAT IS NOT WHAT I AM CONCERNED ABOUT.

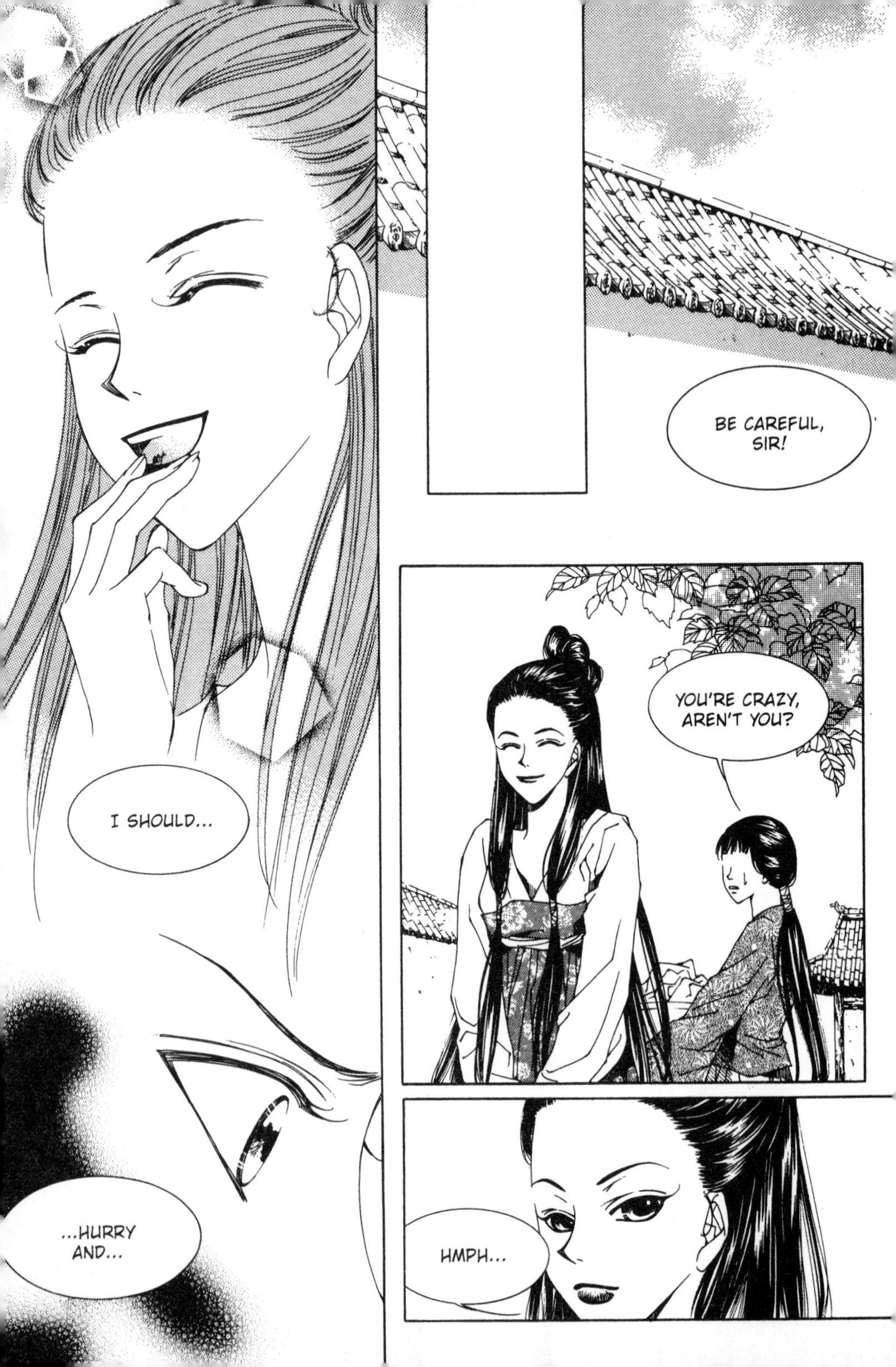
I SHOULD...
...HURRY AND...
BE CAREFUL, SIR!
YOU'RE CRAZY, AREN'T YOU?
HMPH...

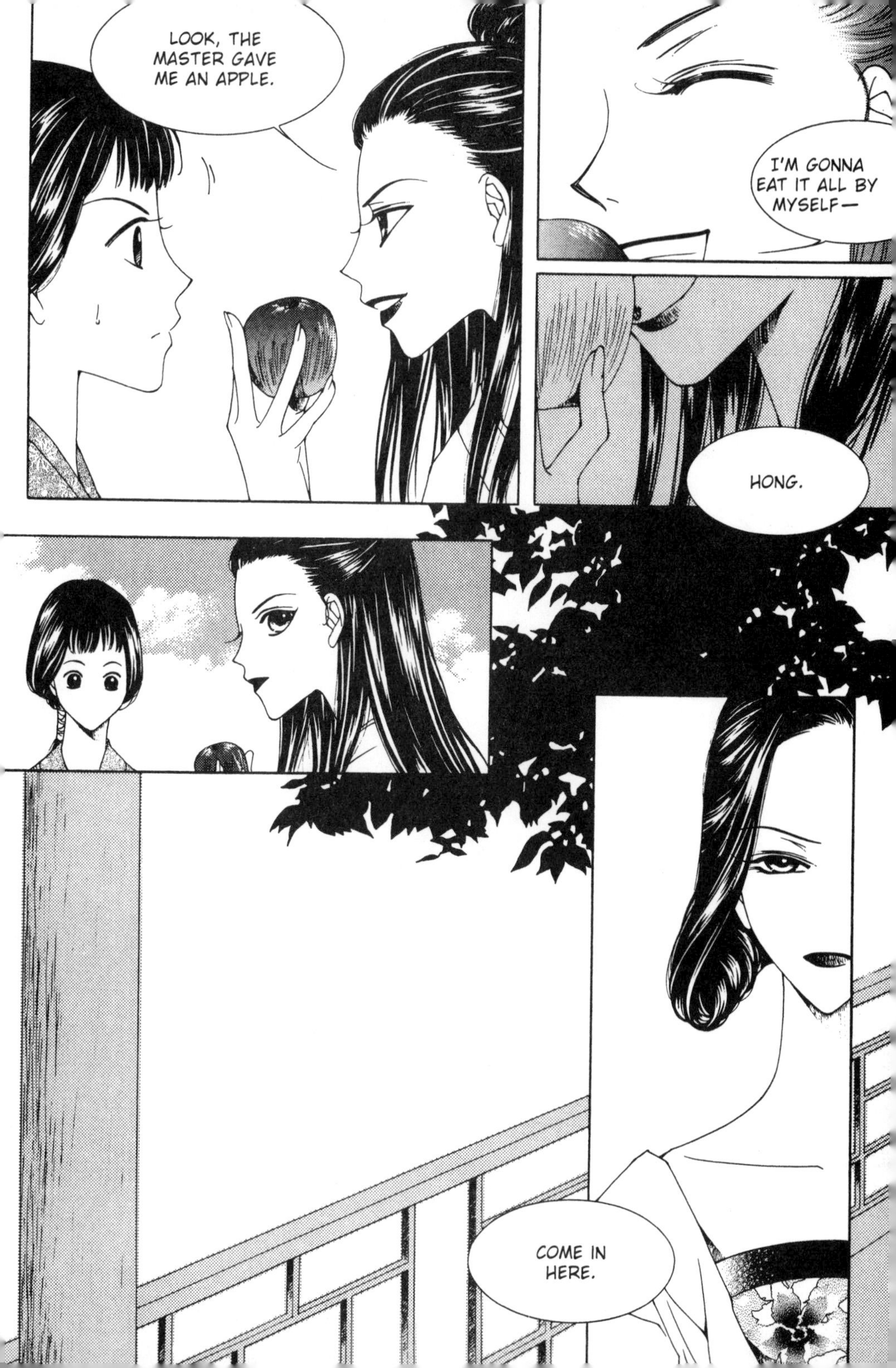
LOOK, THE MASTER GAVE ME AN APPLE.
I'M GONNA EAT IT ALL BY MYSELF—
HONG.
COME IN HERE.

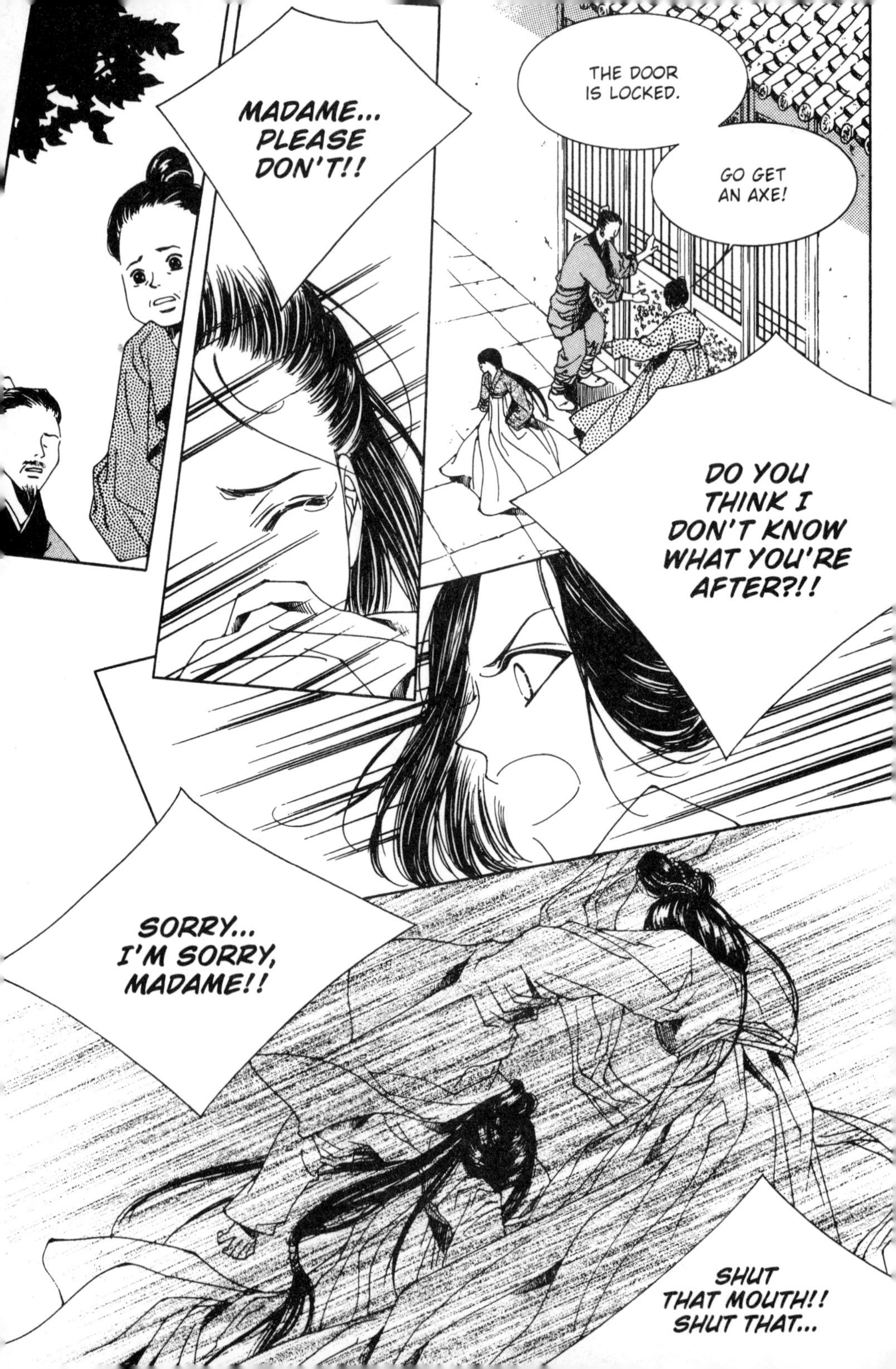
MADAME... PLEASE DON'T!!
THE DOOR IS LOCKED.
GO GET AN AXE!
DO YOU THINK I DON'T KNOW WHAT YOU'RE AFTER?!!
SORRY... I'M SORRY, MADAME!!
SHUT THAT MOUTH!! SHUT THAT...

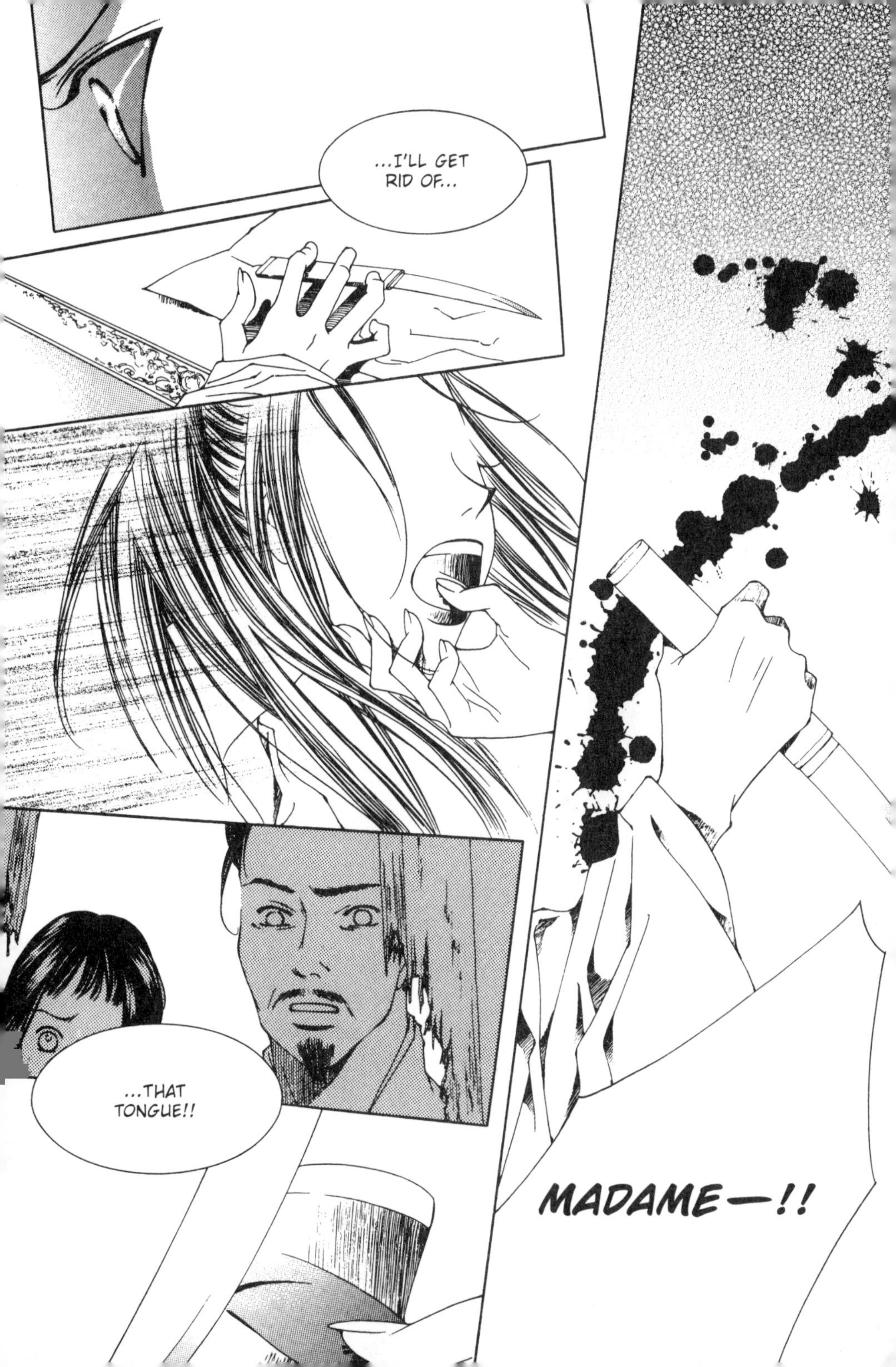
...I'LL GET RID OF...
...THAT TONGUE!!
MADAME—!!

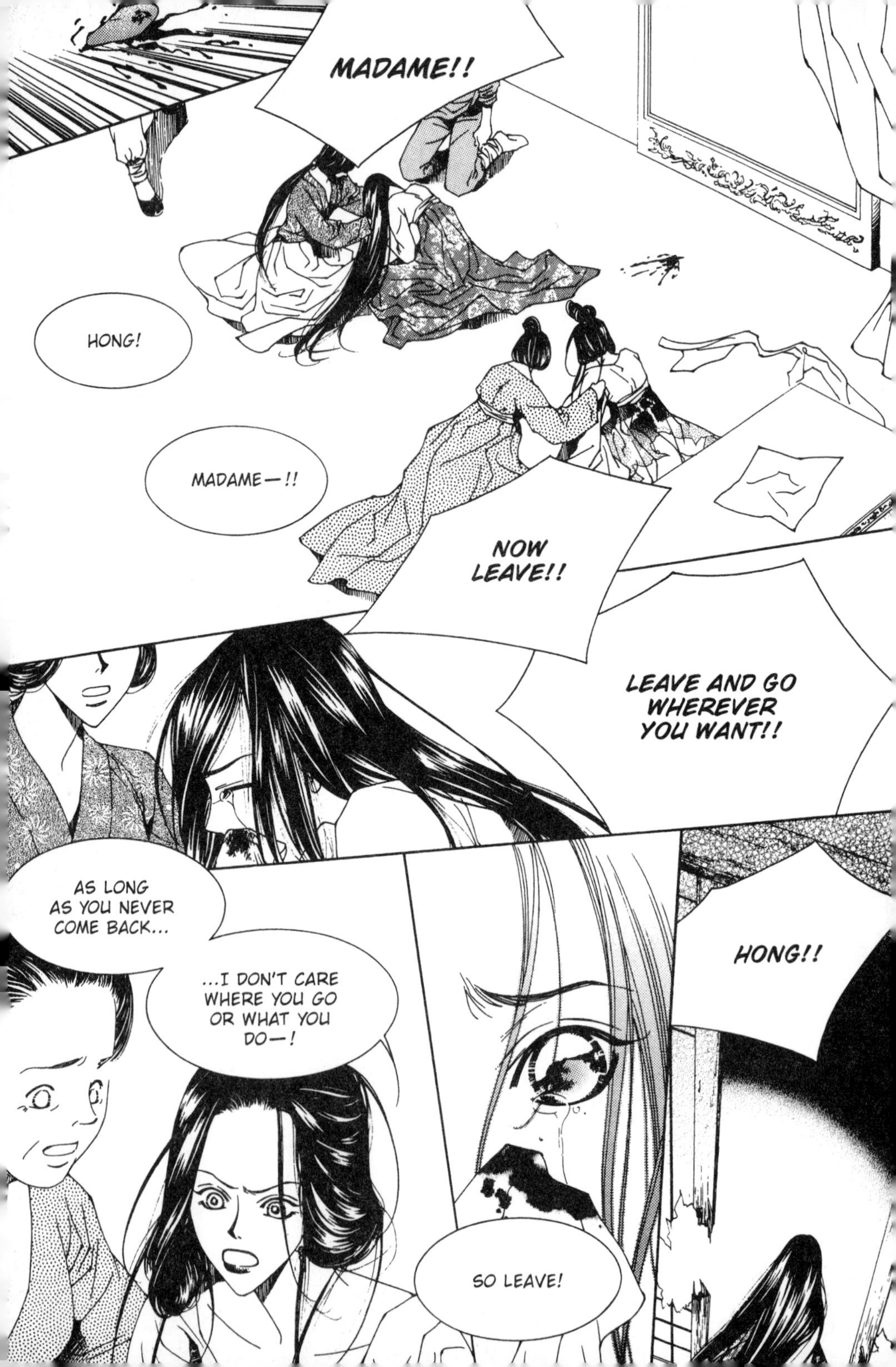
MADAME!!
HONG!
MADAME—!!
NOW LEAVE!!
LEAVE AND GO WHEREVER YOU WANT!!
AS LONG AS YOU NEVER COME BACK...
...I DON'T CARE WHERE YOU GO OR WHAT YOU DO—!
HONG!!
SO LEAVE!

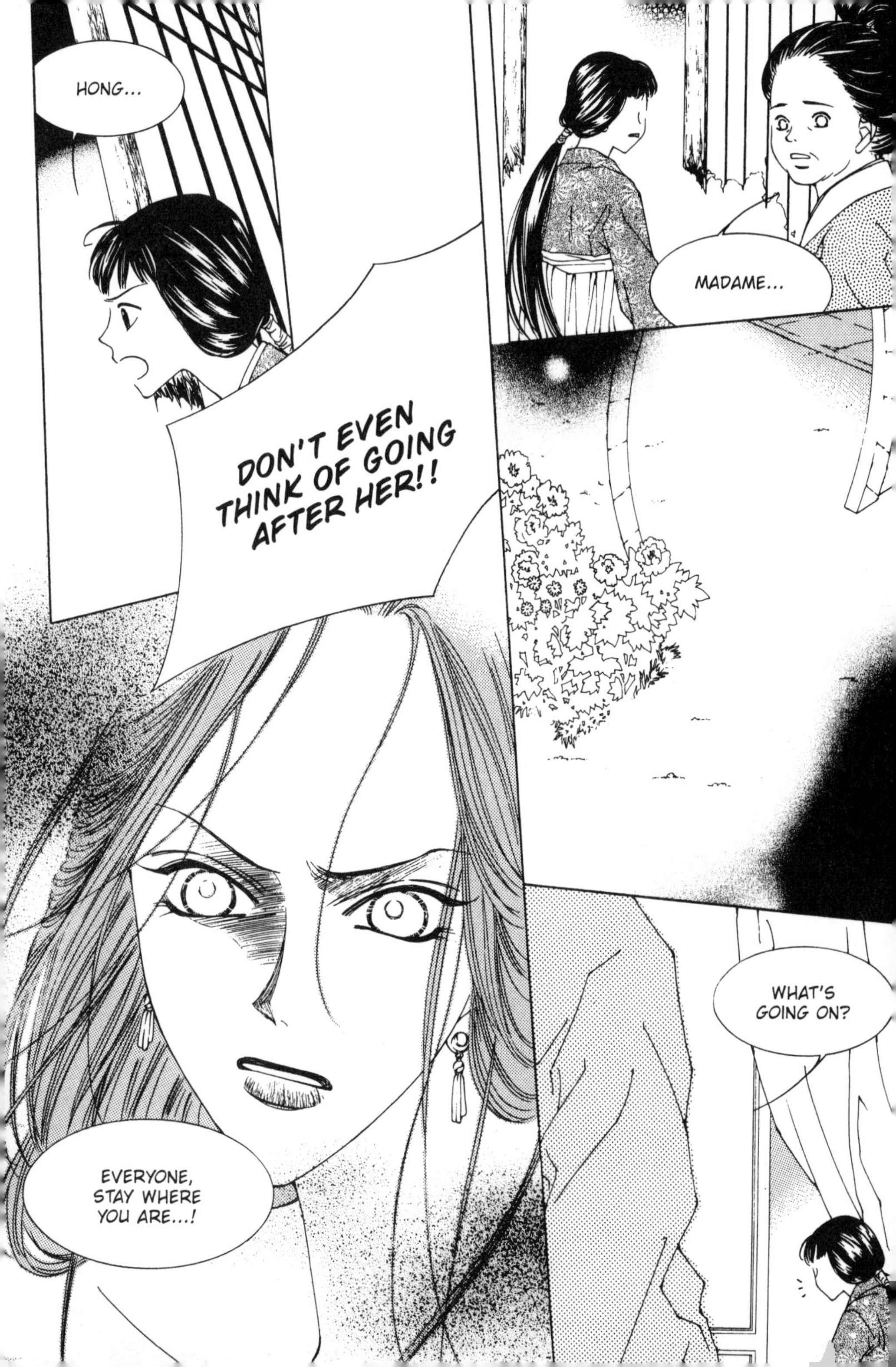
HONG...
DON'T EVEN THINK OF GOING AFTER HER!!
MADAME...
EVERYONE, STAY WHERE YOU ARE...!
WHAT'S GOING ON?

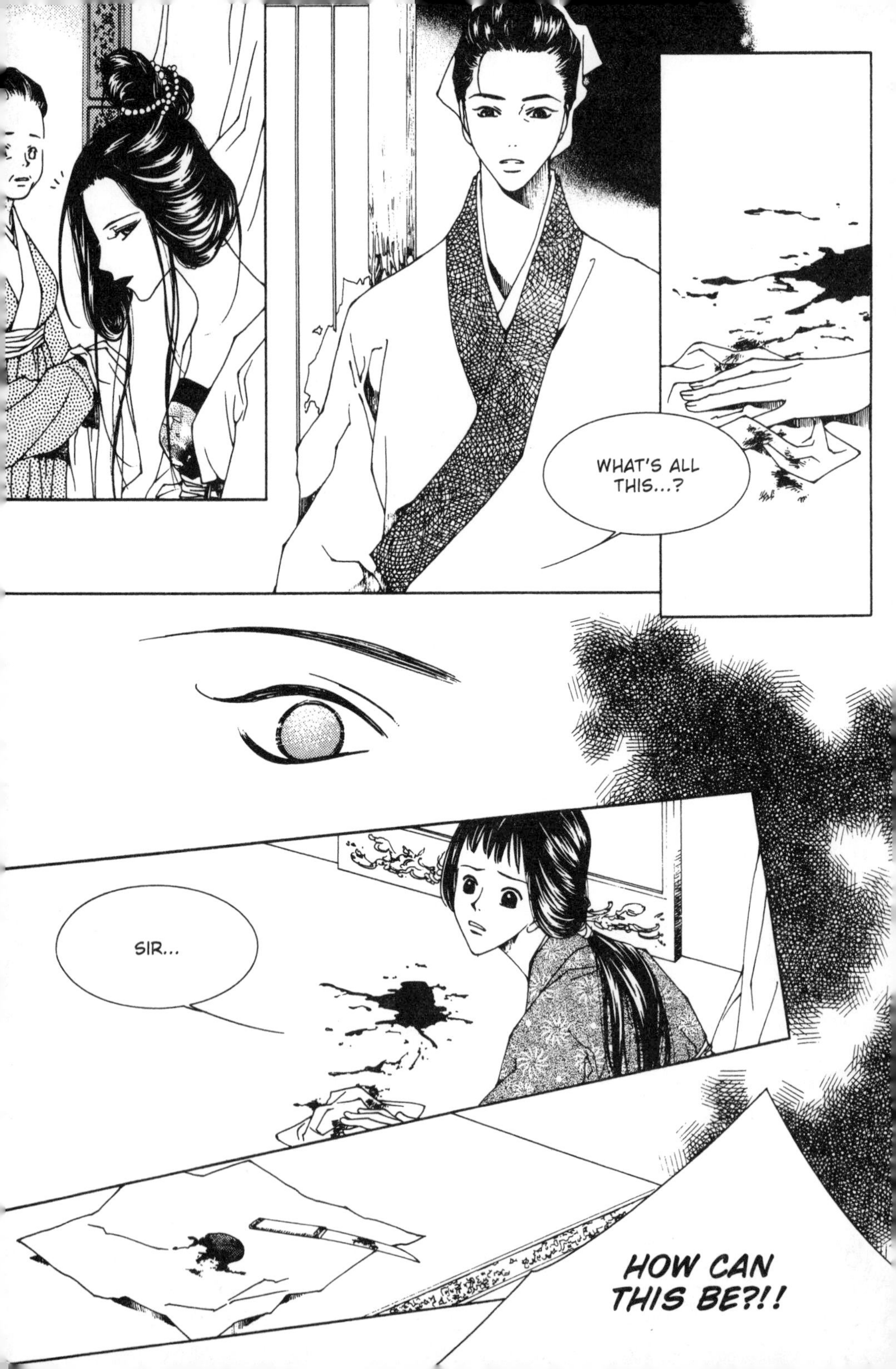
WHAT'S ALL THIS...?
SIR...
HOW CAN THIS BE?!!

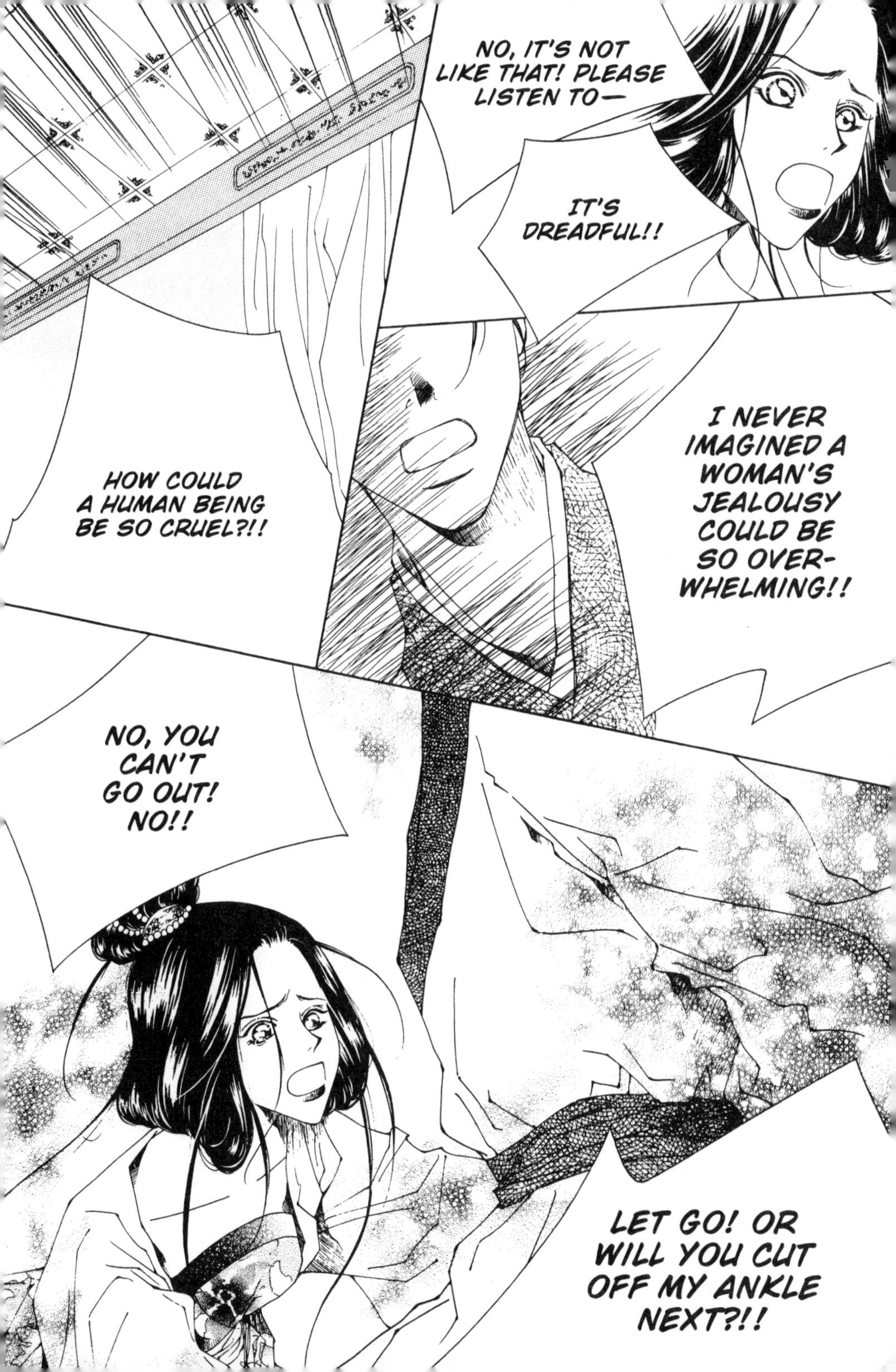
NO, IT'S NOT LIKE THAT! PLEASE LISTEN TO—
IT'S DREADFUL!!
HOW COULD A HUMAN BEING BE SO CRUEL?!!
I NEVER IMAGINED A WOMAN'S JEALOUSY COULD BE SO OVER-WHELMING!!
NO, YOU CAN'T GO OUT! NO!!
LET GO! OR WILL YOU CUT OFF MY ANKLE NEXT?!!

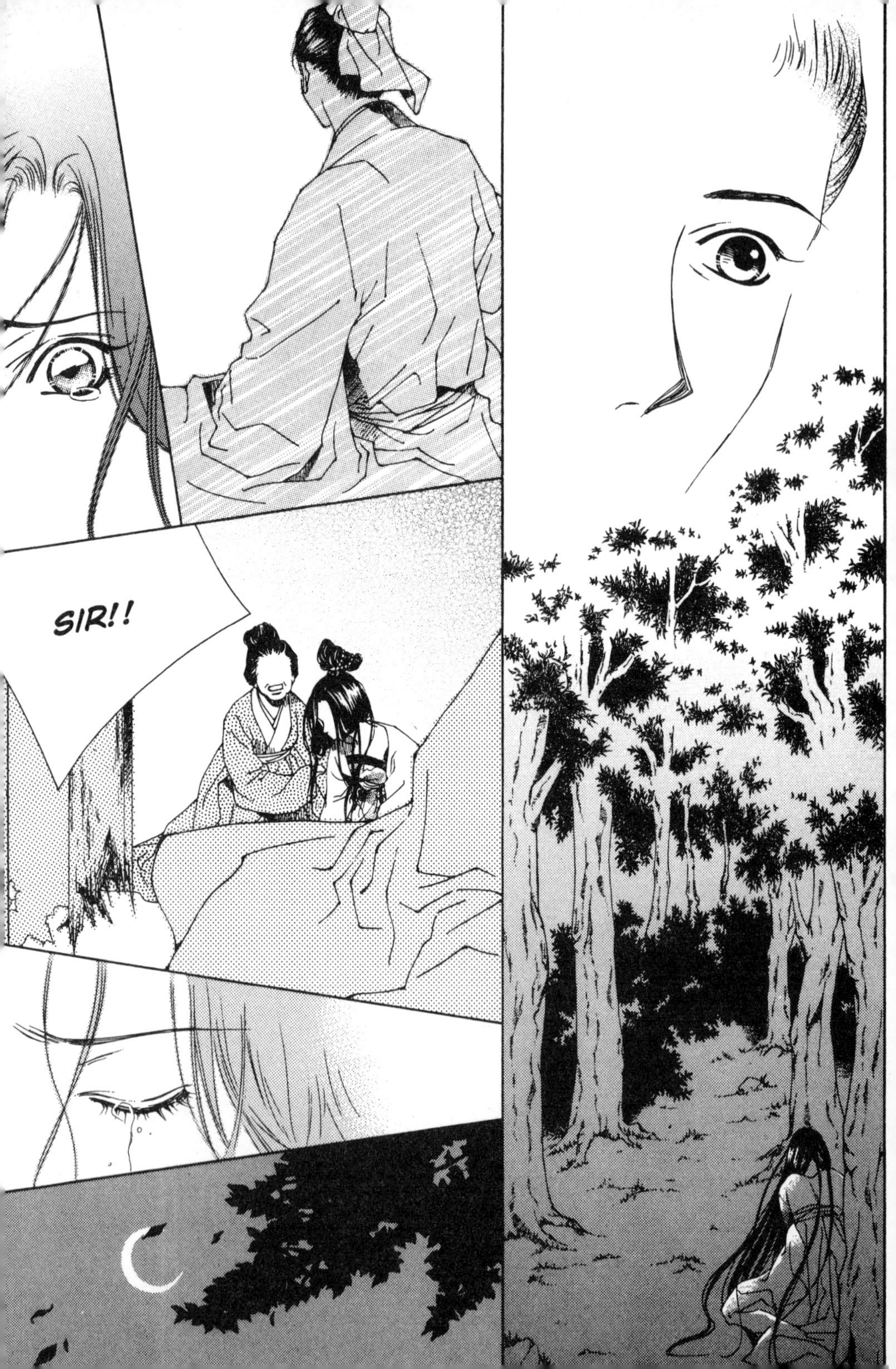
SIR!!

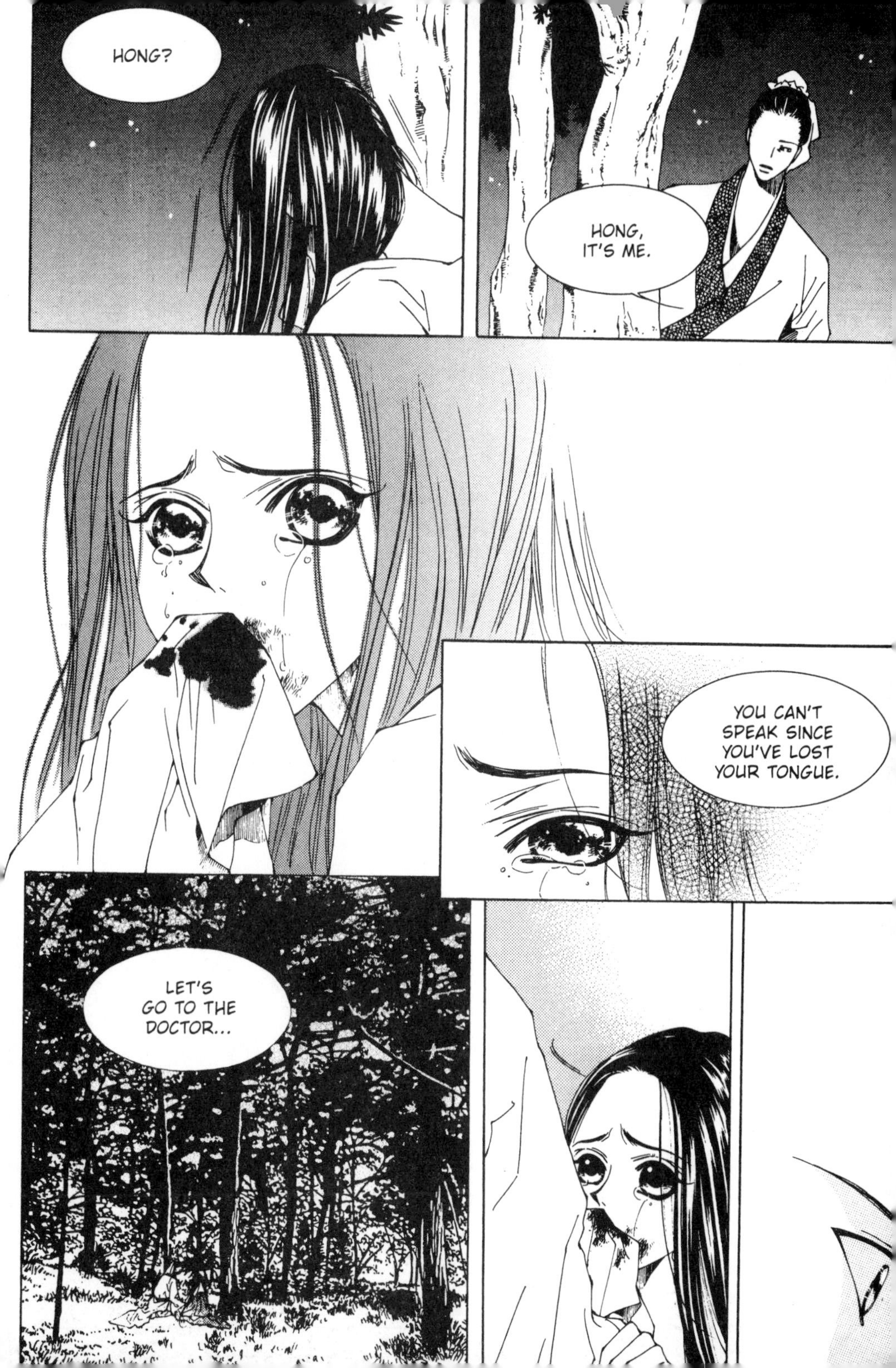
HONG?
HONG, IT'S ME.
YOU CAN'T SPEAK SINCE YOU'VE LOST YOUR TONGUE.
LET'S GO TO THE DOCTOR...

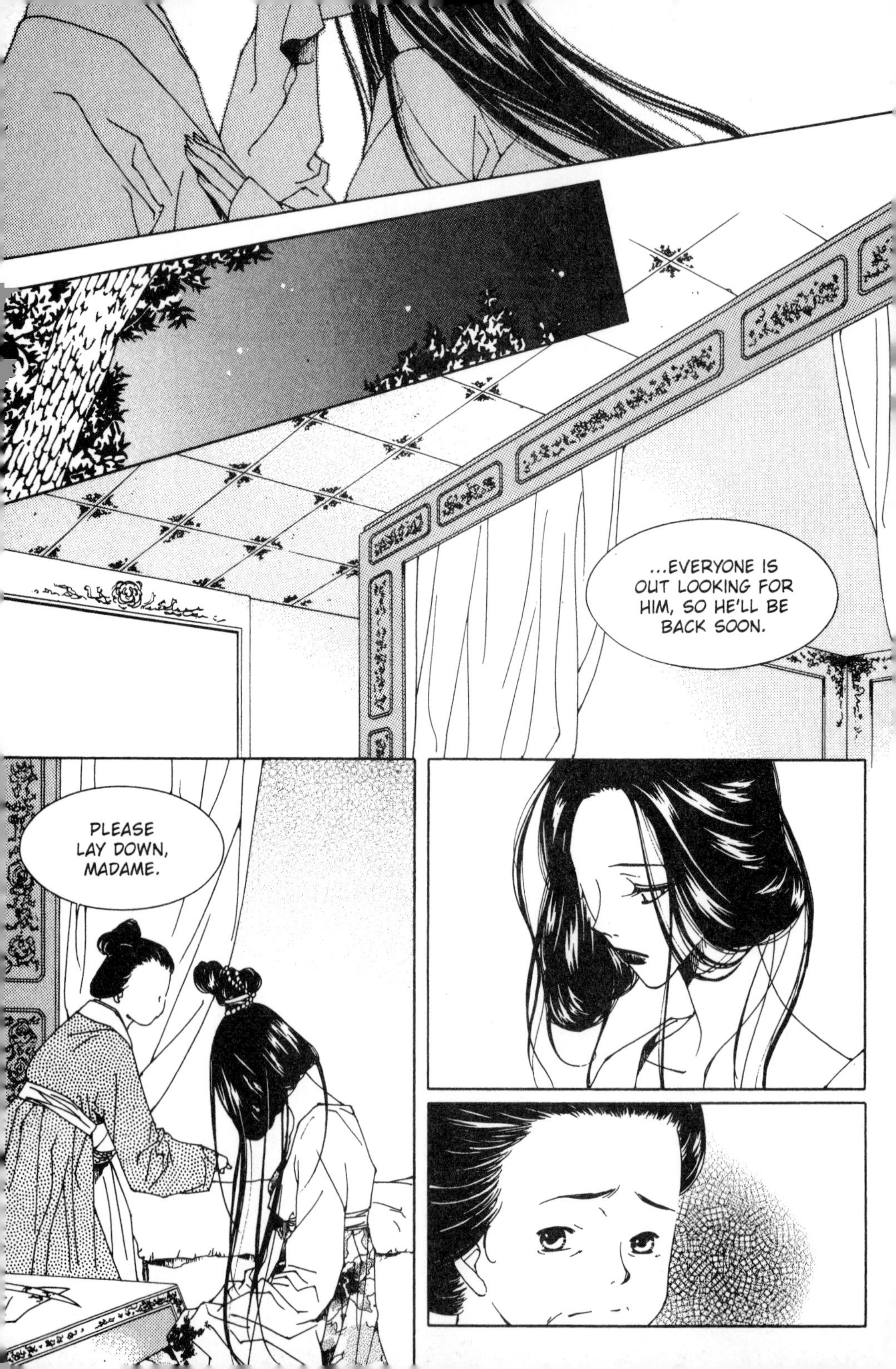
...EVERYONE IS OUT LOOKING FOR HIM, SO HE'LL BE BACK SOON.
PLEASE LAY DOWN, MADAME.

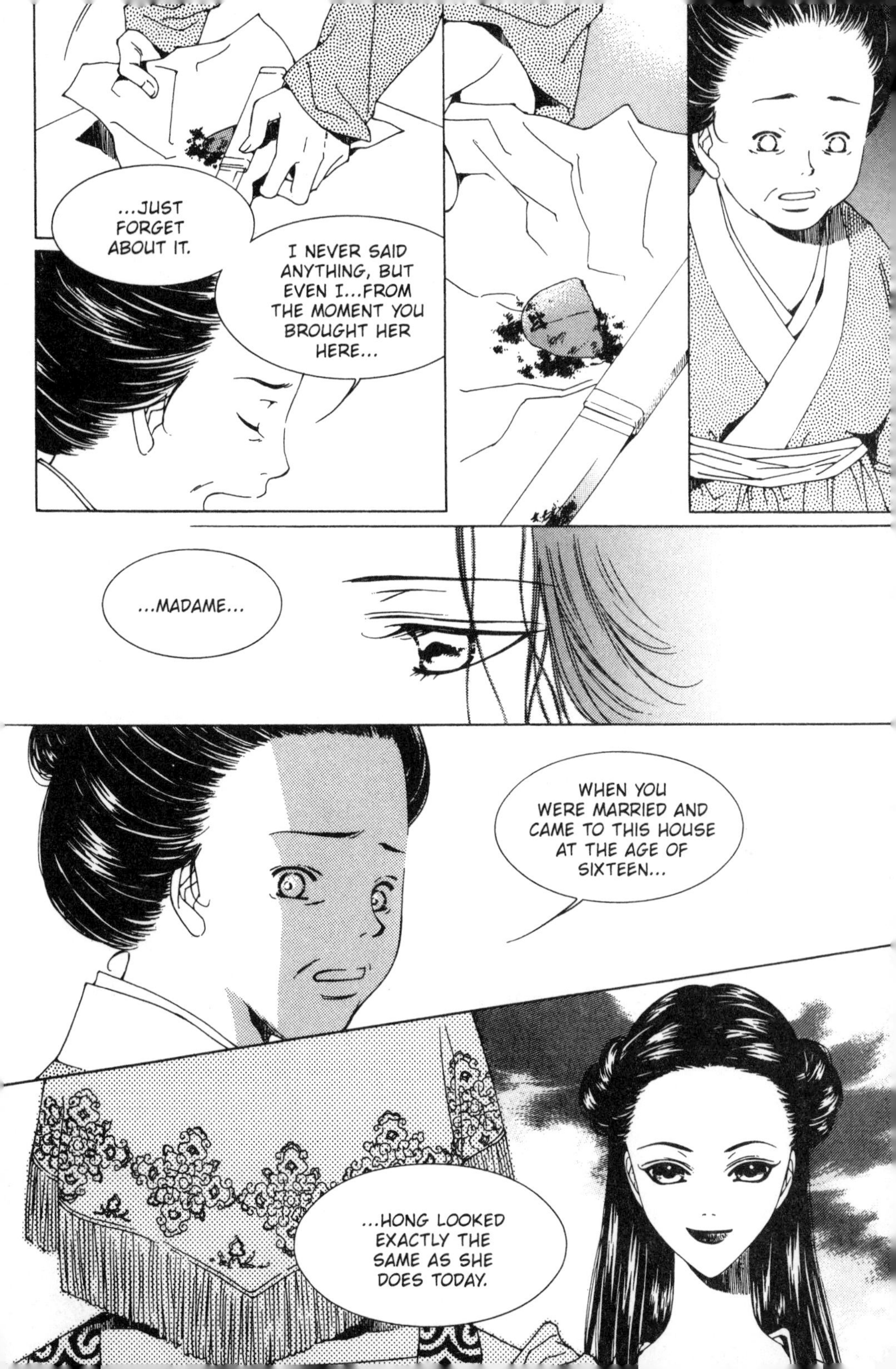
...JUST FORGET ABOUT IT.
I NEVER SAID ANYTHING, BUT EVEN I...FROM THE MOMENT YOU BROUGHT HER HERE...
...MADAME...
WHEN YOU WERE MARRIED AND CAME TO THIS HOUSE AT THE AGE OF SIXTEEN...
...HONG LOOKED EXACTLY THE SAME AS SHE DOES TODAY.

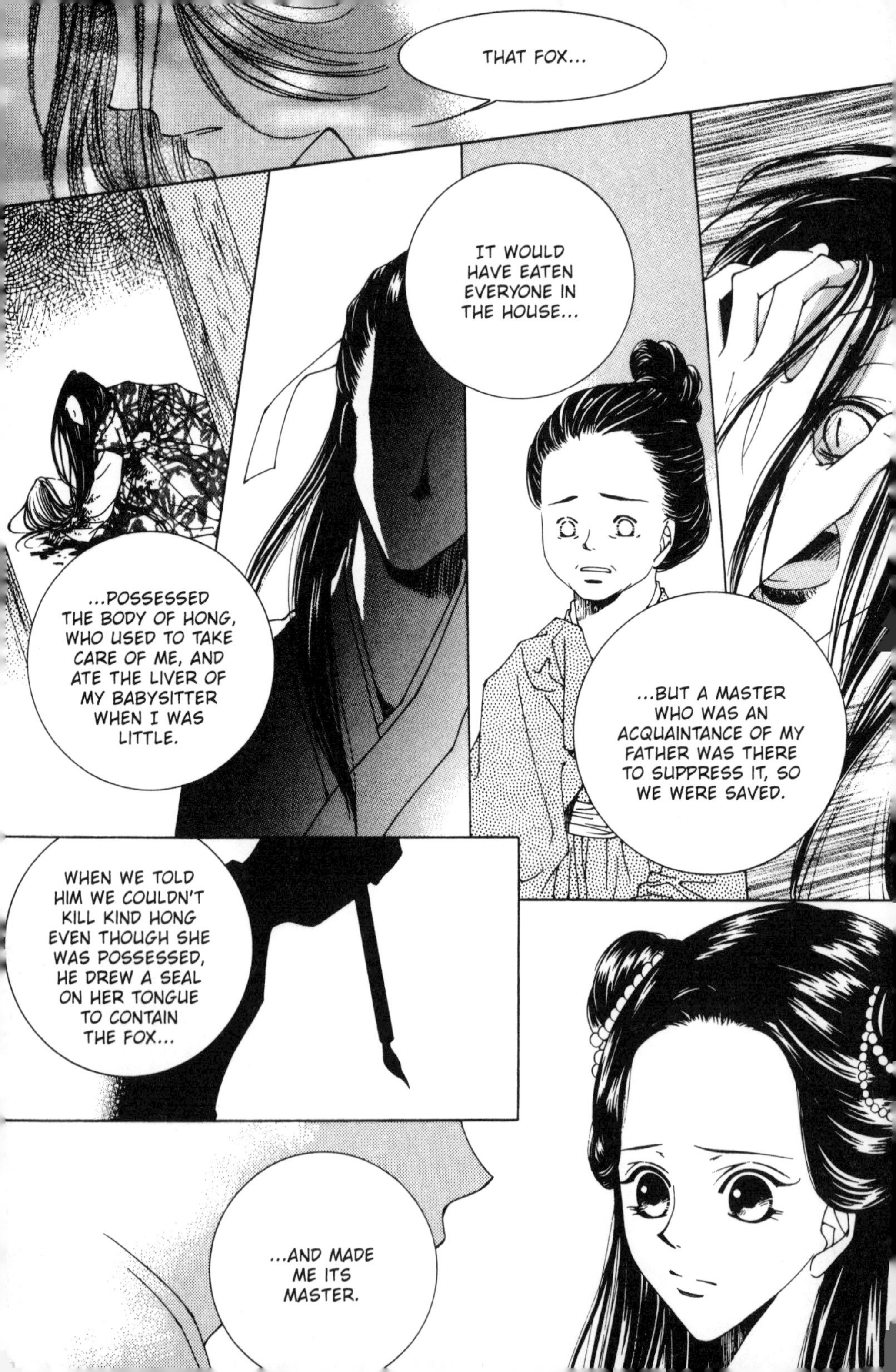
THAT FOX...
...POSSESSED THE BODY OF HONG, WHO USED TO TAKE CARE OF ME, AND ATE THE LIVER OF MY BABYSITTER WHEN I WAS LITTLE.
IT WOULD HAVE EATEN EVERYONE IN THE HOUSE...
...BUT A MASTER WHO WAS AN ACQUAINTANCE OF MY FATHER WAS THERE TO SUPPRESS IT, SO WE WERE SAVED.
WHEN WE TOLD HIM WE COULDN'T KILL KIND HONG EVEN THOUGH SHE WAS POSSESSED, HE DREW A SEAL ON HER TONGUE TO CONTAIN THE FOX...
...AND MADE ME ITS MASTER.

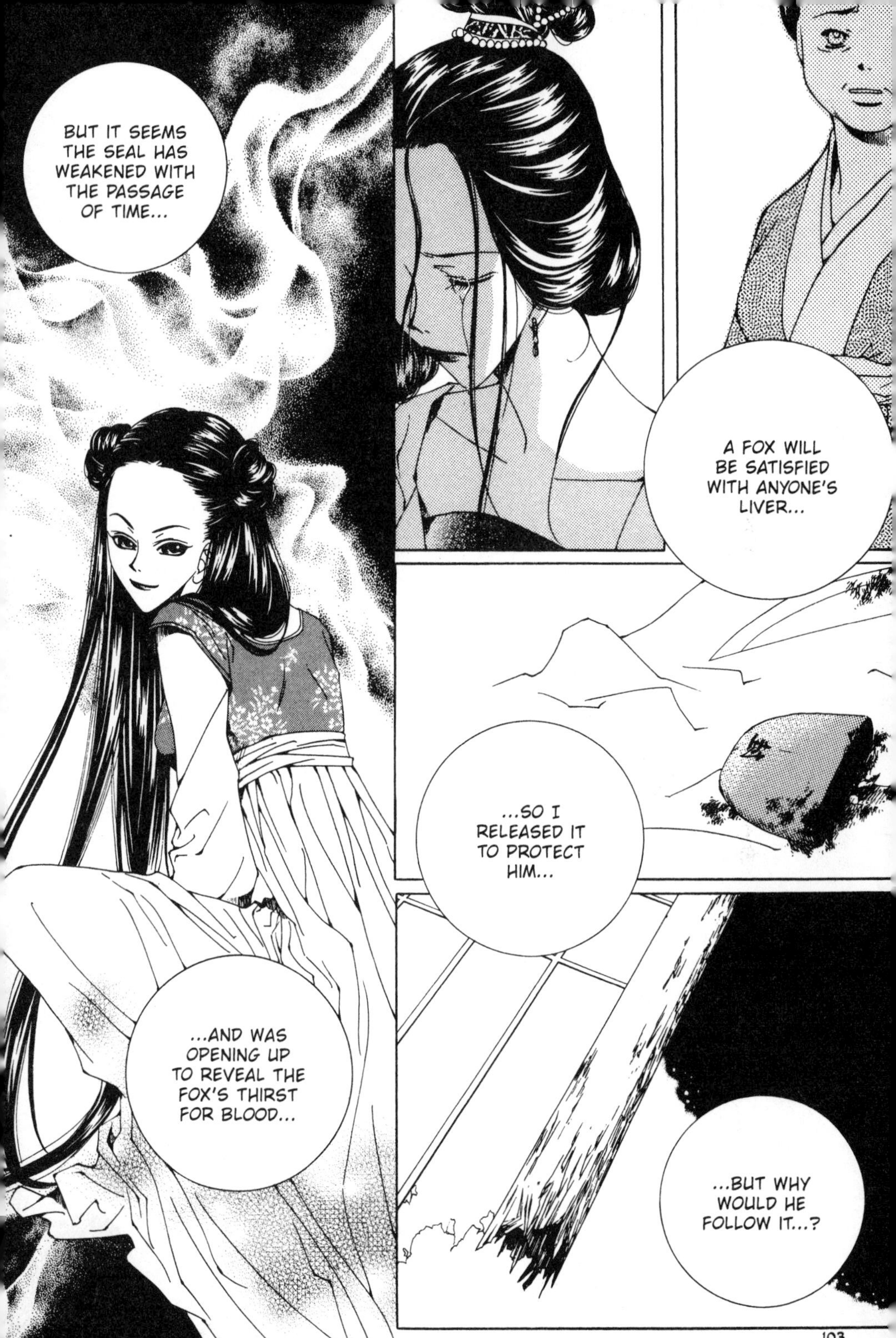
BUT IT SEEMS THE SEAL HAS WEAKENED WITH THE PASSAGE OF TIME...
...AND WAS OPENING UP TO REVEAL THE FOX'S THIRST FOR BLOOD...
A FOX WILL BE SATISFIED WITH ANYONE'S LIVER...
...SO I RELEASED IT TO PROTECT HIM...
...BUT WHY WOULD HE FOLLOW IT...?

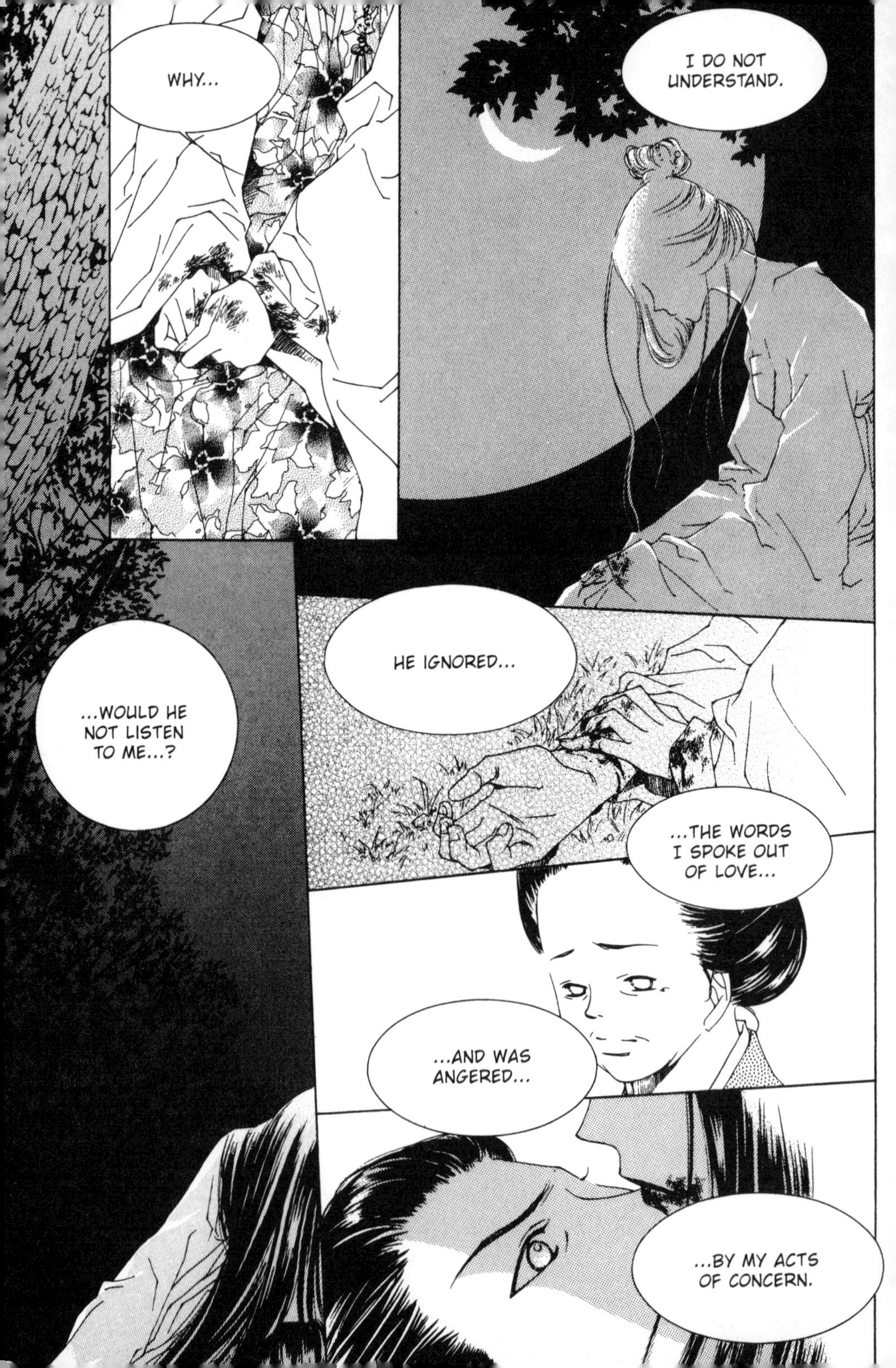
WHY...
I DO NOT UNDERSTAND.
...WOULD HE NOT LISTEN TO ME...?
HE IGNORED...
...THE WORDS I SPOKE OUT OF LOVE...
...AND WAS ANGERED...
...BY MY ACTS OF CONCERN.

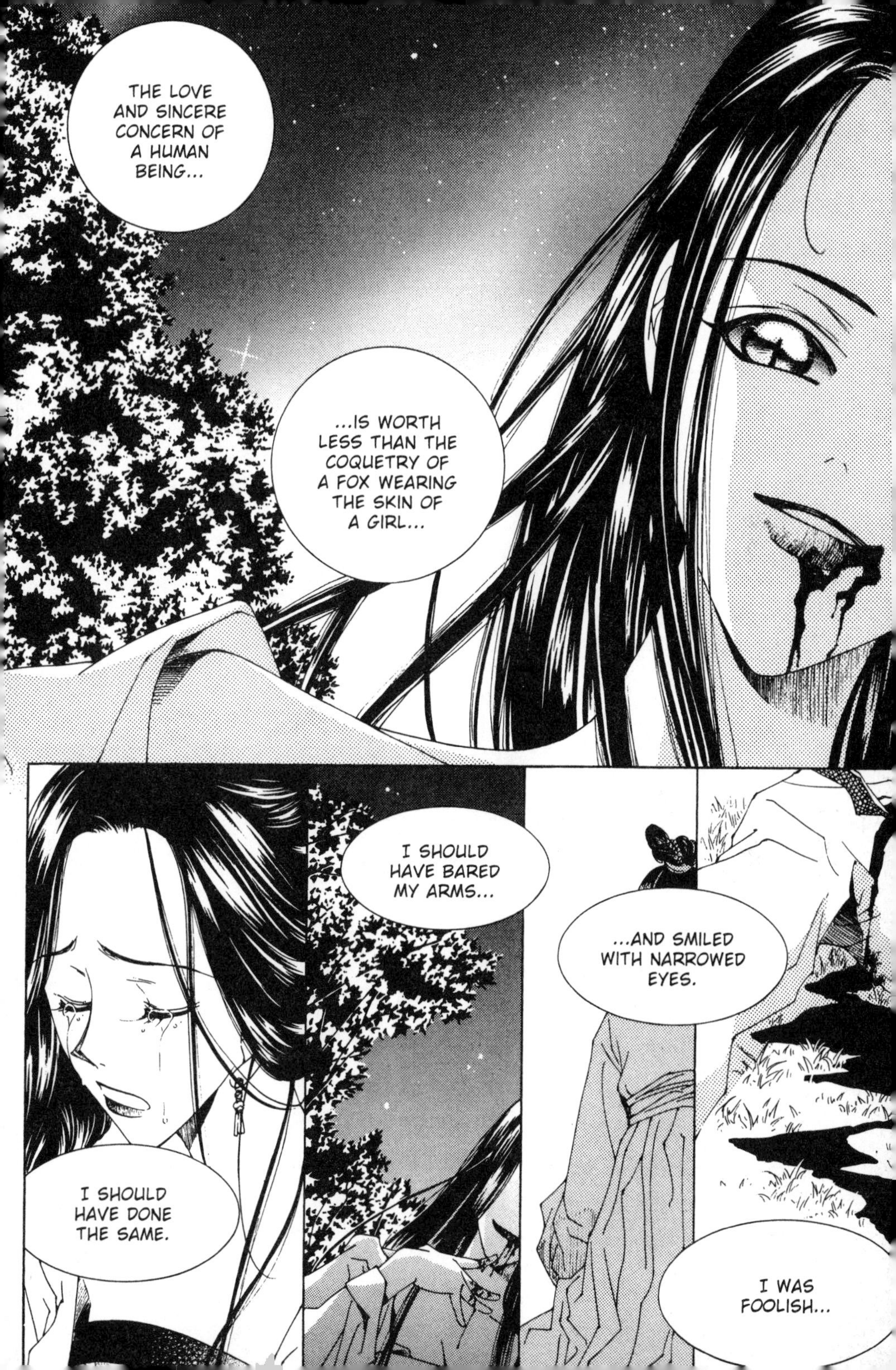
THE LOVE AND SINCERE CONCERN OF A HUMAN BEING...
...IS WORTH LESS THAN THE COQUETRY OF A FOX WEARING THE SKIN OF A GIRL...
I SHOULD HAVE DONE THE SAME.
I SHOULD HAVE BARED MY ARMS...
...AND SMILED WITH NARROWED EYES.
I WAS FOOLISH...

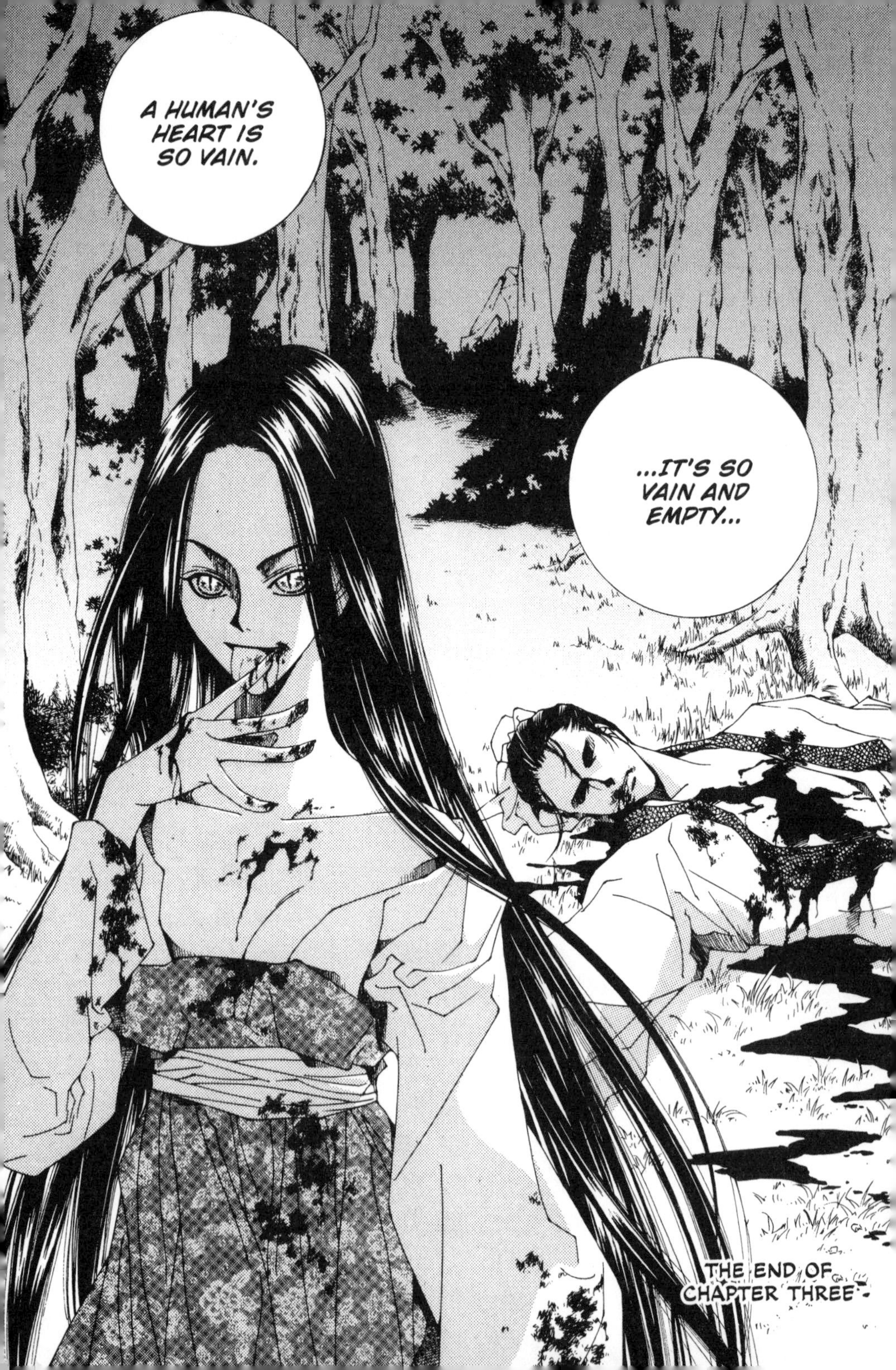
A HUMAN'S HEART IS SO VAIN.
...IT'S SO VAIN AND EMPTY...
THE END OF CHAPTER THREE

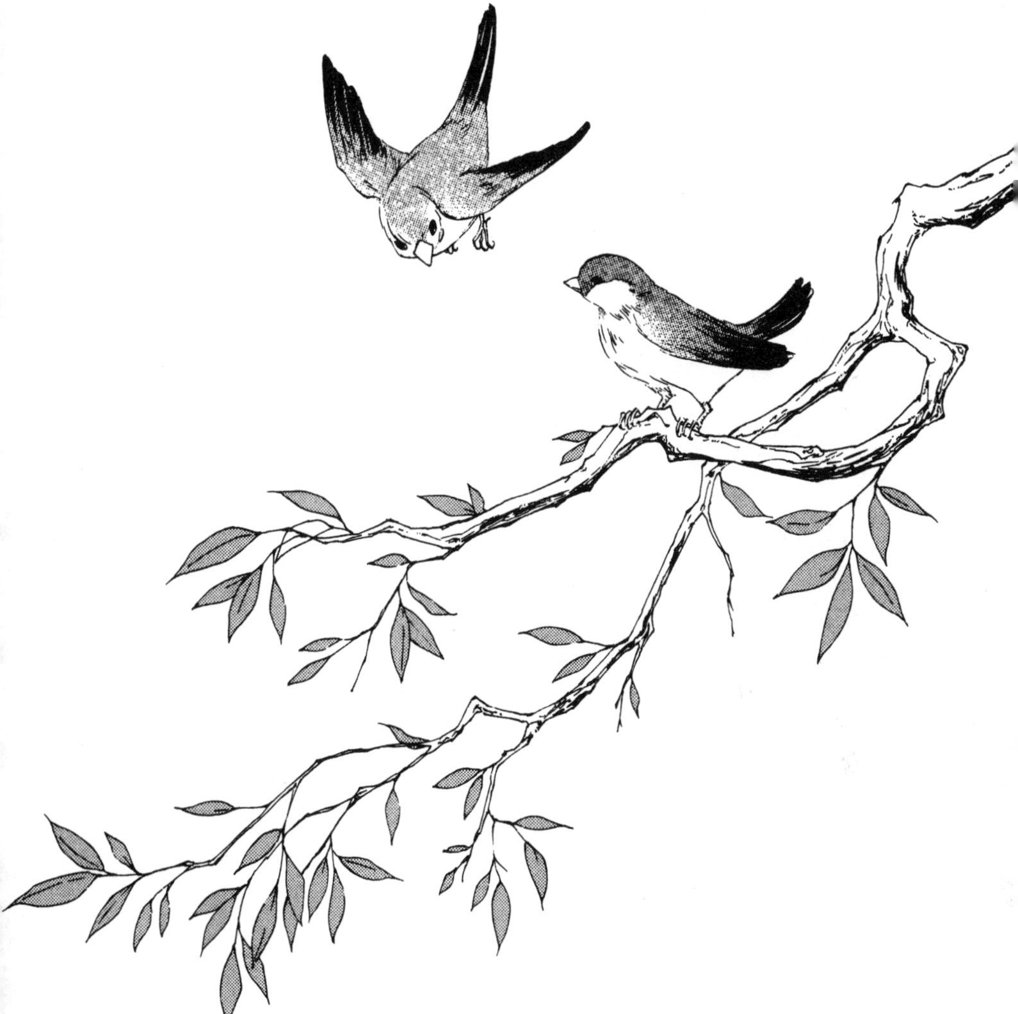

CHAPTER FOUR
BIRD

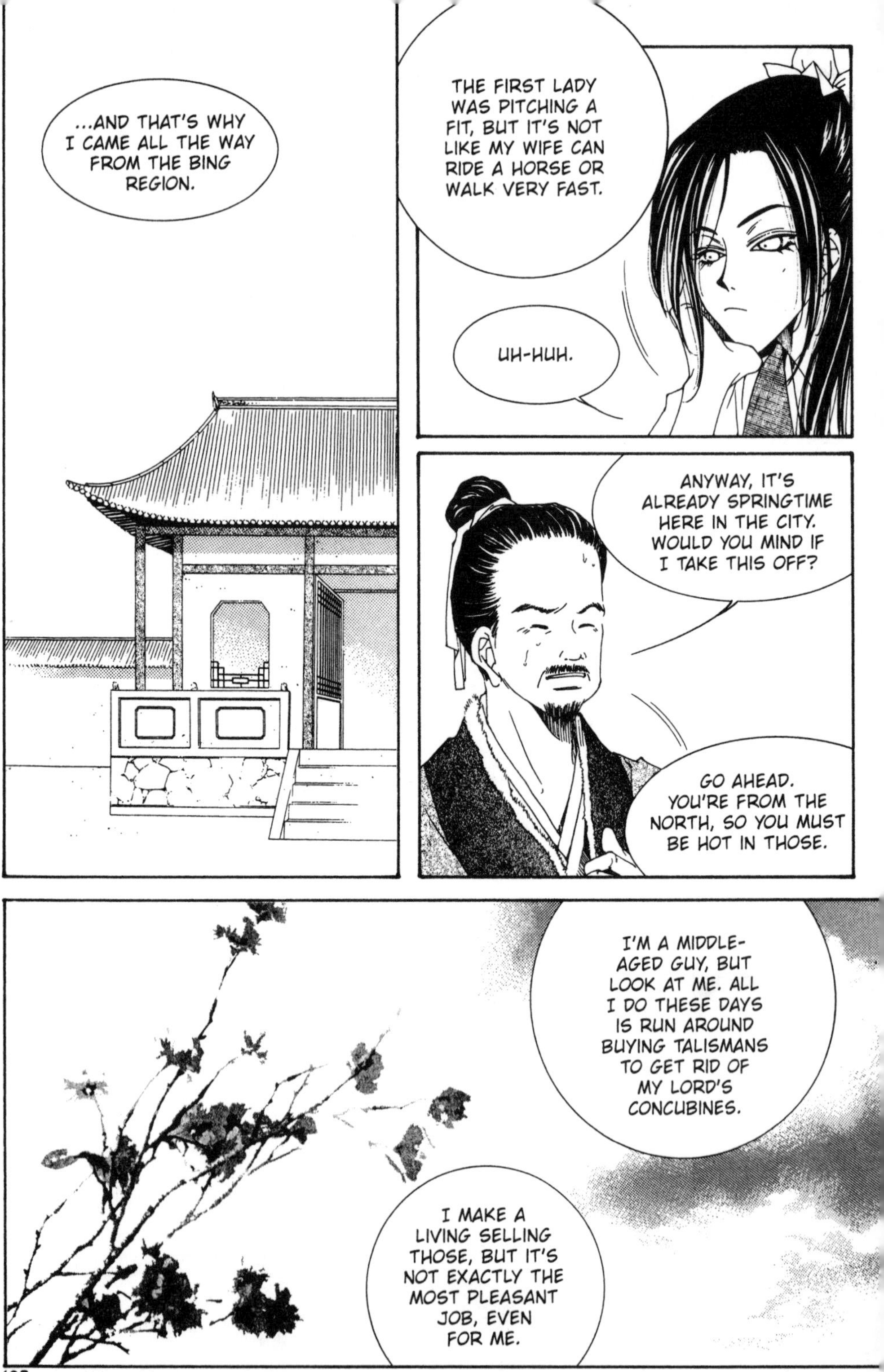
...AND THAT'S WHY I CAME ALL THE WAY FROM THE BING REGION.
THE FIRST LADY WAS PITCHING A FIT, BUT IT'S NOT LIKE MY WIFE CAN RIDE A HORSE OR WALK VERY FAST.
UH-HUH.
ANYWAY, IT'S ALREADY SPRINGTIME HERE IN THE CITY. WOULD YOU MIND IF I TAKE THIS OFF?
GO AHEAD. YOU'RE FROM THE NORTH, SO YOU MUST BE HOT IN THOSE.
I'M A MIDDLE-AGED GUY, BUT LOOK AT ME. ALL I DO THESE DAYS IS RUN AROUND BUYING TALISMANS TO GET RID OF MY LORD'S CONCUBINES.
I MAKE A LIVING SELLING THOSE, BUT IT'S NOT EXACTLY THE MOST PLEASANT JOB, EVEN FOR ME.

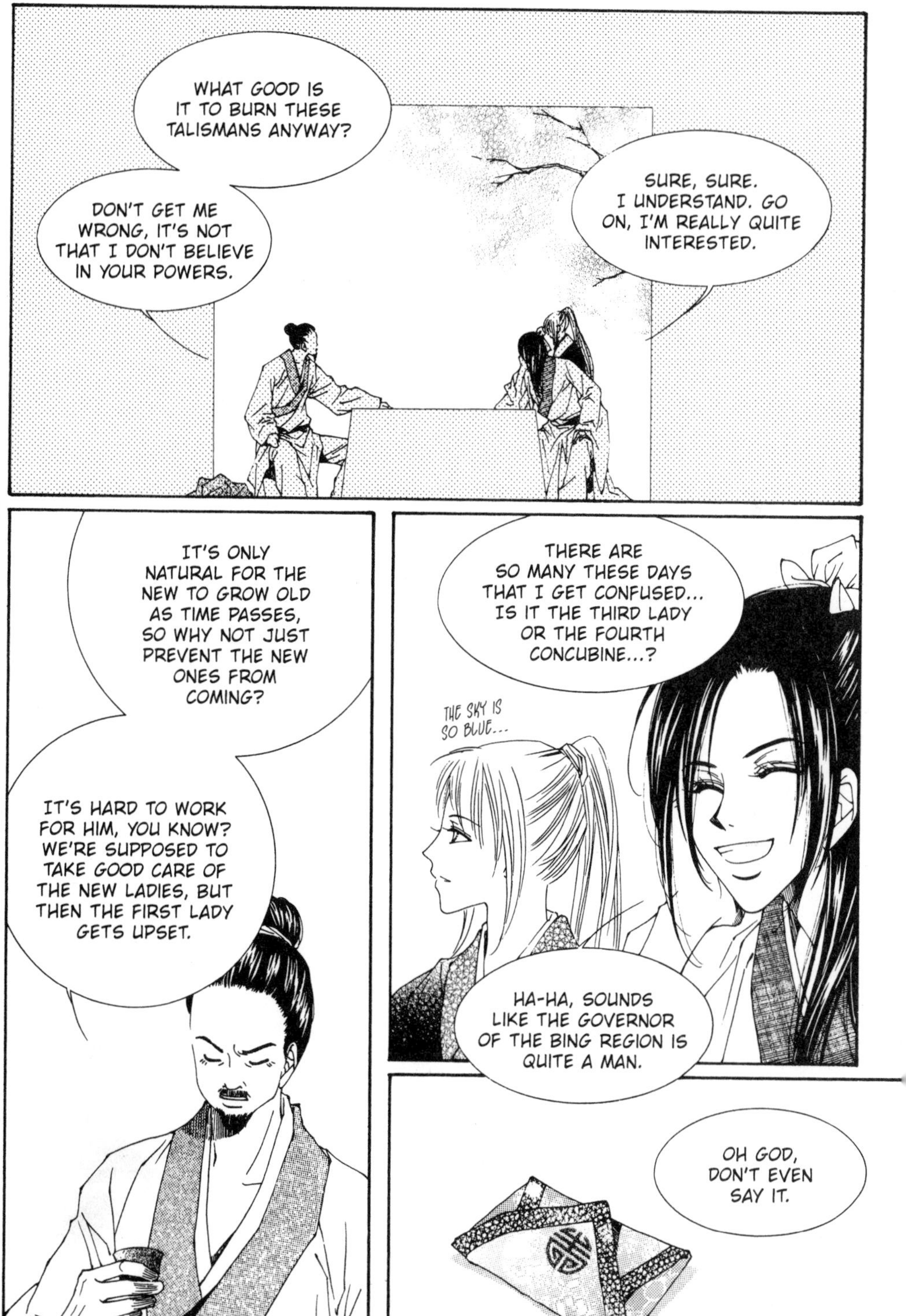
WHAT GOOD IS IT TO BURN THESE TALISMANS ANYWAY?
DON'T GET ME WRONG, IT'S NOT THAT I DON'T BELIEVE IN YOUR POWERS.
SURE, SURE. I UNDERSTAND. GO ON, I'M REALLY QUITE INTERESTED.
IT'S ONLY NATURAL FOR THE NEW TO GROW OLD AS TIME PASSES, SO WHY NOT JUST PREVENT THE NEW ONES FROM COMING?
IT'S HARD TO WORK FOR HIM, YOU KNOW? WE'RE SUPPOSED TO TAKE GOOD CARE OF THE NEW LADIES, BUT THEN THE FIRST LADY GETS UPSET.
THERE ARE SO MANY THESE DAYS THAT I GET CONFUSED... IS IT THE THIRD LADY OR THE FOURTH CONCUBINE...?
THE SKY IS SO BLUE...
HA-HA, SOUNDS LIKE THE GOVERNOR OF THE BING REGION IS QUITE A MAN.
OH GOD, DON'T EVEN SAY IT.

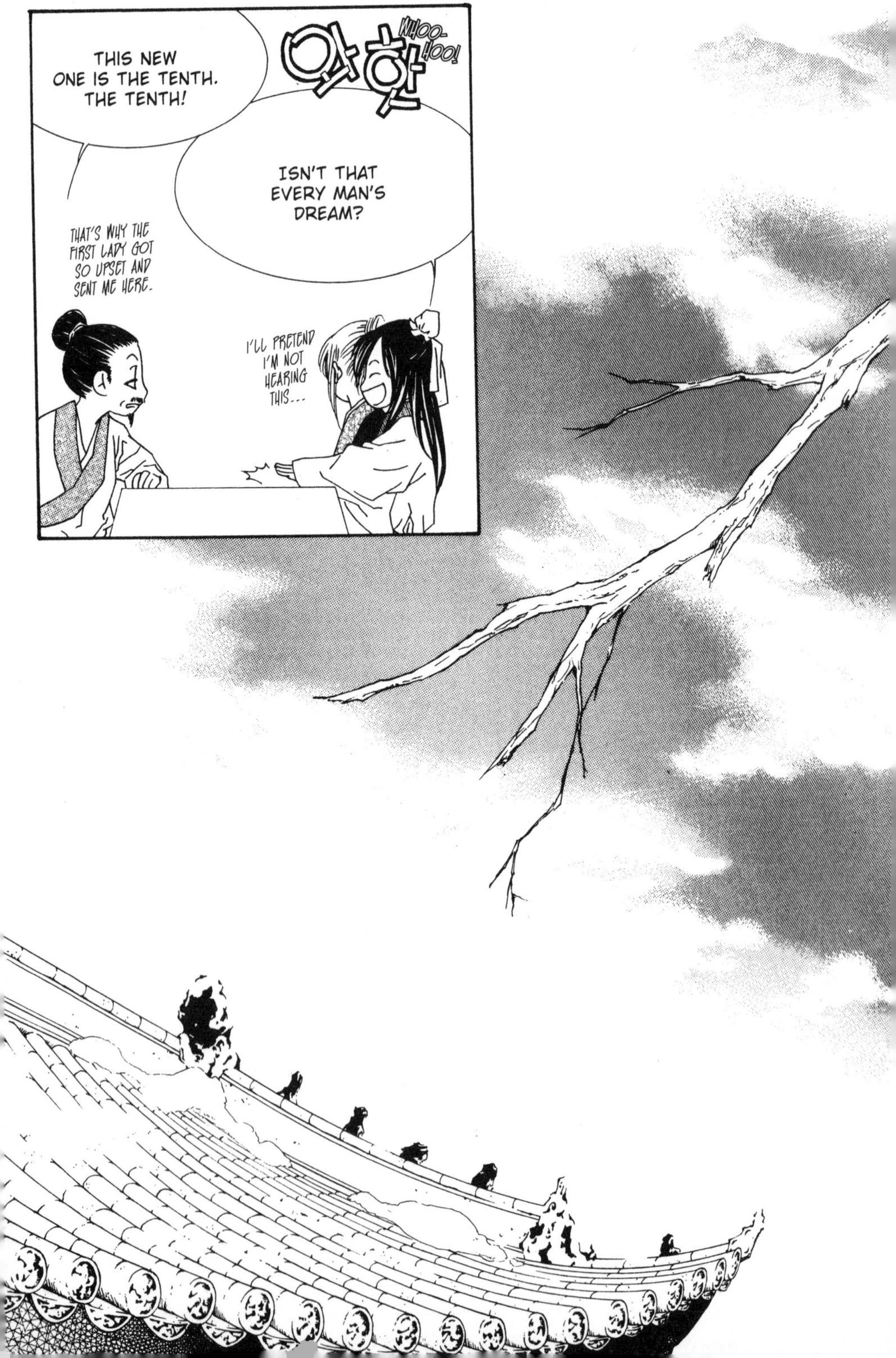
THIS NEW ONE IS THE TENTH. THE TENTH!
왁핫
WHOO-HOO!
ISN'T THAT EVERY MAN'S DREAM?
THAT'S WHY THE FIRST LADY GOT SO UPSET AND SENT ME HERE.
I'LL PRETEND I'M NOT HEARING THIS...

MA'AM, LOOK AT THIS. IT'S VERY FINE SILK.

IF WE MAKE A DRESS OUT OF IT, IT WOULD LOO—

STOP RIGHT THERE.

DON'T TOUCH IT. YOU'LL GET IT DIRTY.

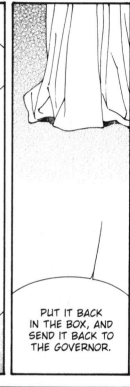

PUT IT BACK IN THE BOX, AND SEND IT BACK TO THE GOVERNOR.

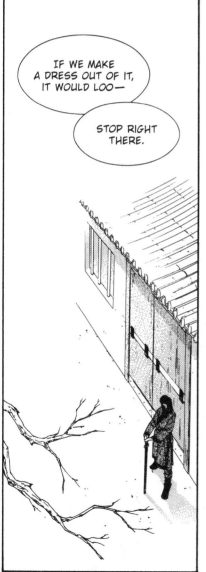

......

BUT MA'AM...

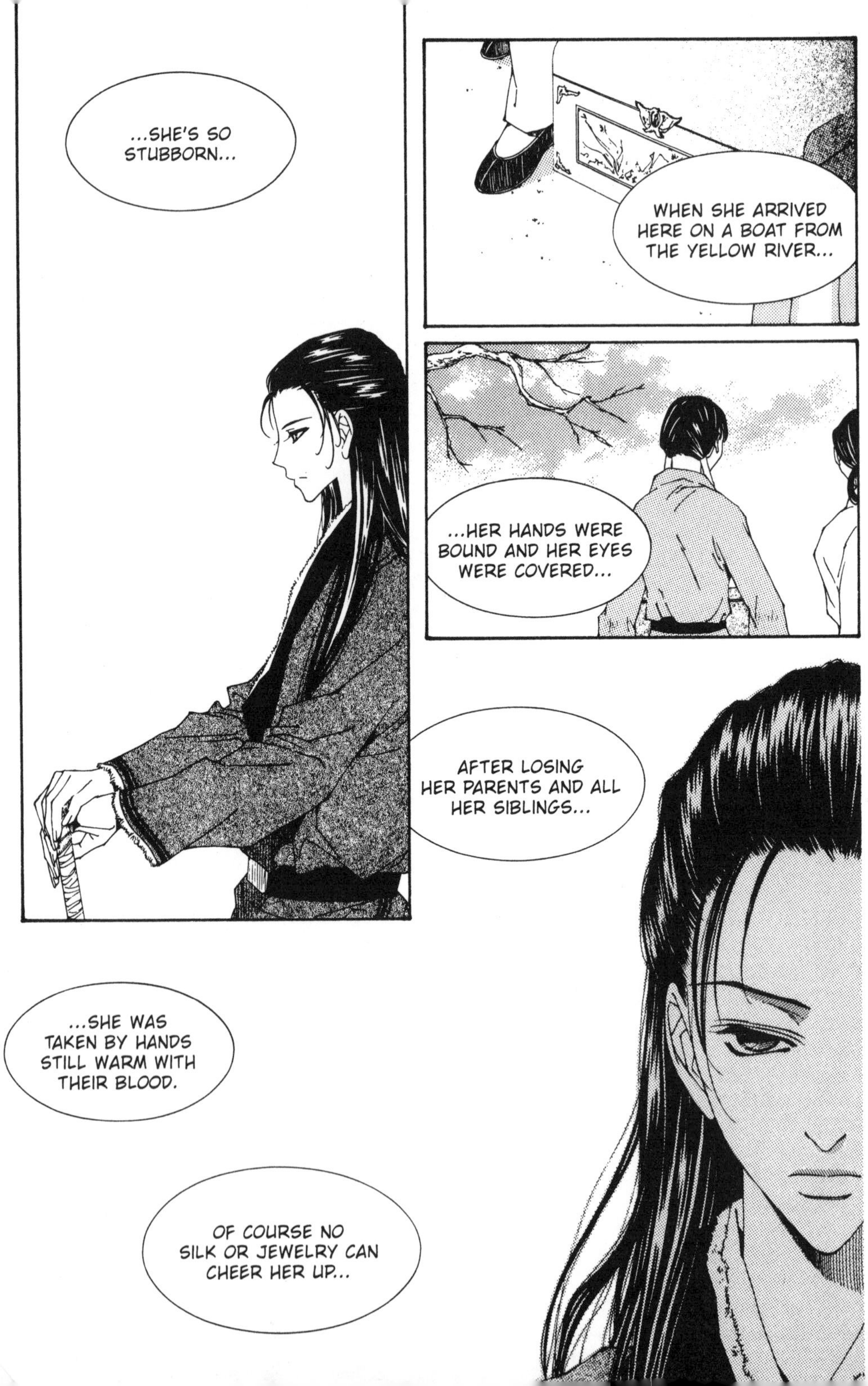
...SHE'S SO STUBBORN...
WHEN SHE ARRIVED HERE ON A BOAT FROM THE YELLOW RIVER...
...HER HANDS WERE BOUND AND HER EYES WERE COVERED...
AFTER LOSING HER PARENTS AND ALL HER SIBLINGS...
...SHE WAS TAKEN BY HANDS STILL WARM WITH THEIR BLOOD.
OF COURSE NO SILK OR JEWELRY CAN CHEER HER UP...

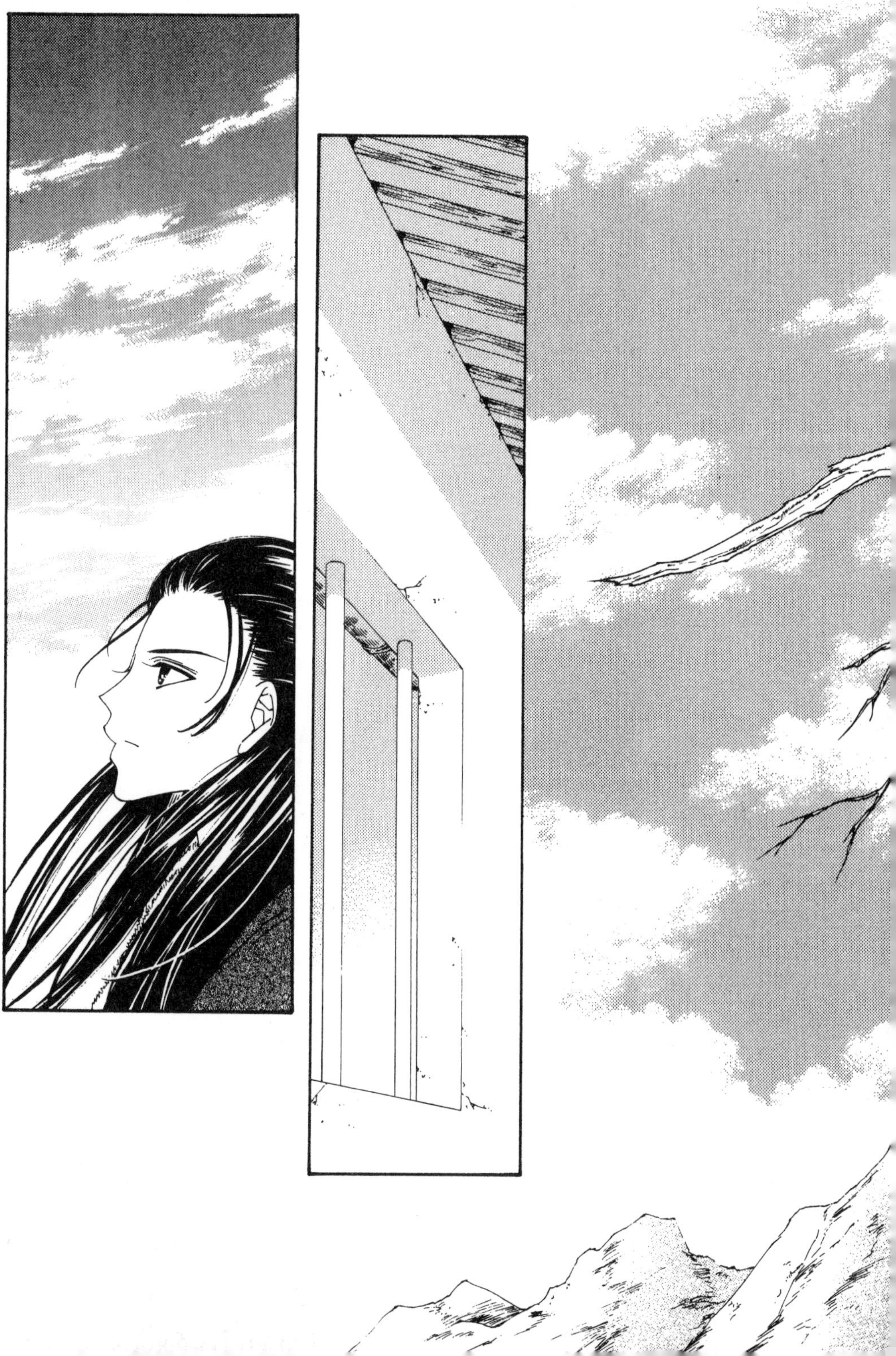

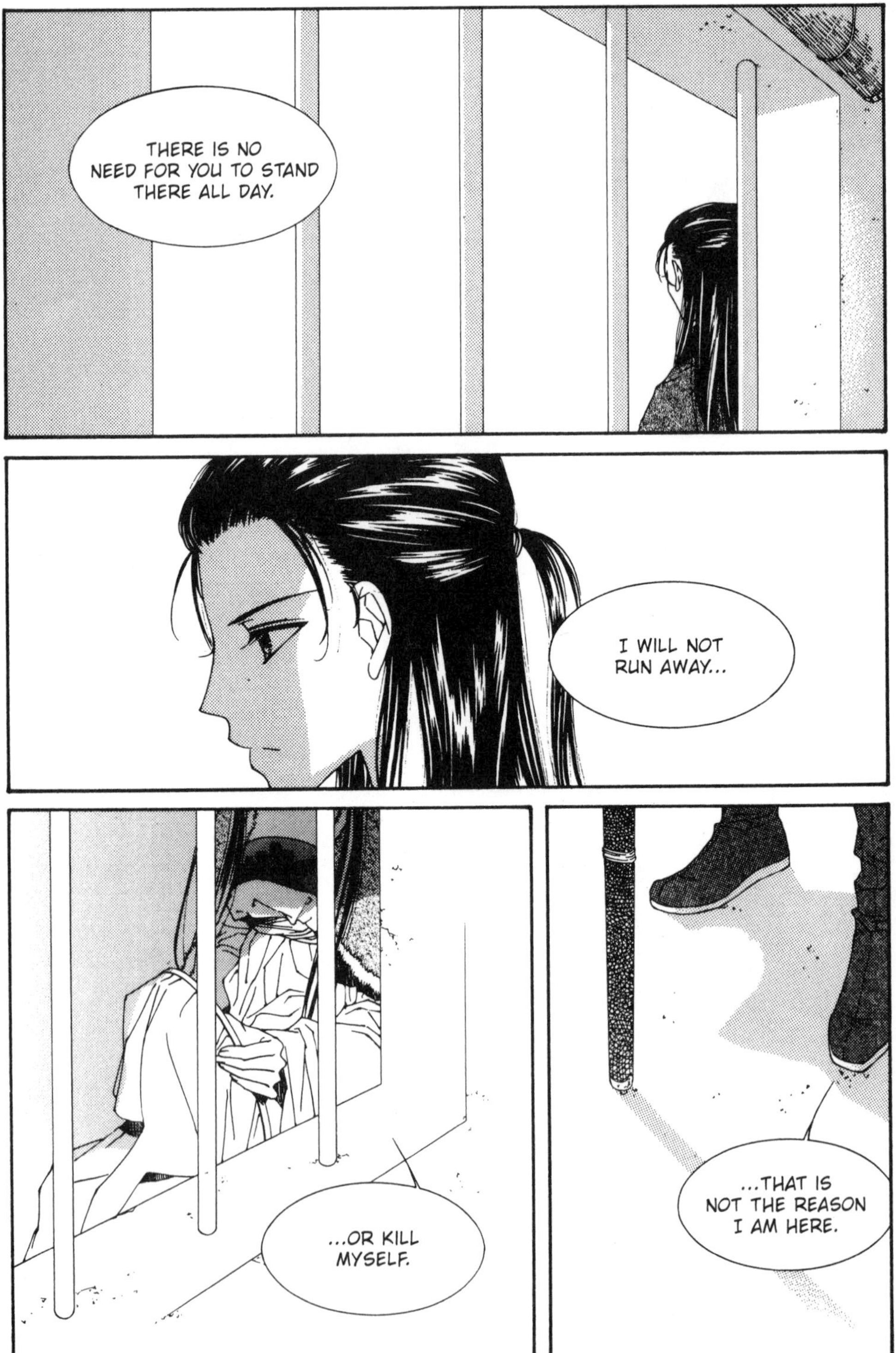
THERE IS NO NEED FOR YOU TO STAND THERE ALL DAY.
I WILL NOT RUN AWAY...
...OR KILL MYSELF.
...THAT IS NOT THE REASON I AM HERE.

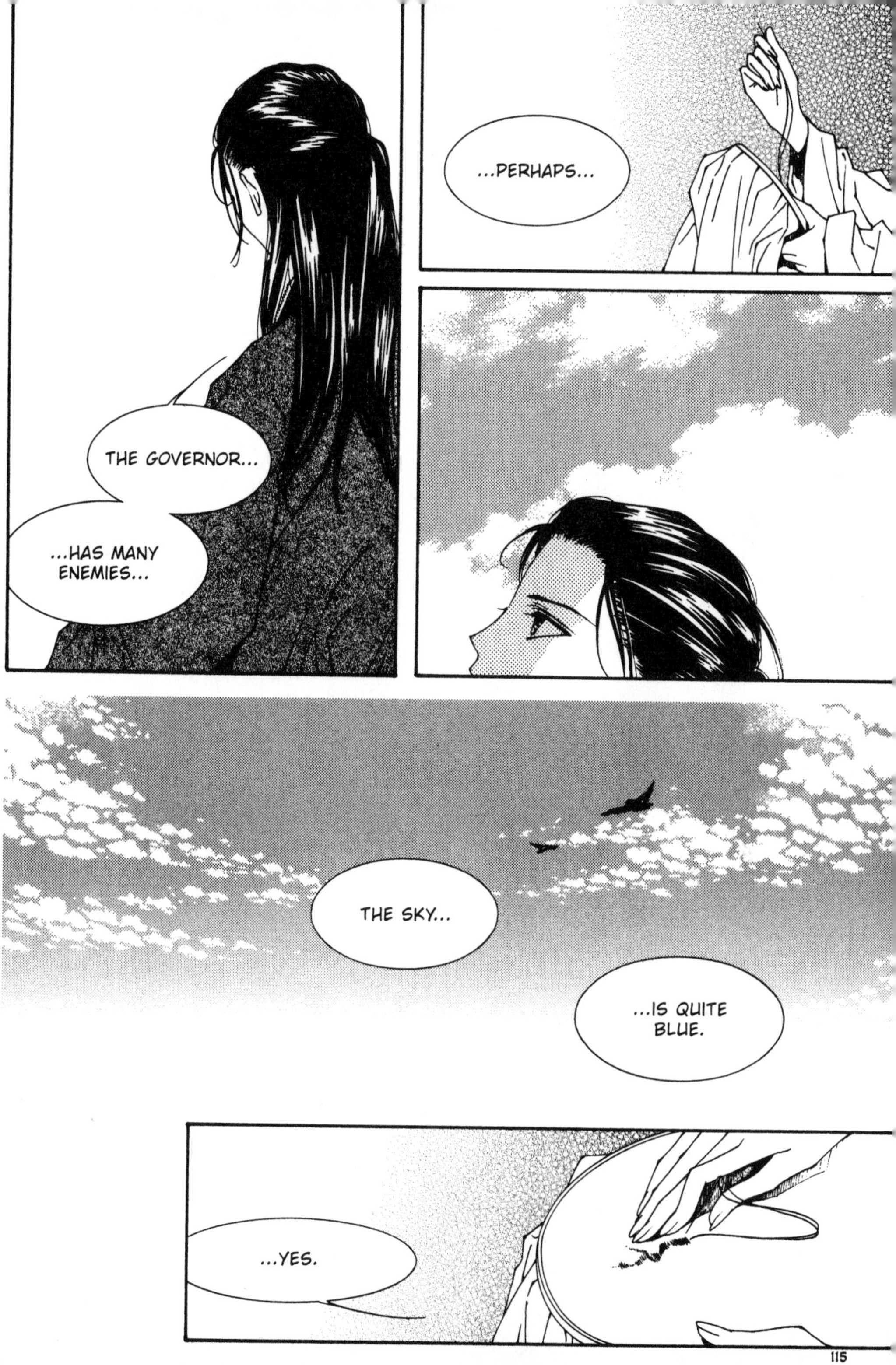
THE GOVERNOR...
...HAS MANY ENEMIES...
...PERHAPS...
THE SKY...
...IS QUITE BLUE.
...YES.

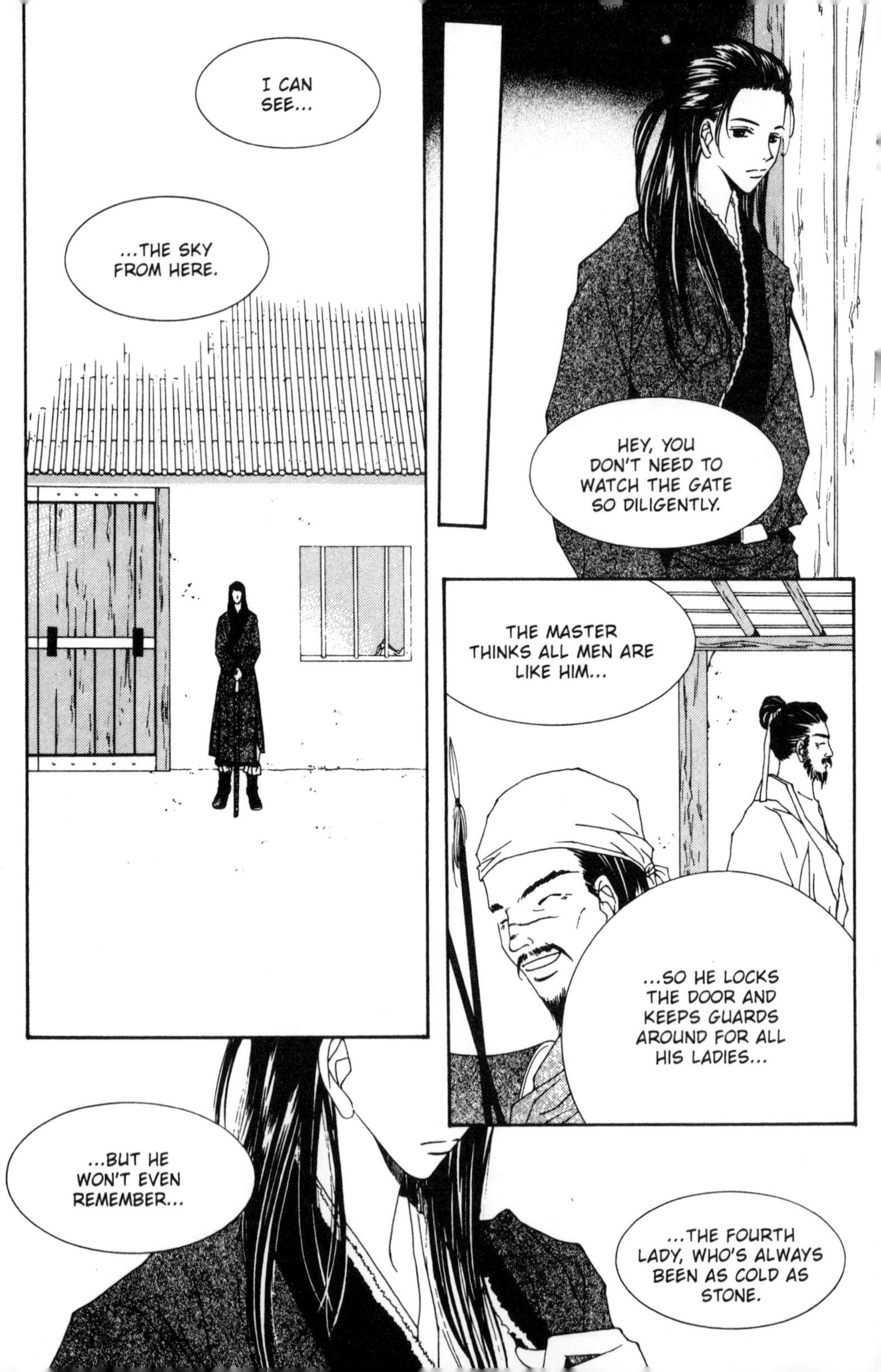
I CAN SEE...
...THE SKY FROM HERE.
HEY, YOU DON'T NEED TO WATCH THE GATE SO DILIGENTLY.
THE MASTER THINKS ALL MEN ARE LIKE HIM...
...SO HE LOCKS THE DOOR AND KEEPS GUARDS AROUND FOR ALL HIS LADIES...
...BUT HE WON'T EVEN REMEMBER...
...THE FOURTH LADY, WHO'S ALWAYS BEEN AS COLD AS STONE.

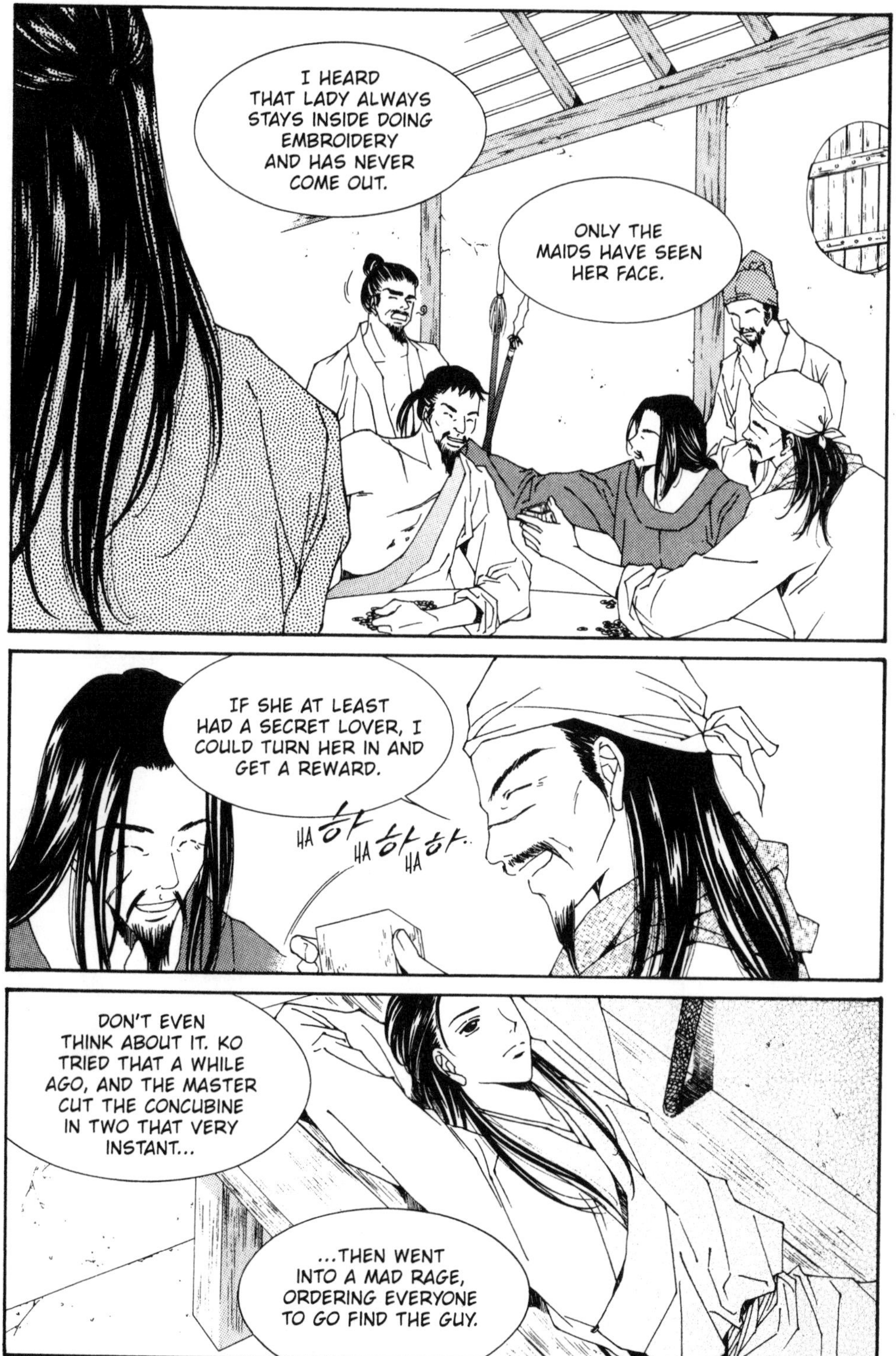
I HEARD THAT LADY ALWAYS STAYS INSIDE DOING EMBROIDERY AND HAS NEVER COME OUT.
ONLY THE MAIDS HAVE SEEN HER FACE.
IF SHE AT LEAST HAD A SECRET LOVER, I COULD TURN HER IN AND GET A REWARD.
HA 하 HA 하 HA 하.
DON'T EVEN THINK ABOUT IT. KO TRIED THAT A WHILE AGO, AND THE MASTER CUT THE CONCUBINE IN TWO THAT VERY INSTANT...
...THEN WENT INTO A MAD RAGE, ORDERING EVERYONE TO GO FIND THE GUY.

KO COULDN'T EVEN MENTION A REWARD, HE WAS SHAKING SO BAD.

IT WAS LIKE DONG ZHUO COME BACK TO LIFE.

THE FLOWERS ARE IN BLOOM.

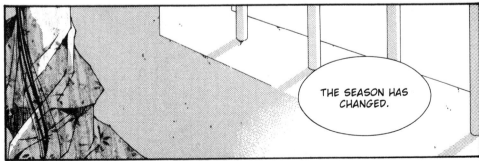

THE SEASON HAS CHANGED.

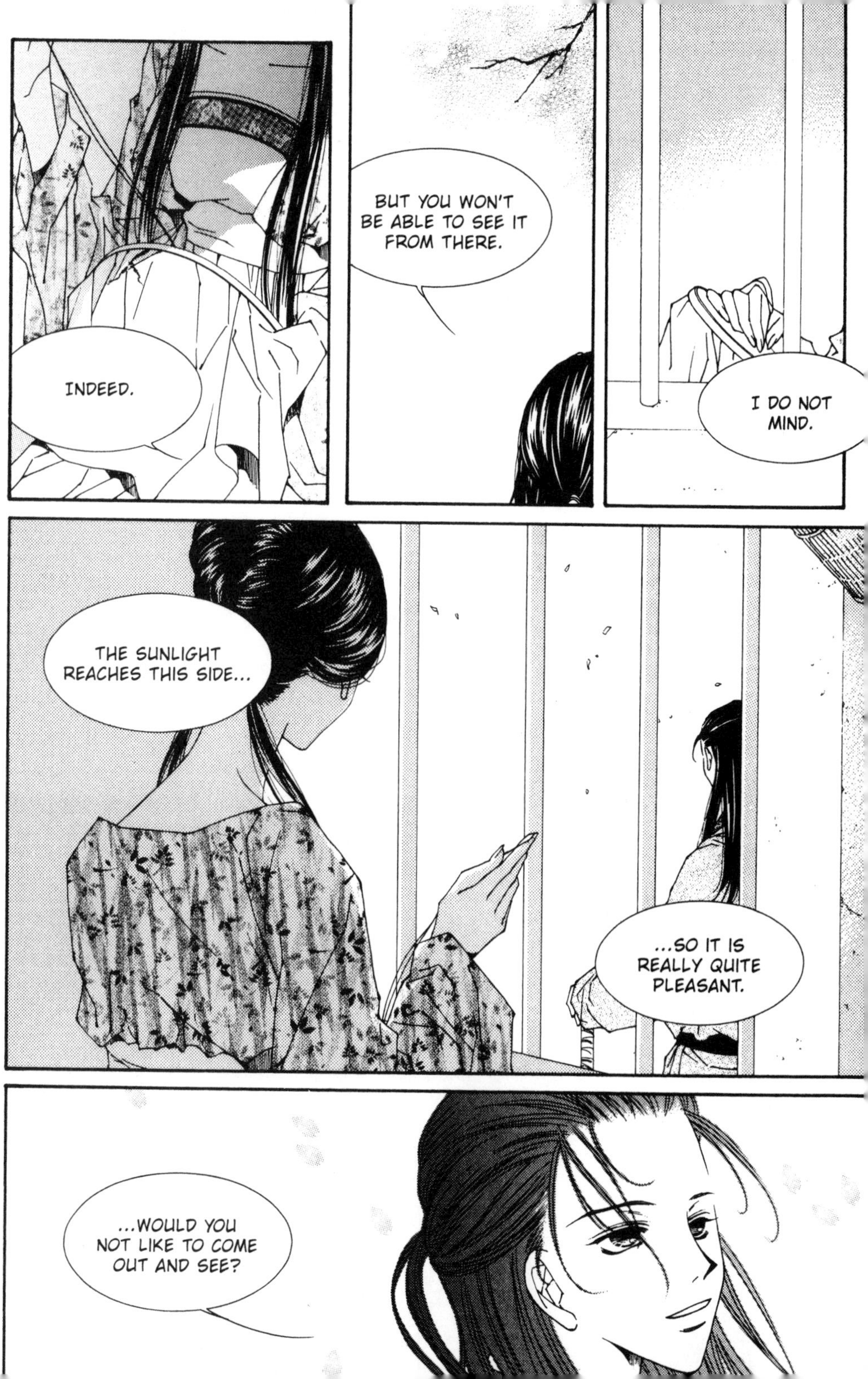
INDEED.
BUT YOU WON'T BE ABLE TO SEE IT FROM THERE.
I DO NOT MIND.
THE SUNLIGHT REACHES THIS SIDE...
...SO IT IS REALLY QUITE PLEASANT.
...WOULD YOU NOT LIKE TO COME OUT AND SEE?

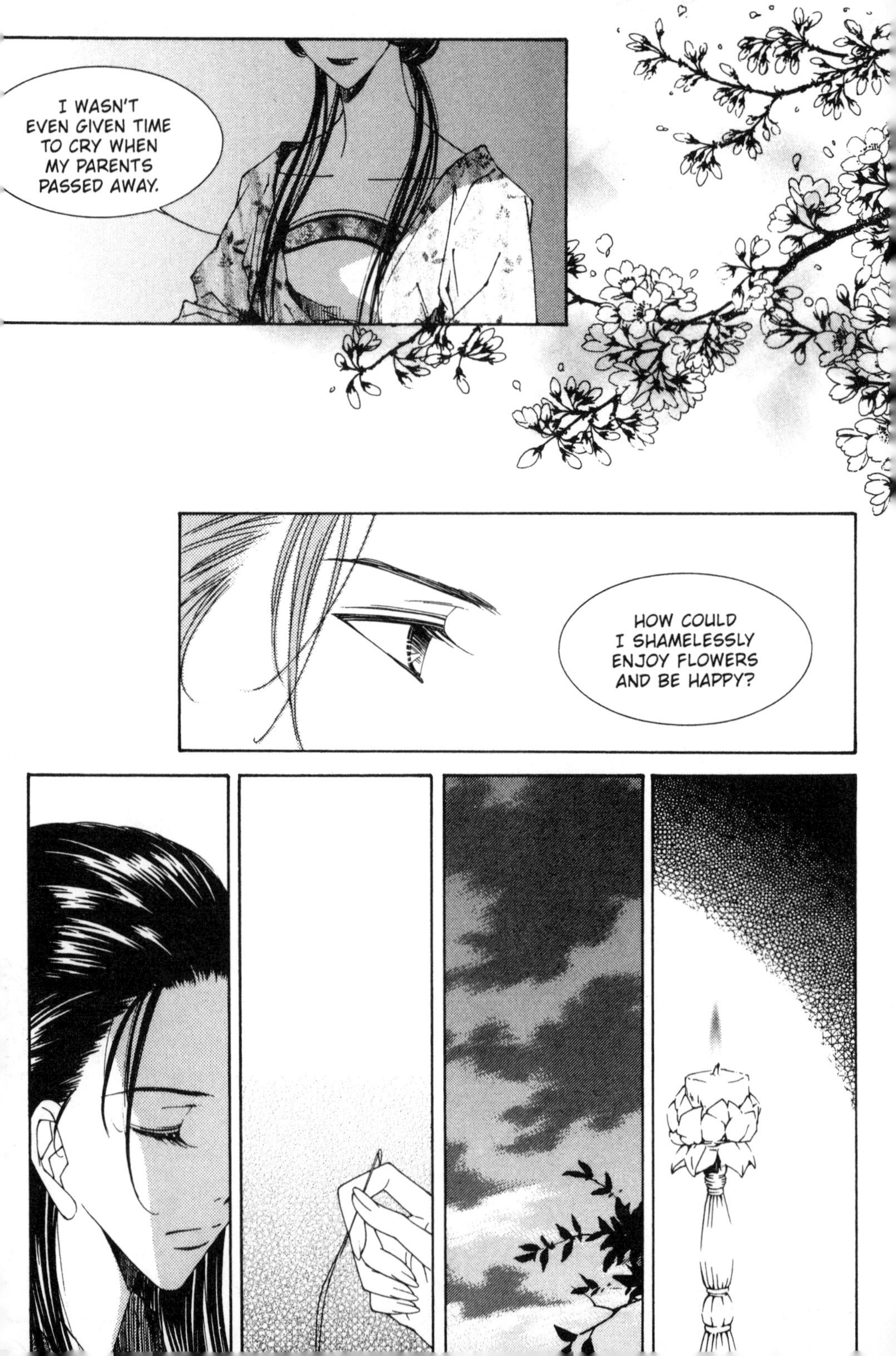
I WASN'T EVEN GIVEN TIME TO CRY WHEN MY PARENTS PASSED AWAY.
HOW COULD I SHAMELESSLY ENJOY FLOWERS AND BE HAPPY?

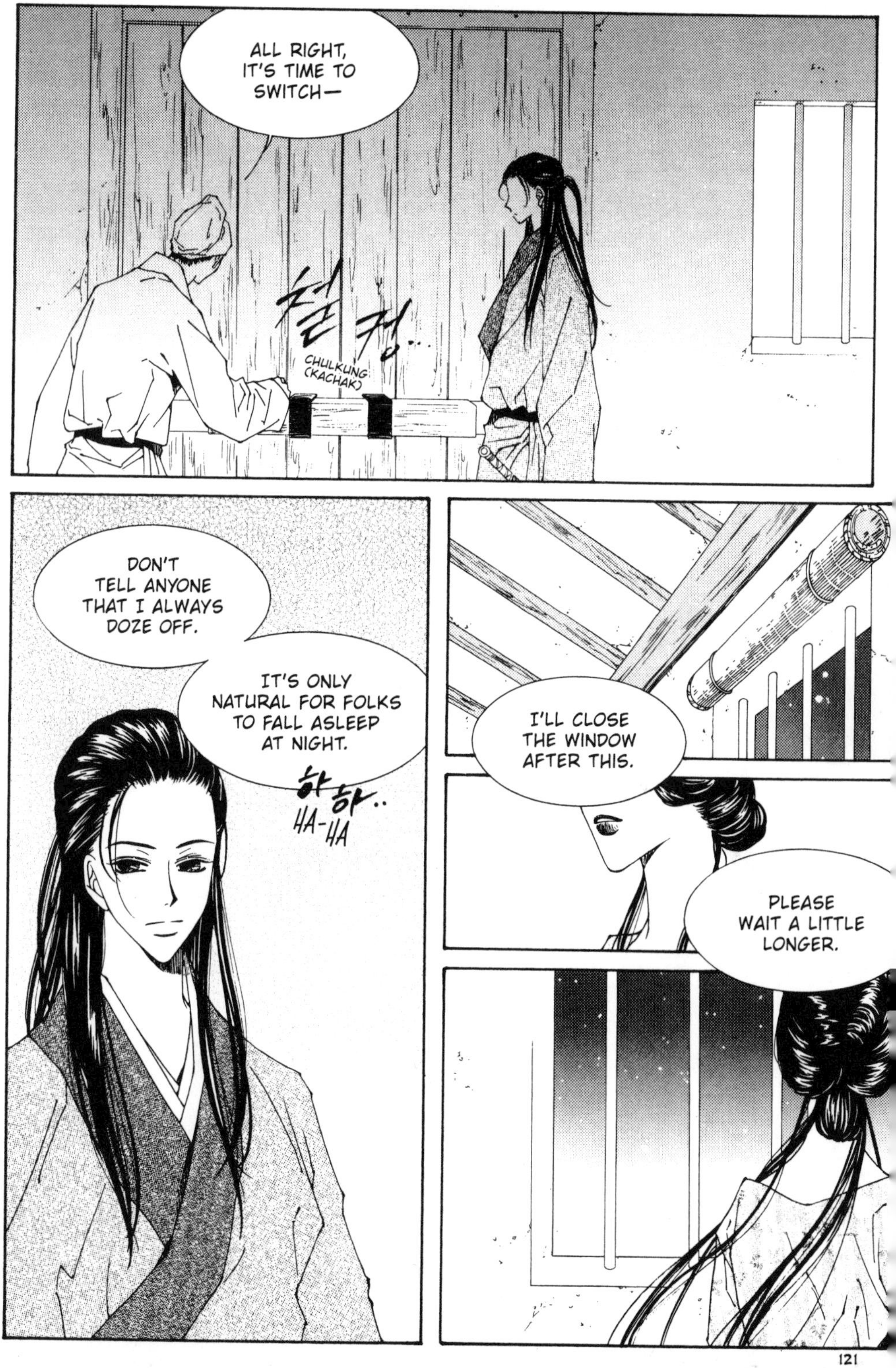
ALL RIGHT, IT'S TIME TO SWITCH—
철컹...
CHULKUNG (KACHAK)
DON'T TELL ANYONE THAT I ALWAYS DOZE OFF.
IT'S ONLY NATURAL FOR FOLKS TO FALL ASLEEP AT NIGHT.
하하..
HA-HA
I'LL CLOSE THE WINDOW AFTER THIS.
PLEASE WAIT A LITTLE LONGER.

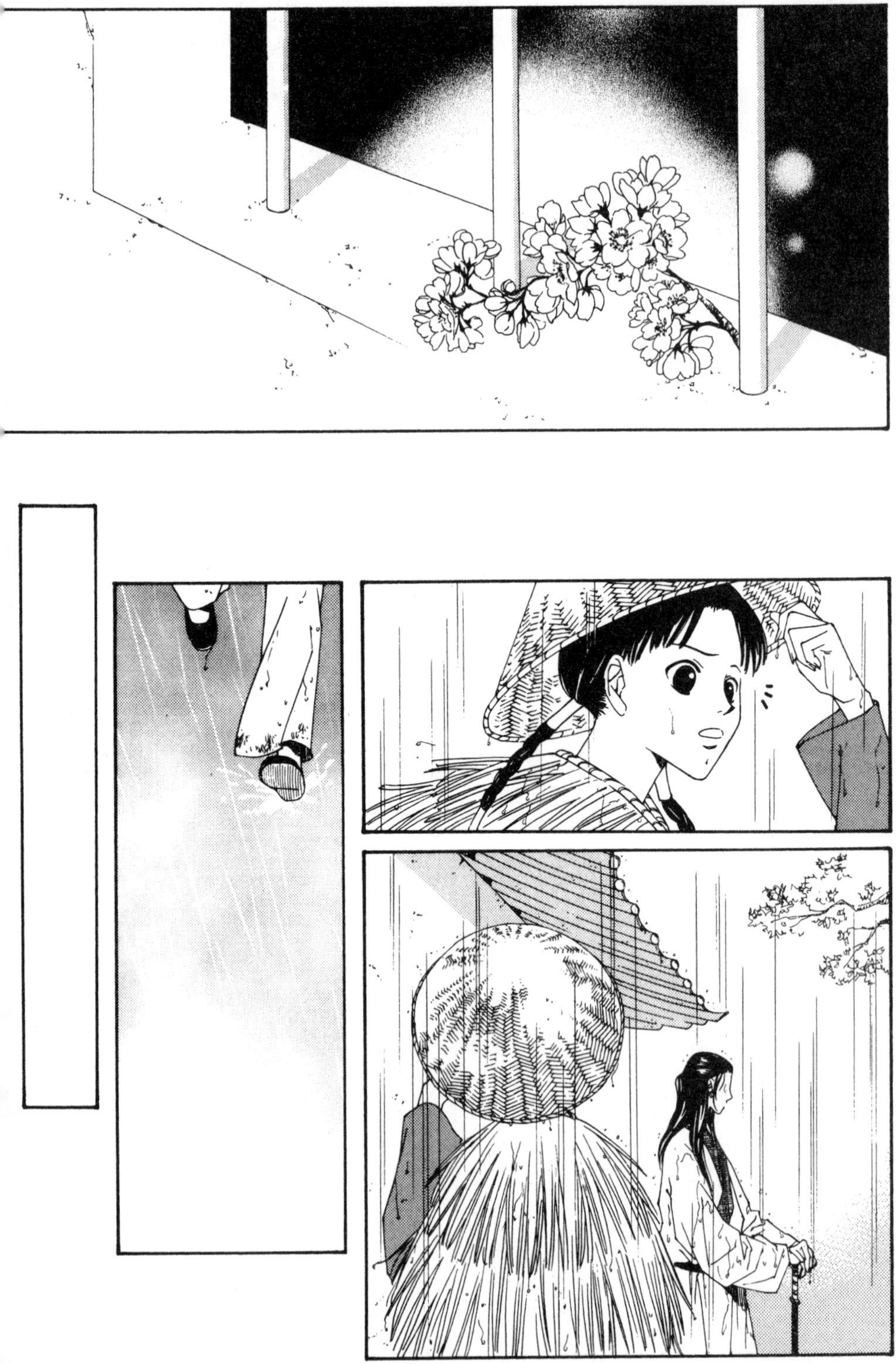

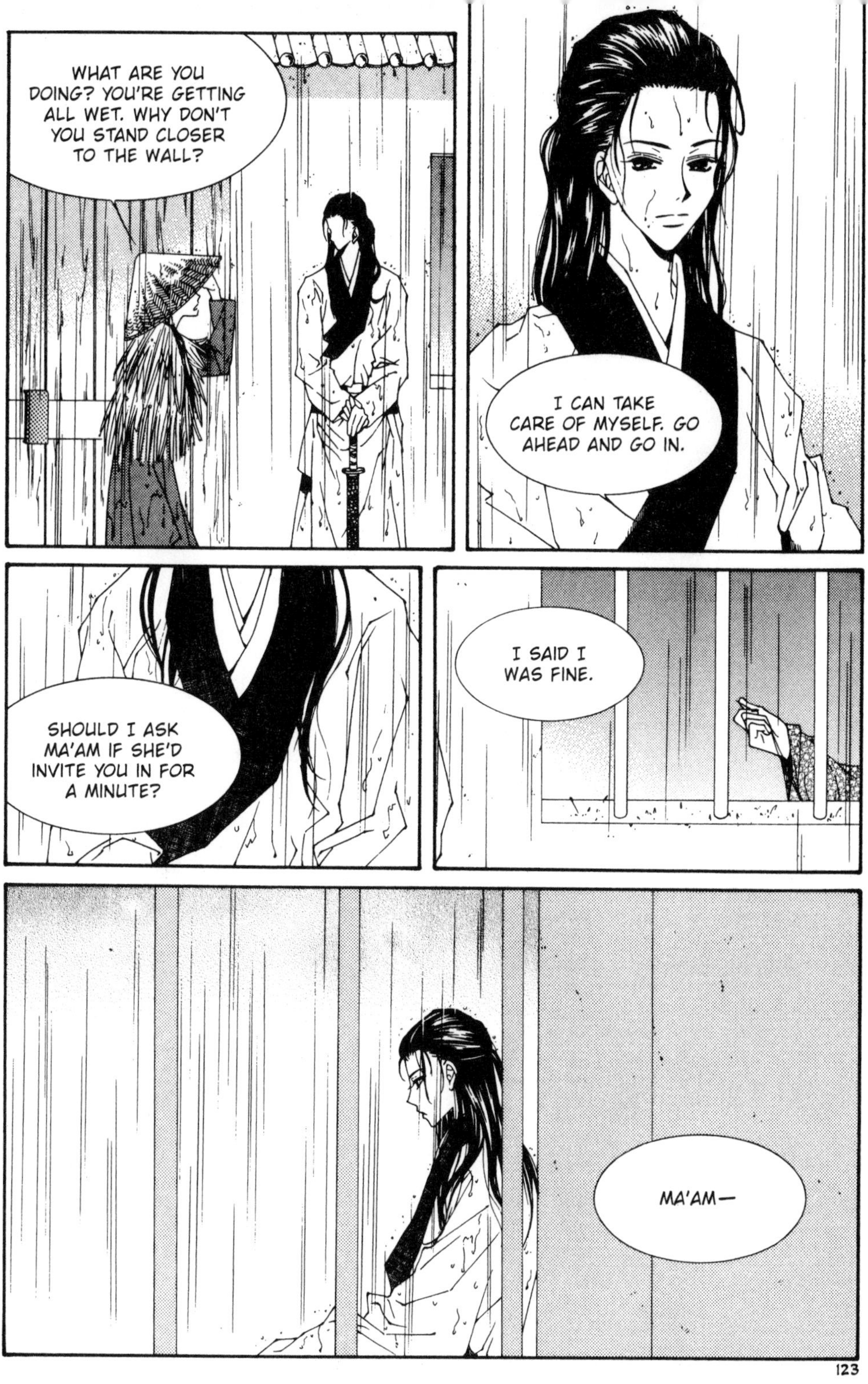
WHAT ARE YOU DOING? YOU'RE GETTING ALL WET. WHY DON'T YOU STAND CLOSER TO THE WALL?
I CAN TAKE CARE OF MYSELF. GO AHEAD AND GO IN.
SHOULD I ASK MA'AM IF SHE'D INVITE YOU IN FOR A MINUTE?
I SAID I WAS FINE.
MA'AM—

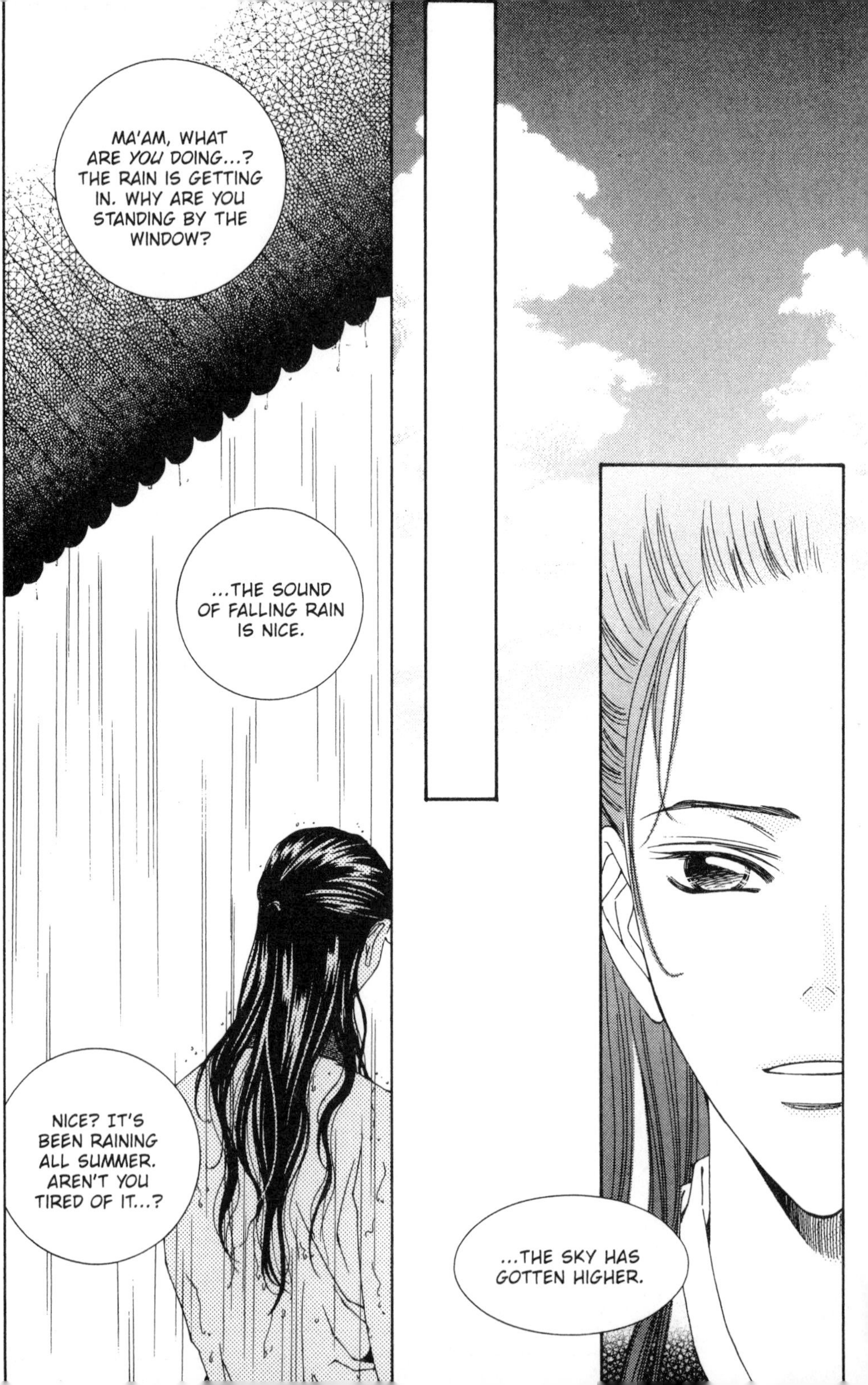
MA'AM, WHAT ARE *YOU* DOING...? THE RAIN IS GETTING IN. WHY ARE YOU STANDING BY THE WINDOW?
...THE SOUND OF FALLING RAIN IS NICE.
NICE? IT'S BEEN RAINING ALL SUMMER. AREN'T YOU TIRED OF IT...?
...THE SKY HAS GOTTEN HIGHER.

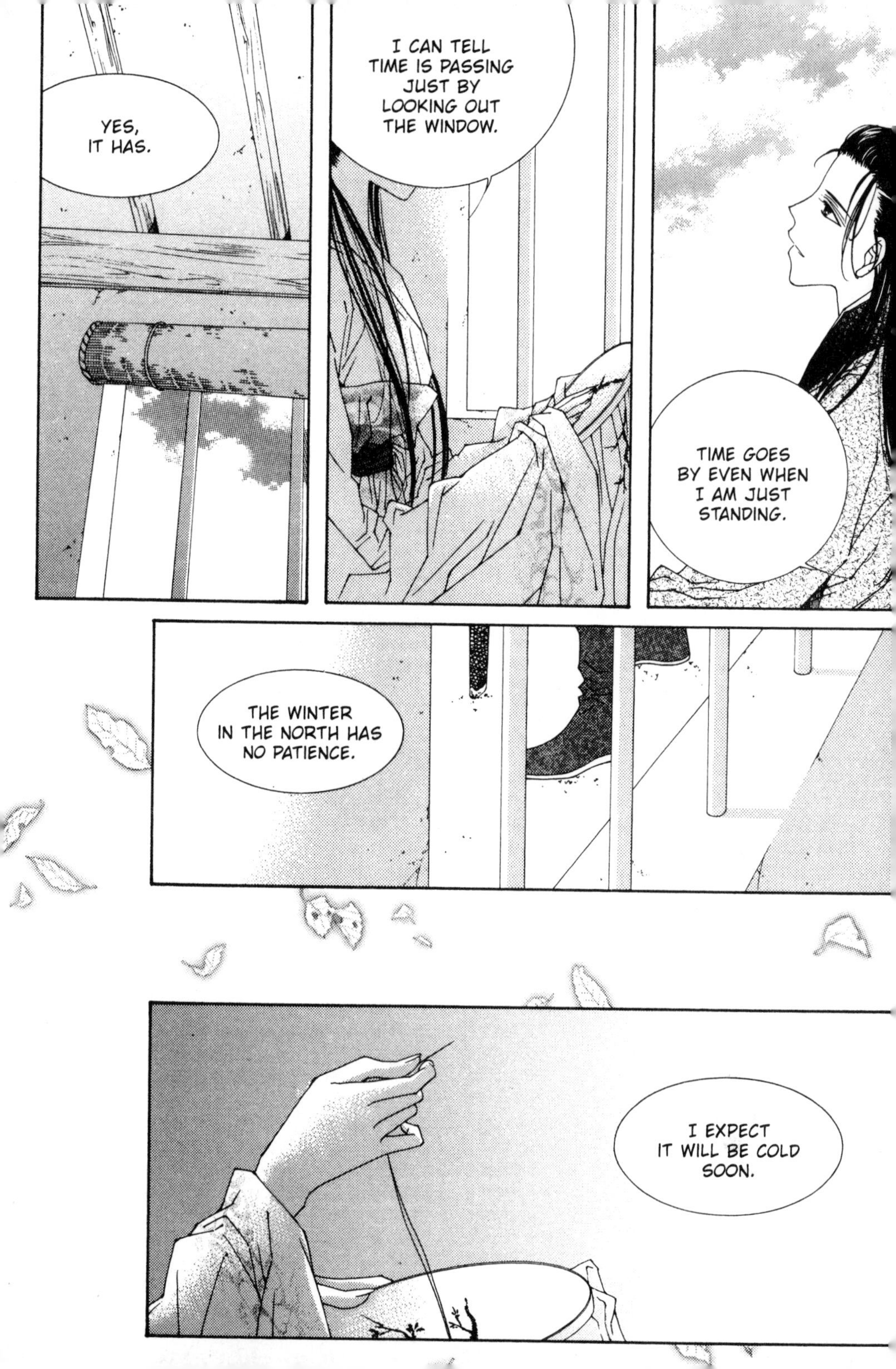
YES, IT HAS.
I CAN TELL TIME IS PASSING JUST BY LOOKING OUT THE WINDOW.
TIME GOES BY EVEN WHEN I AM JUST STANDING.
THE WINTER IN THE NORTH HAS NO PATIENCE.
I EXPECT IT WILL BE COLD SOON.

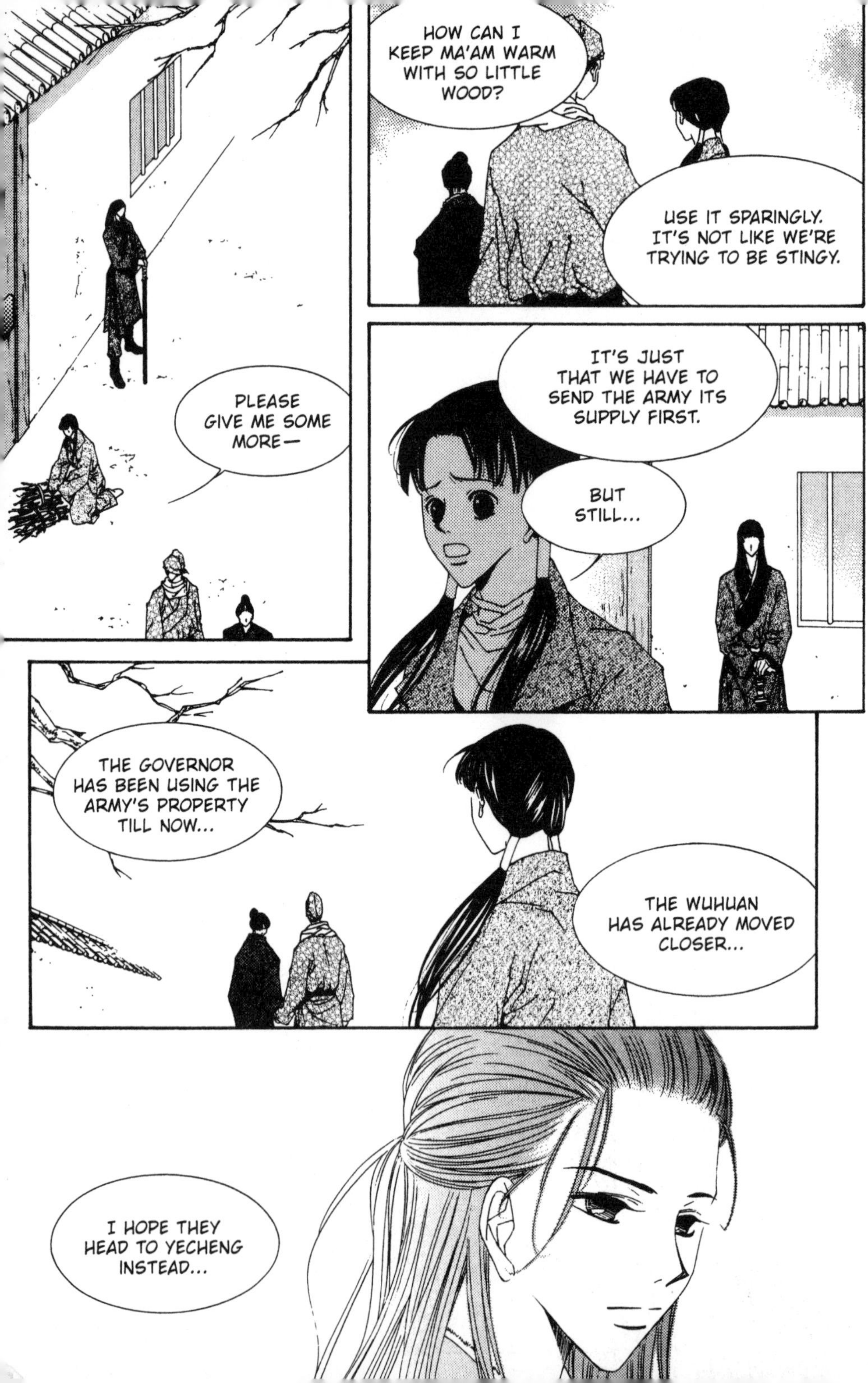
PLEASE GIVE ME SOME MORE—
HOW CAN I KEEP MA'AM WARM WITH SO LITTLE WOOD?
USE IT SPARINGLY. IT'S NOT LIKE WE'RE TRYING TO BE STINGY.
IT'S JUST THAT WE HAVE TO SEND THE ARMY ITS SUPPLY FIRST.
BUT STILL...
THE GOVERNOR HAS BEEN USING THE ARMY'S PROPERTY TILL NOW...
THE WUHUAN HAS ALREADY MOVED CLOSER...
I HOPE THEY HEAD TO YECHENG INSTEAD...

IT HAS BECOME VERY COLD.

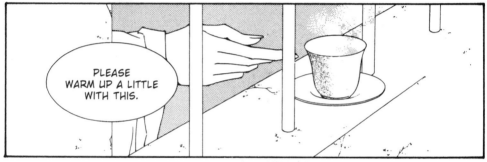

PLEASE WARM UP A LITTLE WITH THIS.

...PLEASE CLOSE THE WINDOW. THIS WIND IS FRIGID.

...THE ROOM IS HOT, SO THE COOL BREEZE FEELS NICE.

...WILL YOU NOT DRINK THIS?

IT HAS GOTTEN COLD. SHOULD I TAKE IT AWAY?

...NO...

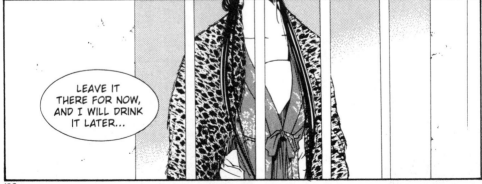

LEAVE IT THERE FOR NOW, AND I WILL DRINK IT LATER...

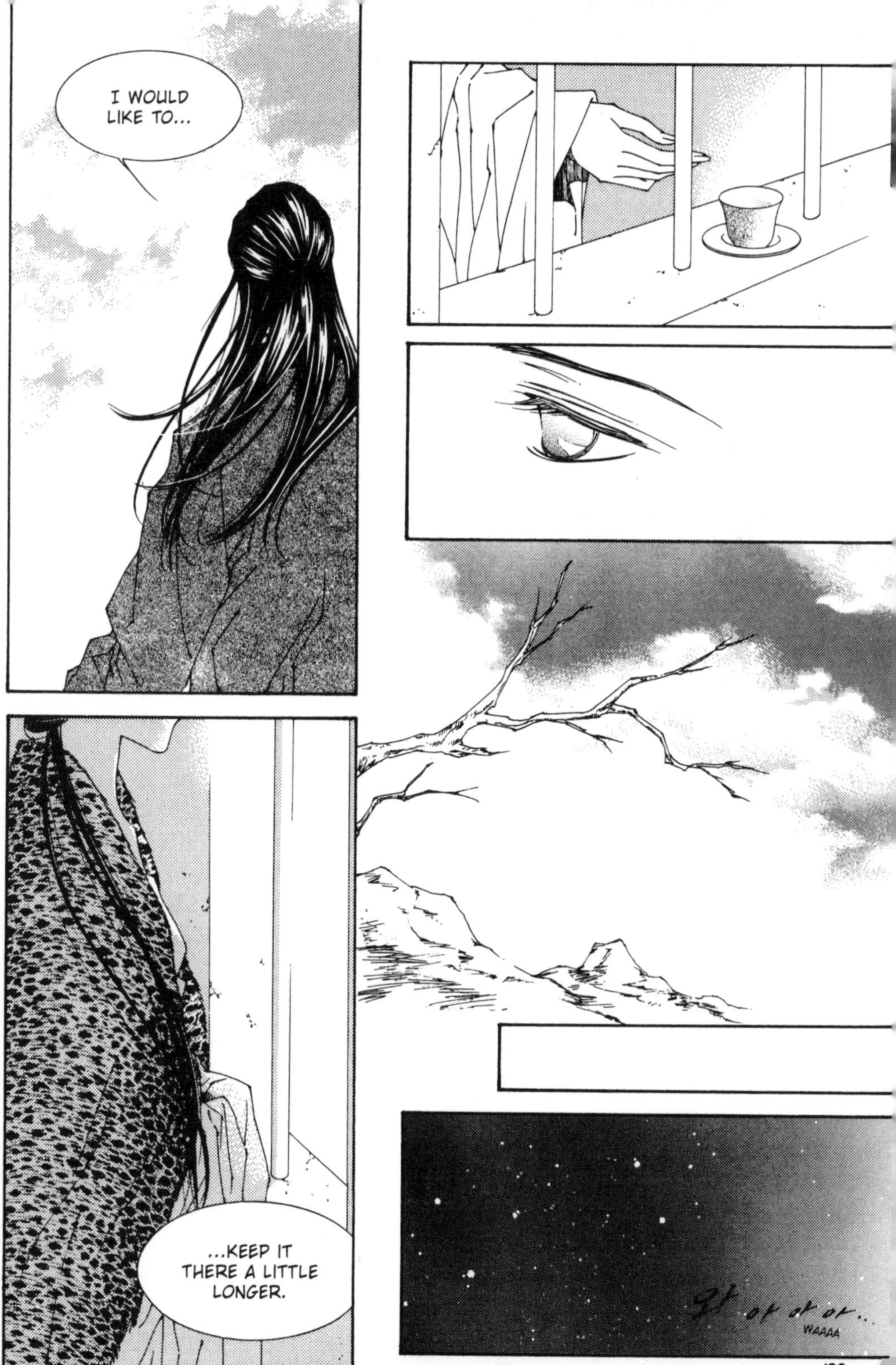
I WOULD LIKE TO...
...KEEP IT THERE A LITTLE LONGER.
와아아아...
WAAAA

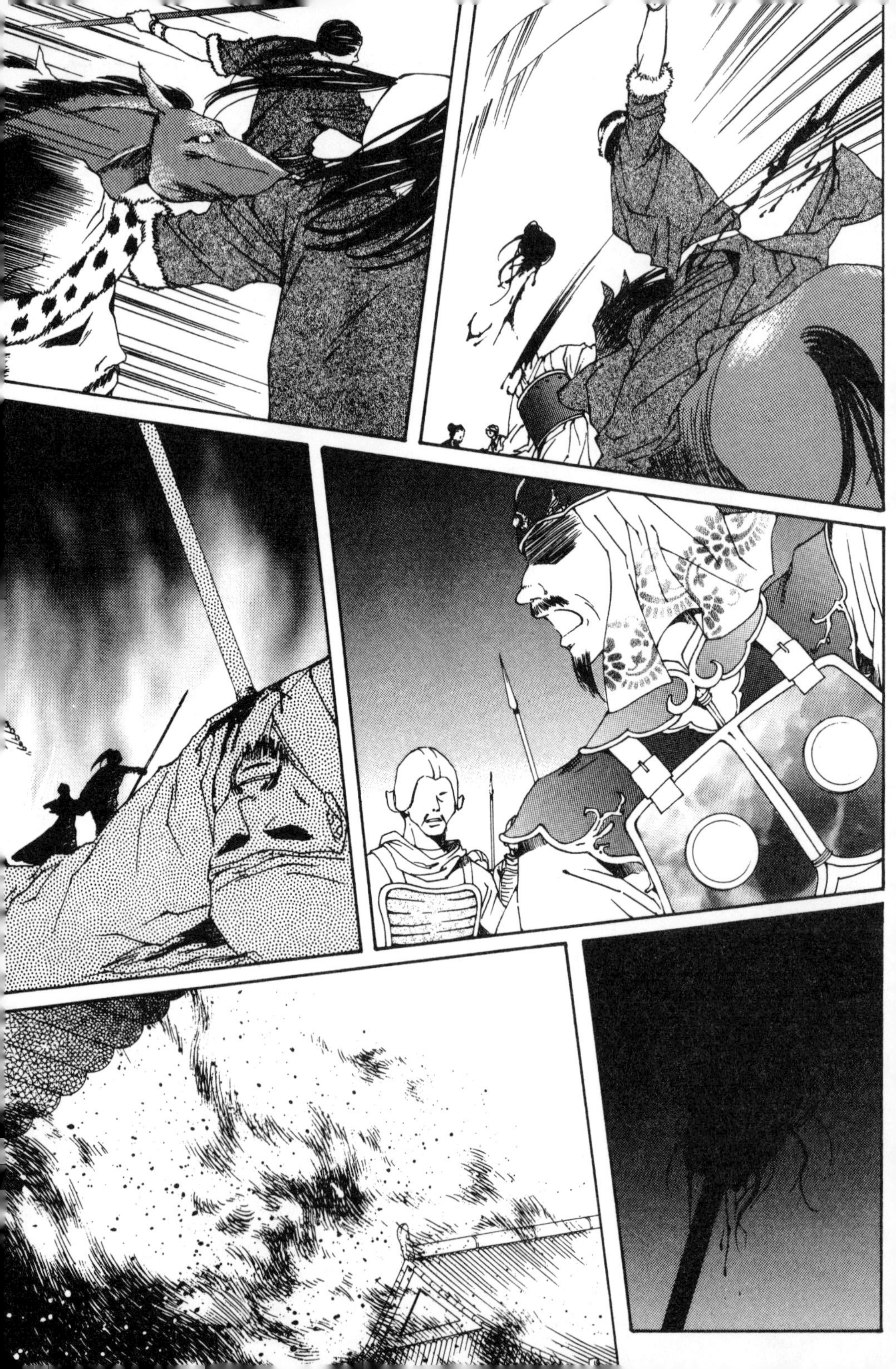

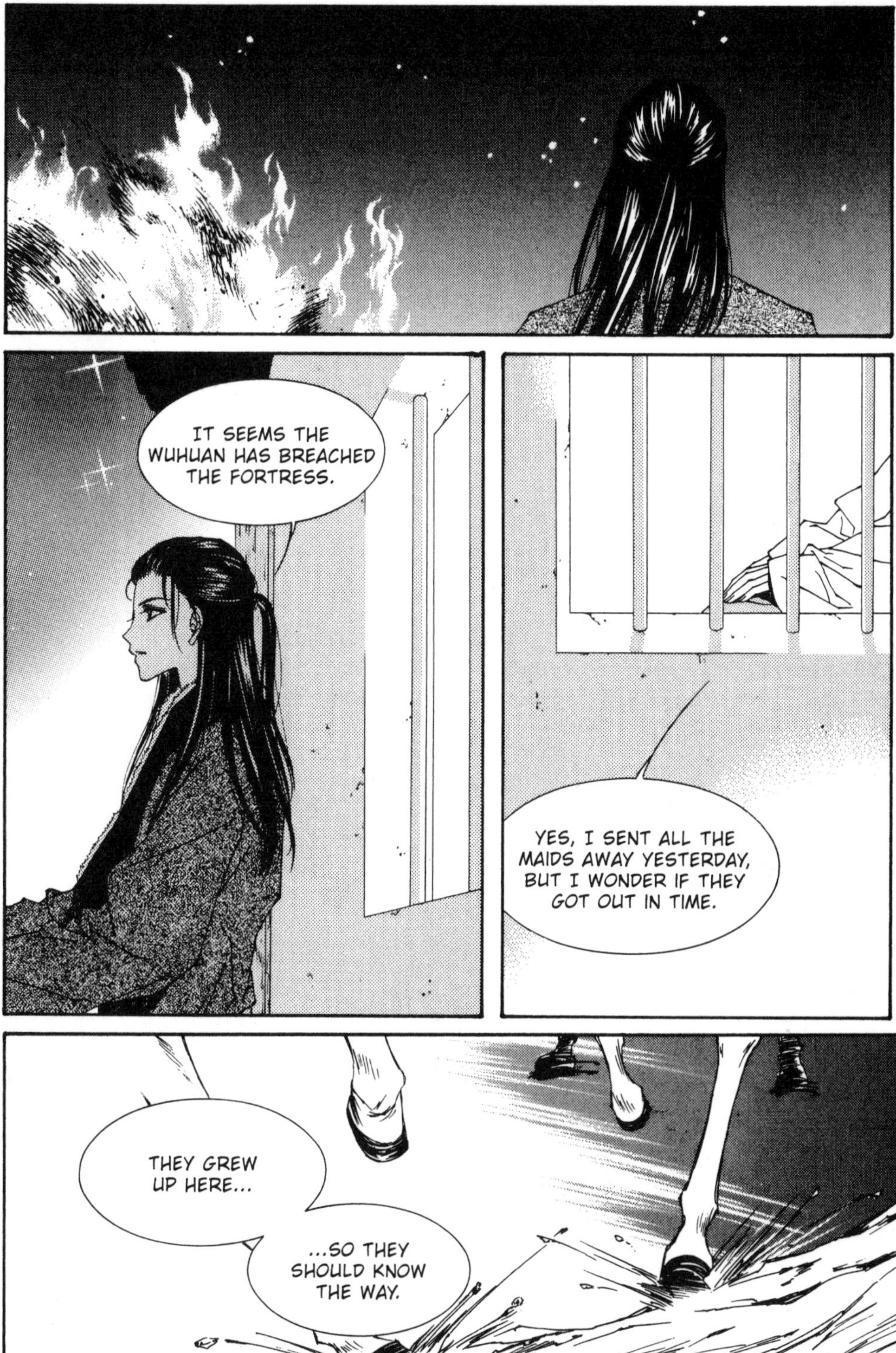
IT SEEMS THE WUHUAN HAS BREACHED THE FORTRESS.
YES, I SENT ALL THE MAIDS AWAY YESTERDAY, BUT I WONDER IF THEY GOT OUT IN TIME.
THEY GREW UP HERE...
...SO THEY SHOULD KNOW THE WAY.

PLEASE ESCAPE. THERE IS GREAT DANGER APPROACHING.

WOULD YOU LIKE TO LEAVE?

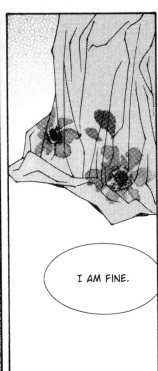

I AM FINE.

MY LIFE IS NOT WORTH THE EFFORT TO CONTINUE LIVING.

THIS IS ENOUGH.

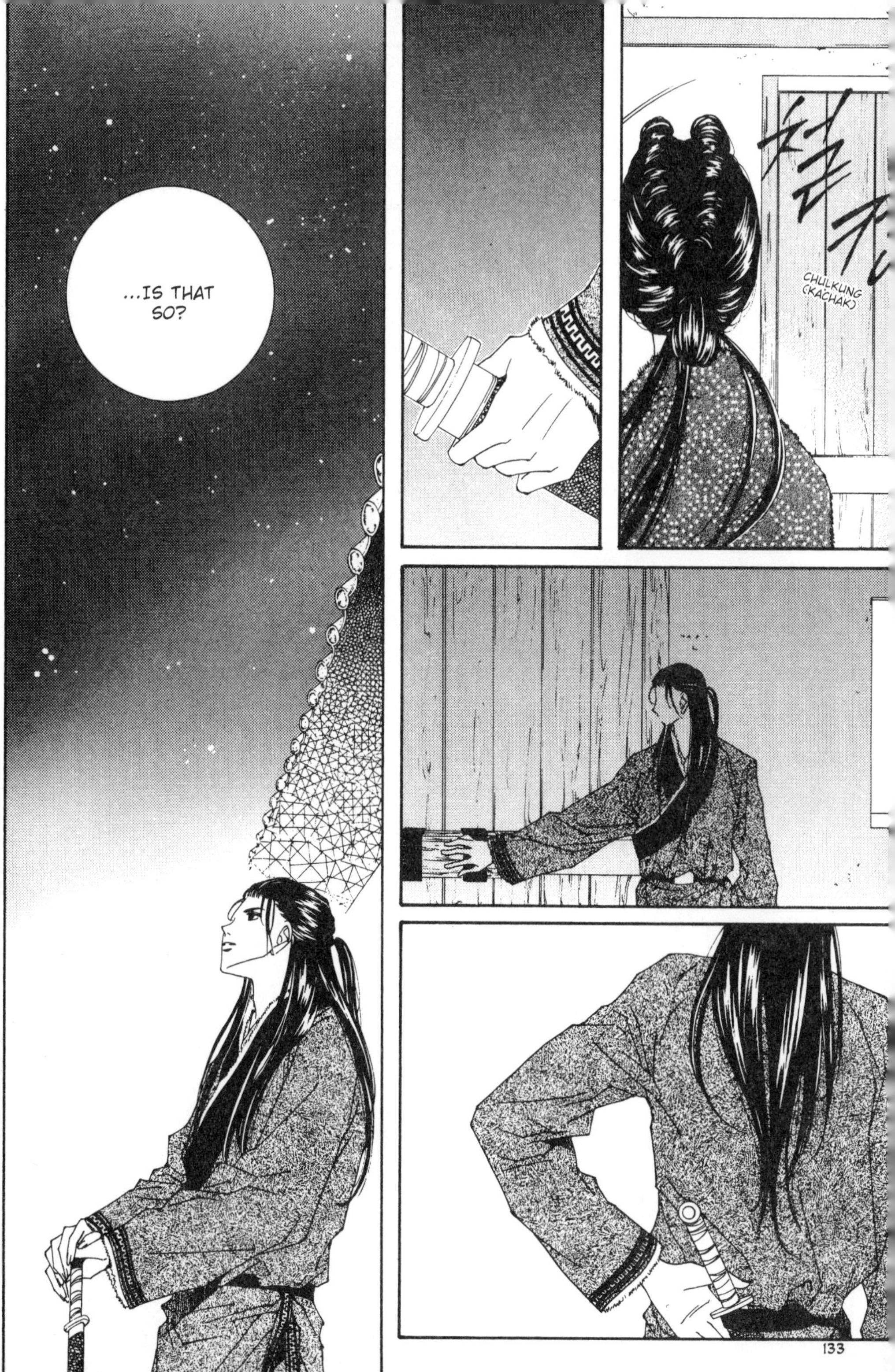
...IS THAT SO?
CHULKUNG (KACHAK)

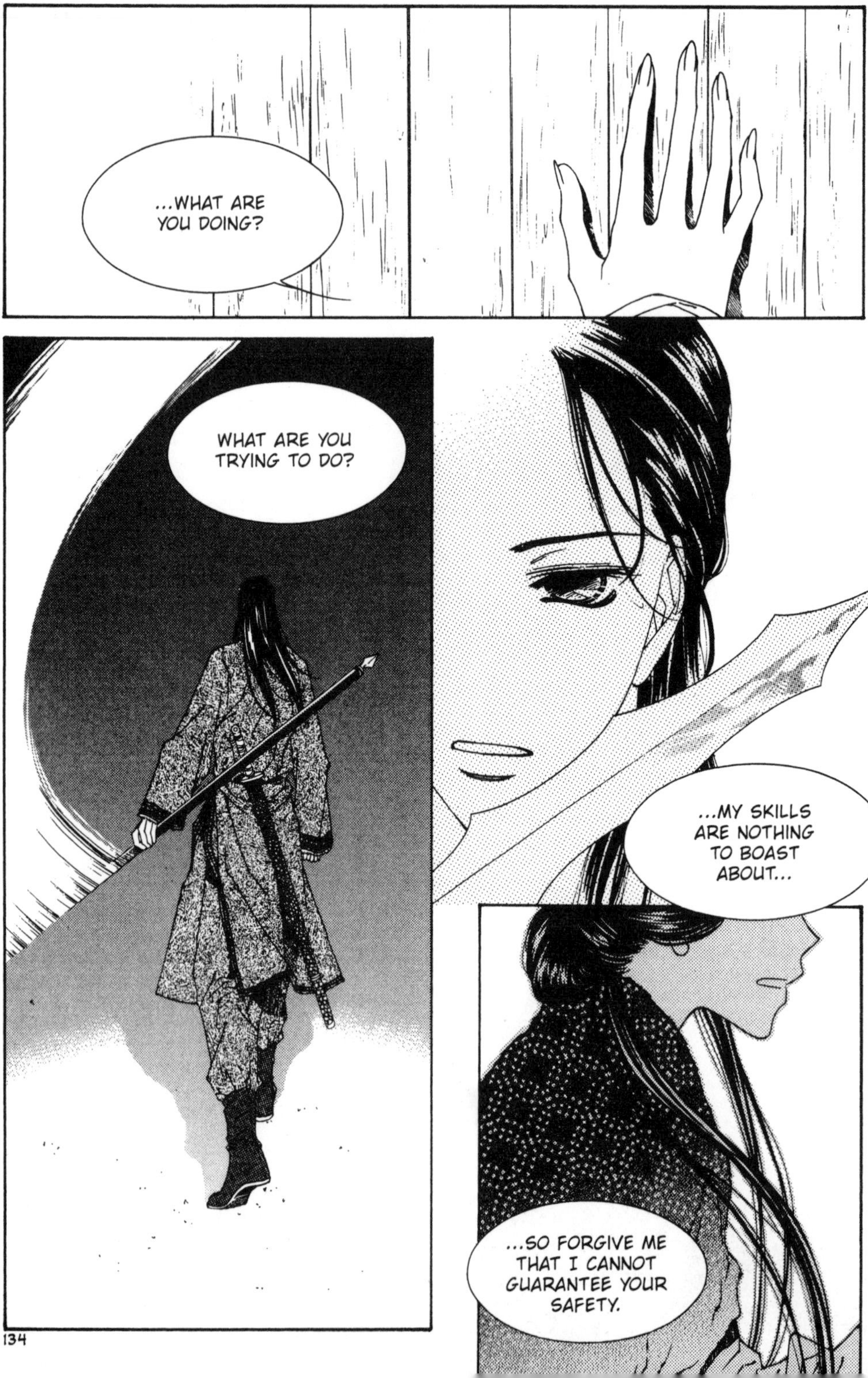
...WHAT ARE YOU DOING?
WHAT ARE YOU TRYING TO DO?
...MY SKILLS ARE NOTHING TO BOAST ABOUT...
...SO FORGIVE ME THAT I CANNOT GUARANTEE YOUR SAFETY.

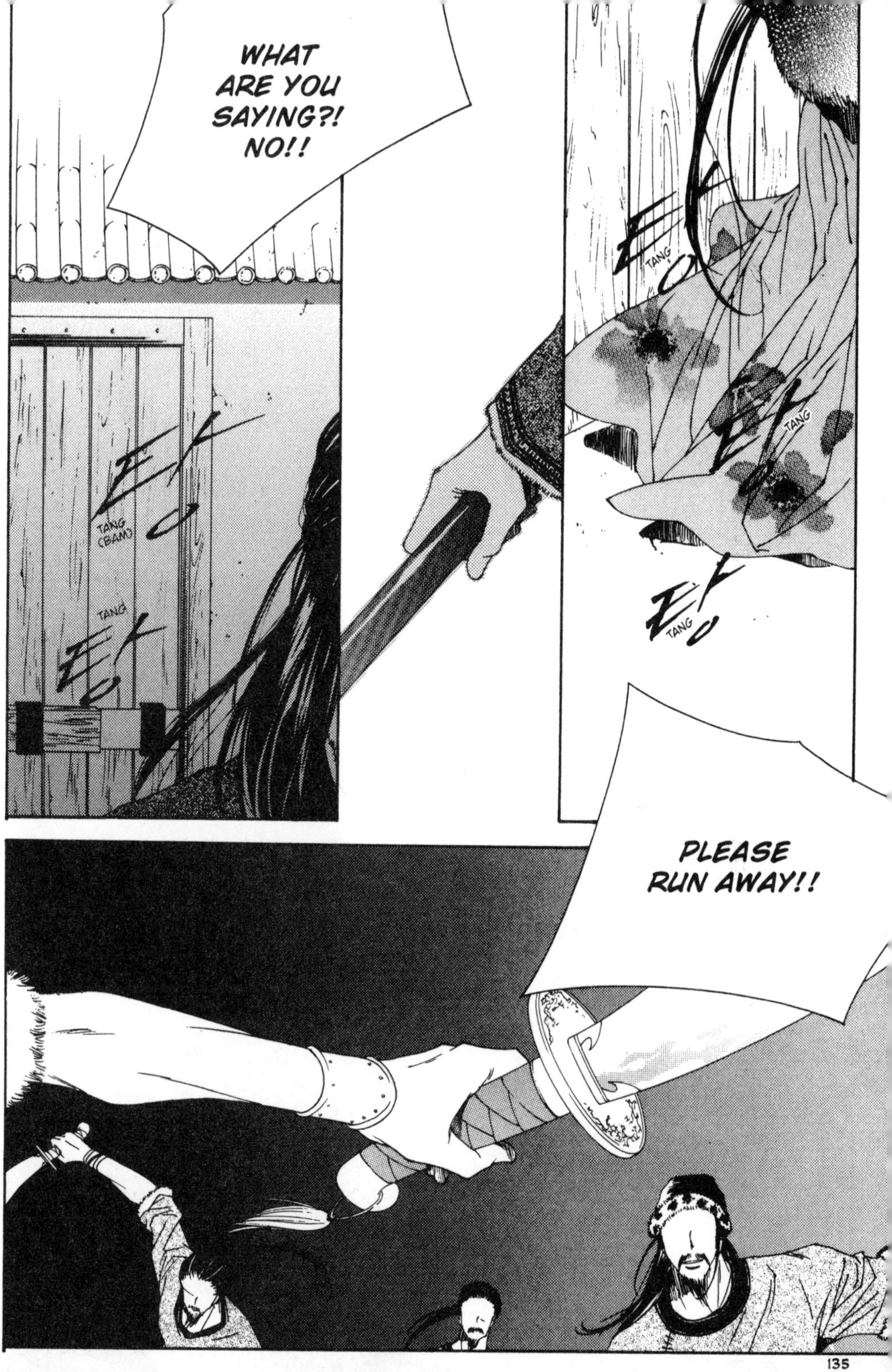
WHAT ARE YOU SAYING?! NO!!
TANG (BAM)
TANG
TANG
TANG
TANG
PLEASE RUN AWAY!!

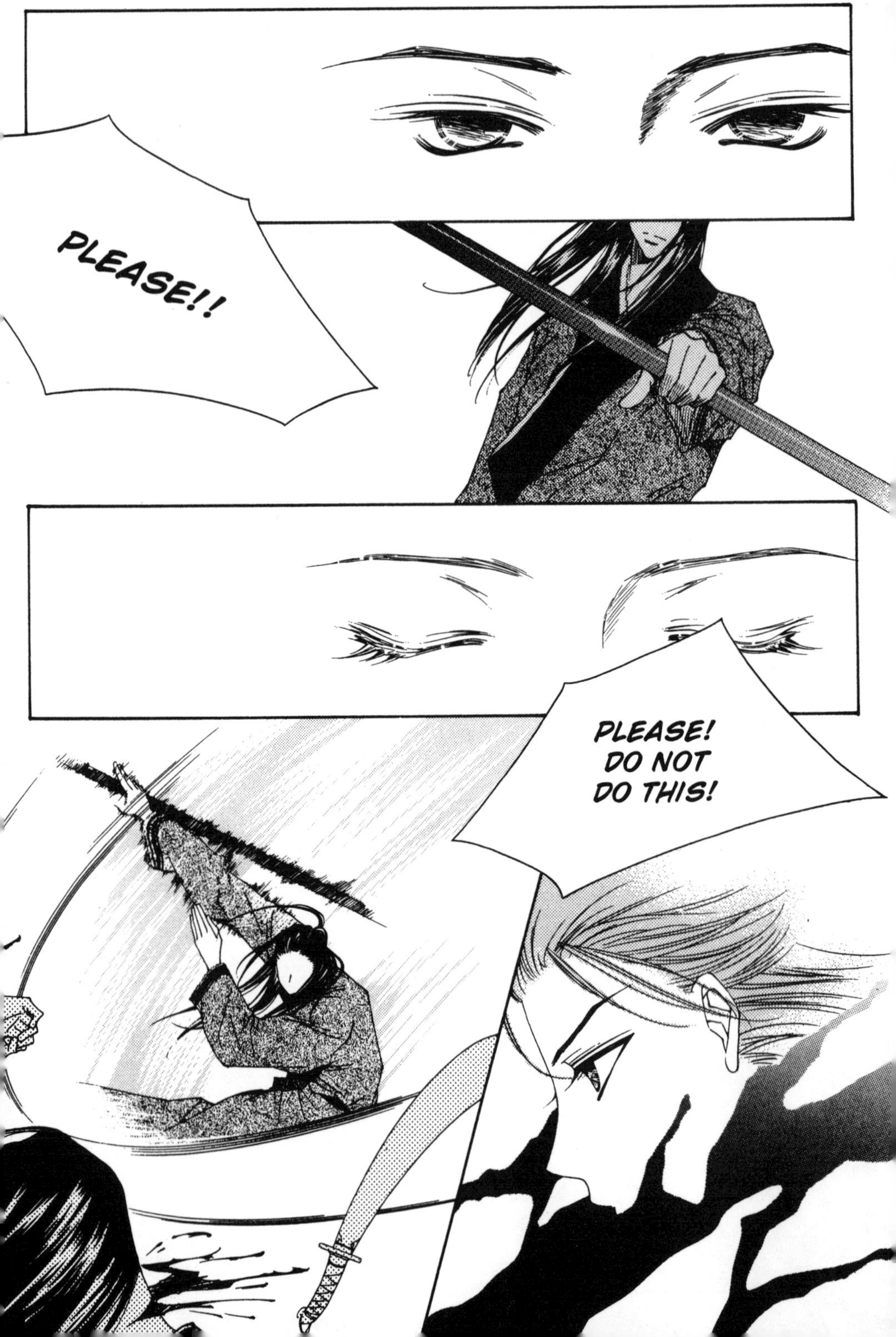
PLEASE!!
PLEASE! DO NOT DO THIS!

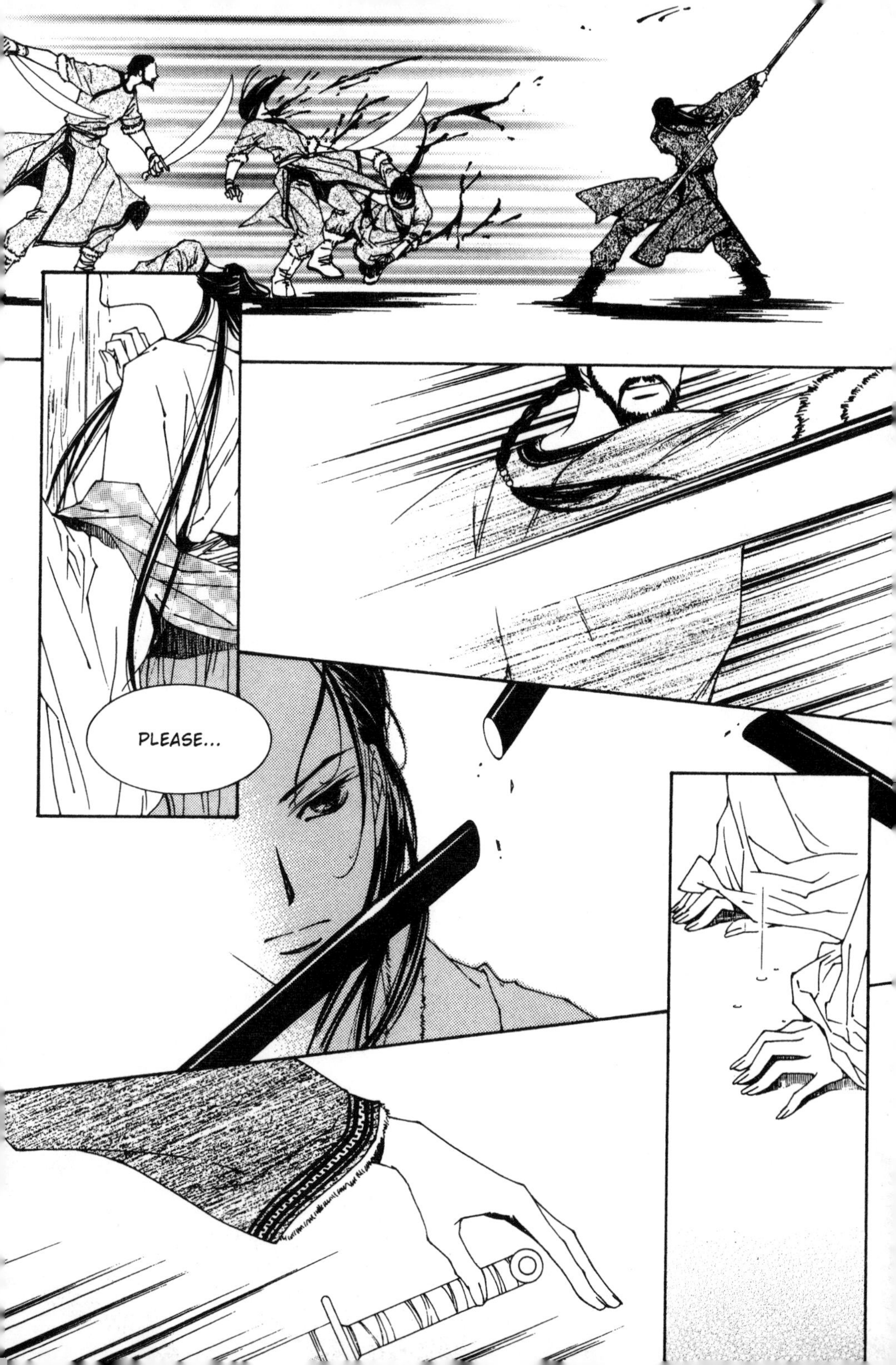
PLEASE...

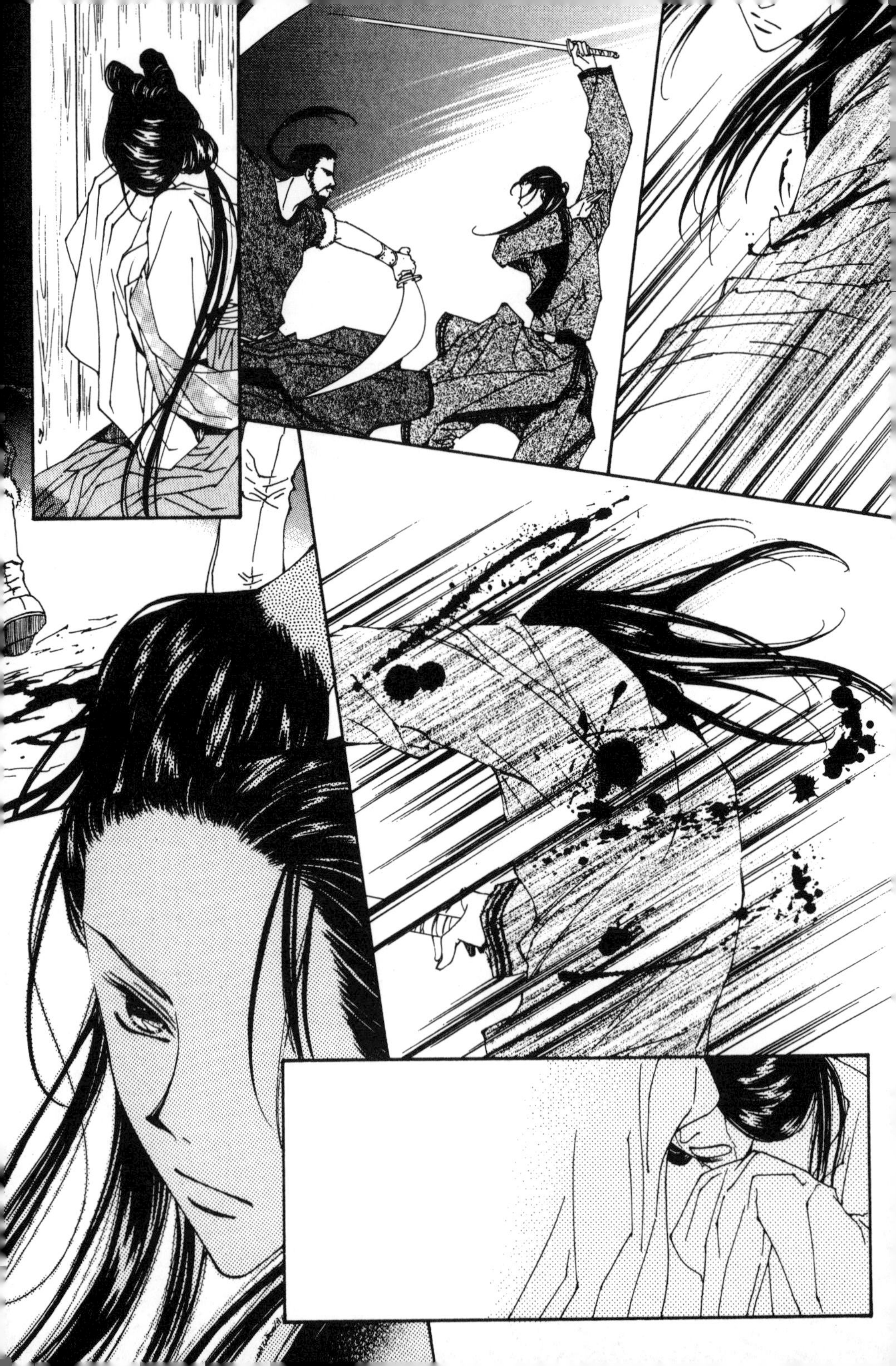

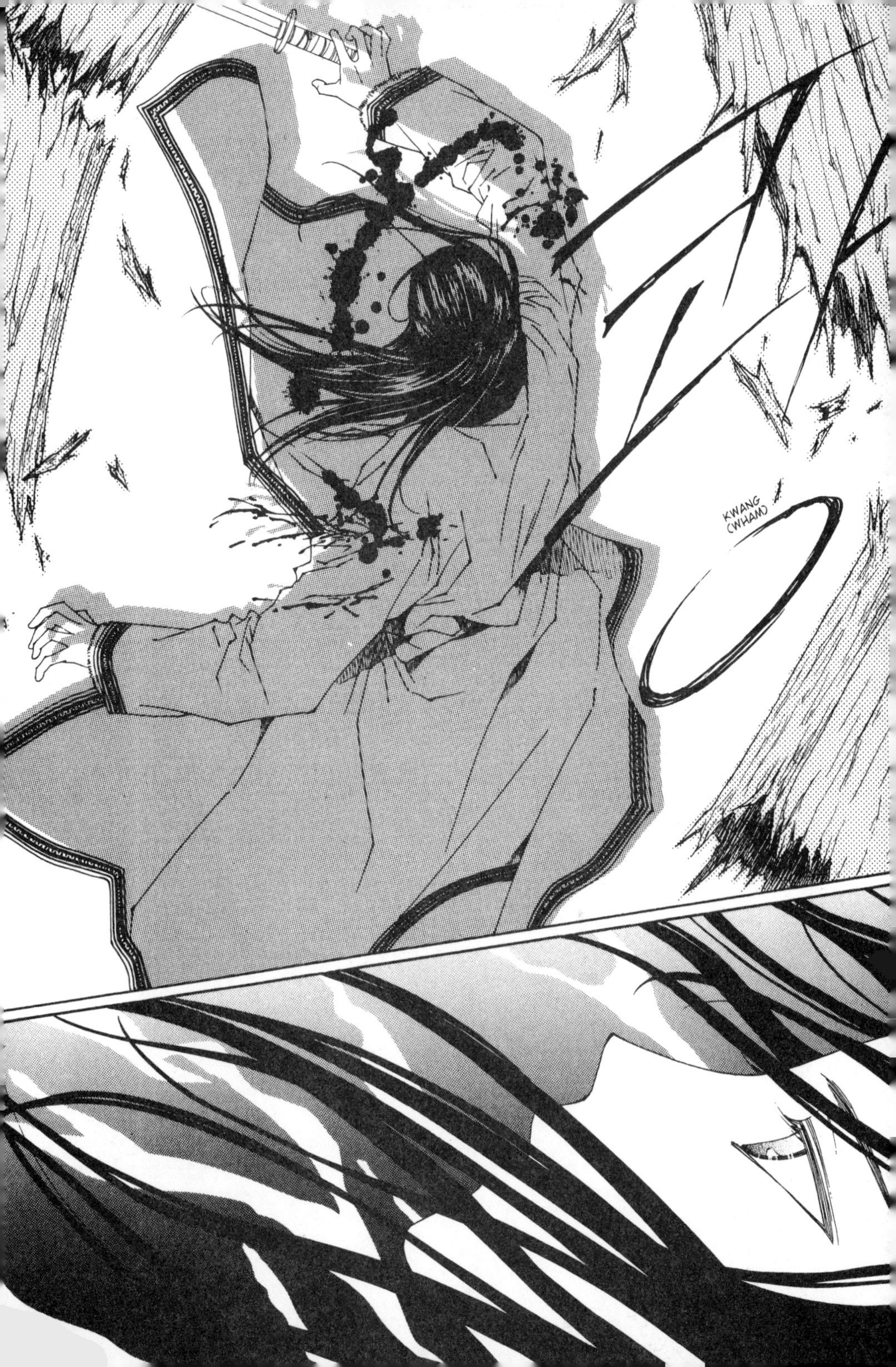
KWANG
(WHAM)

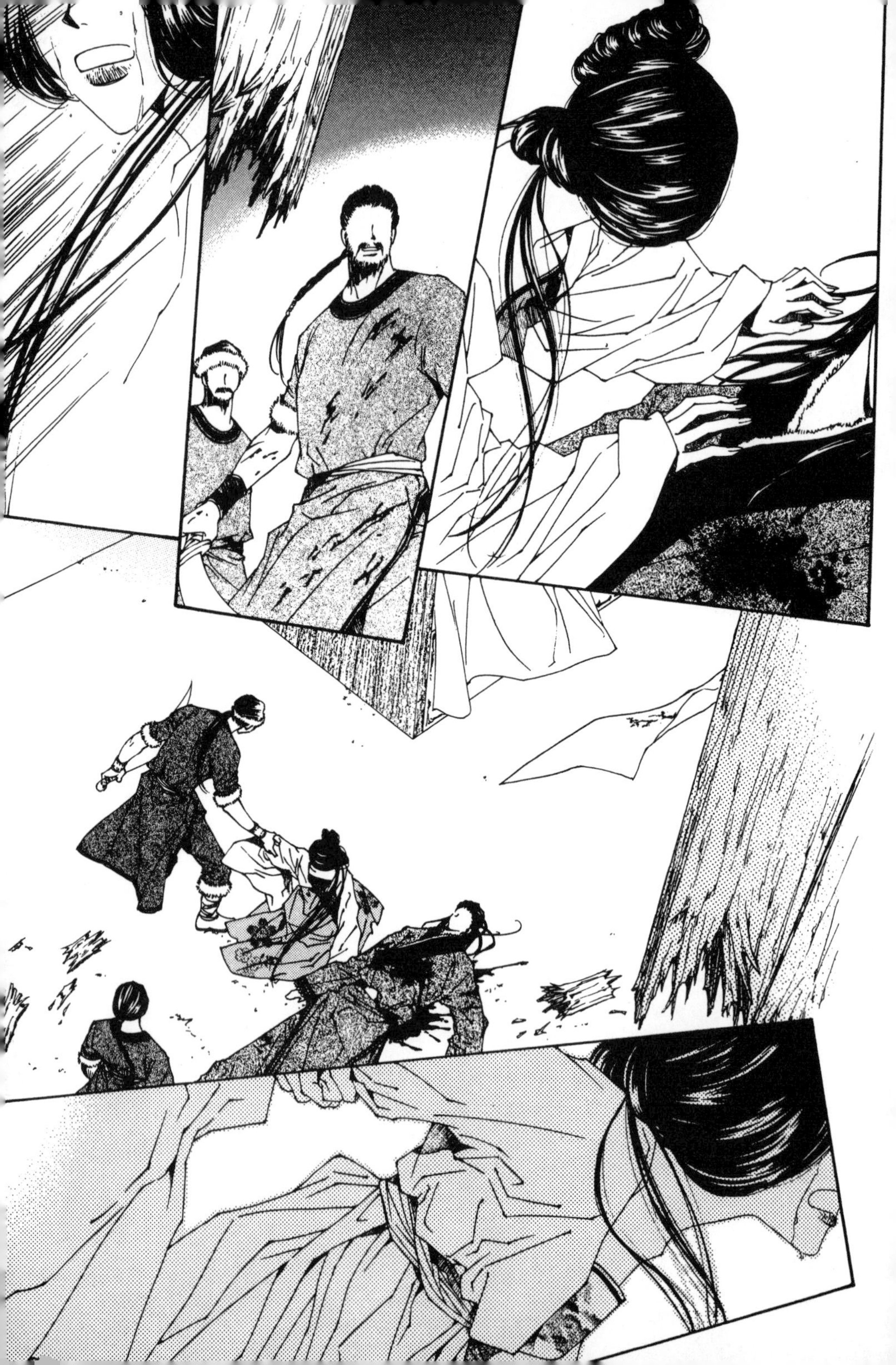

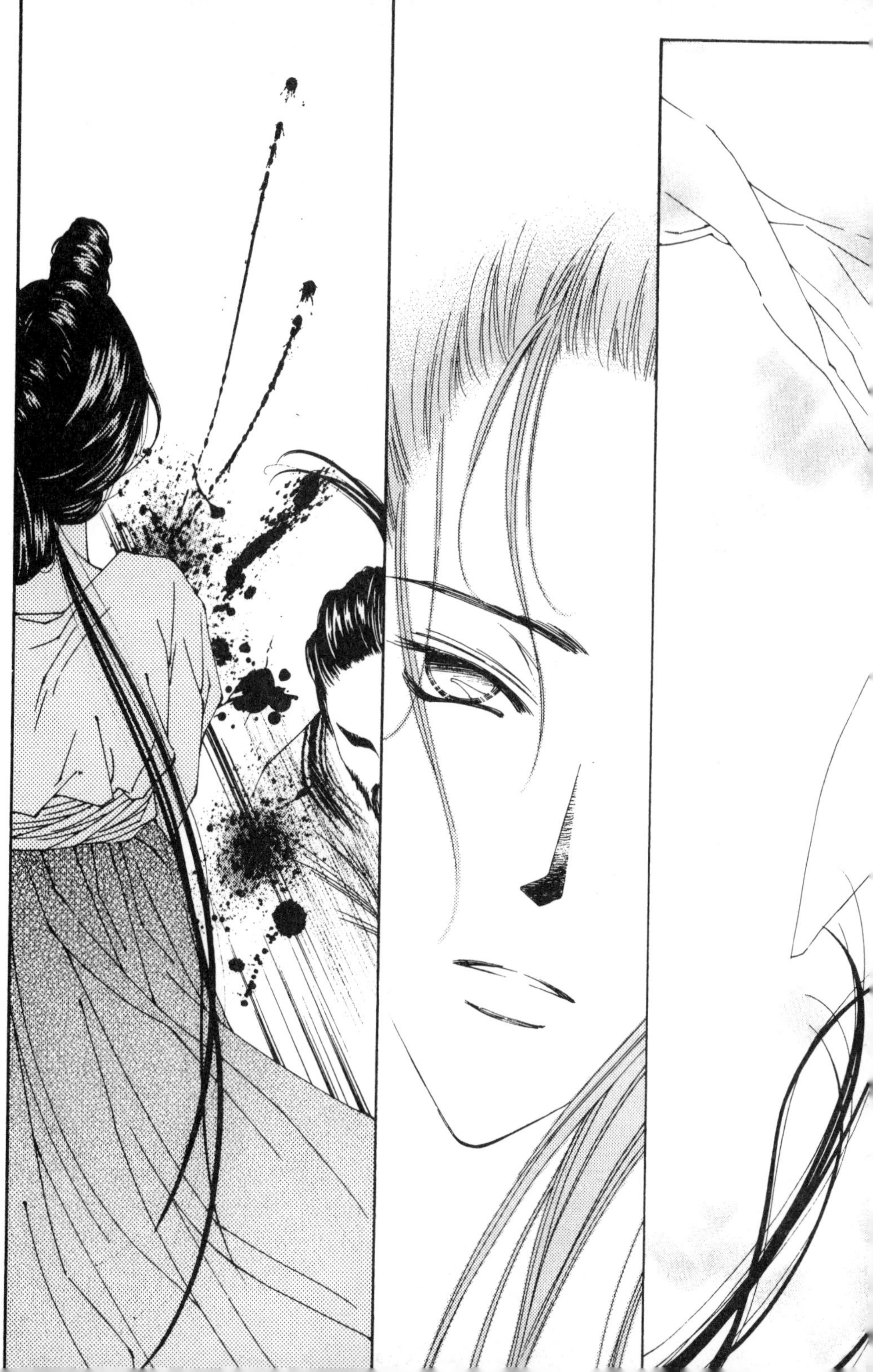

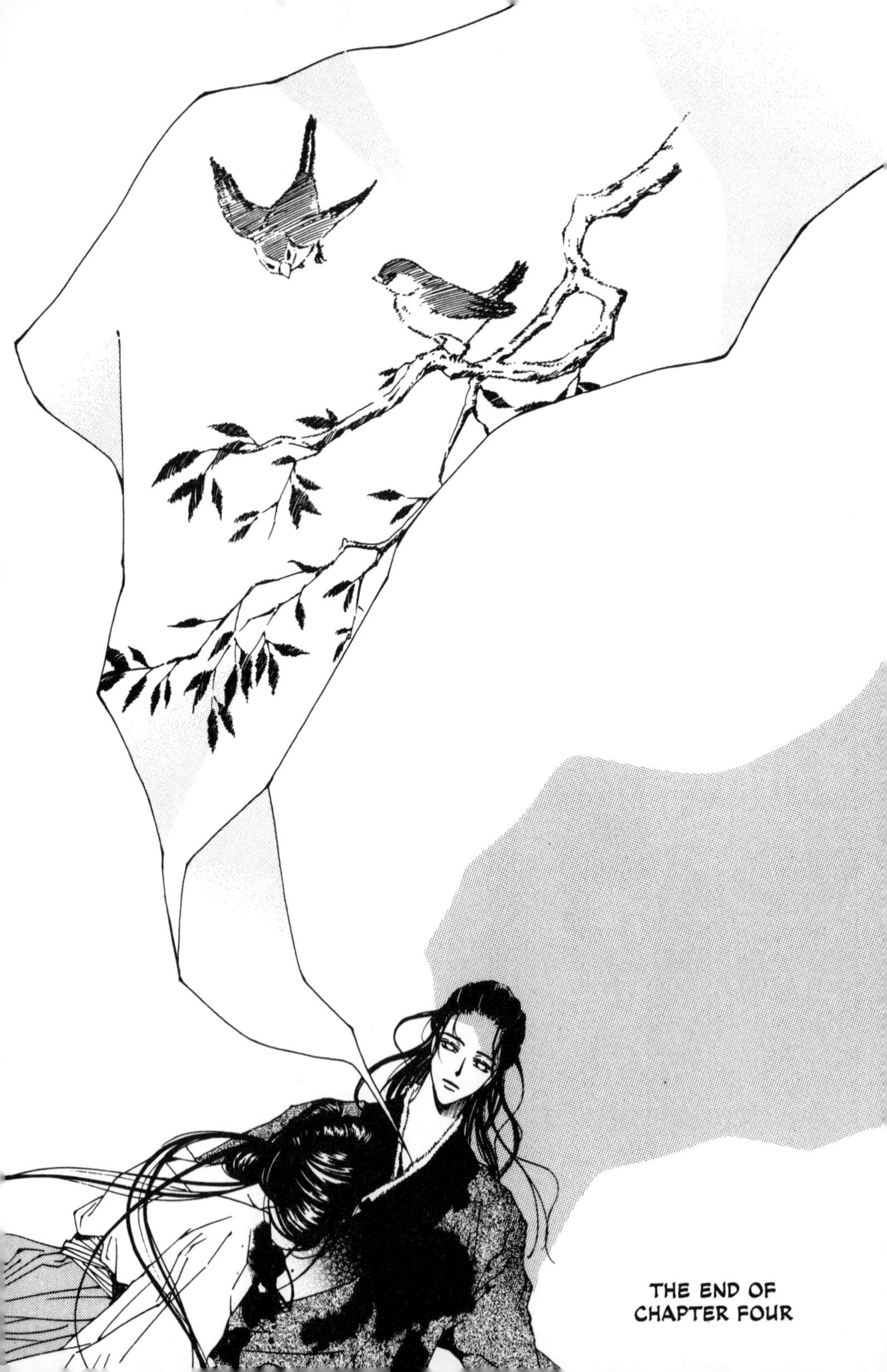
THE END OF
CHAPTER FOUR

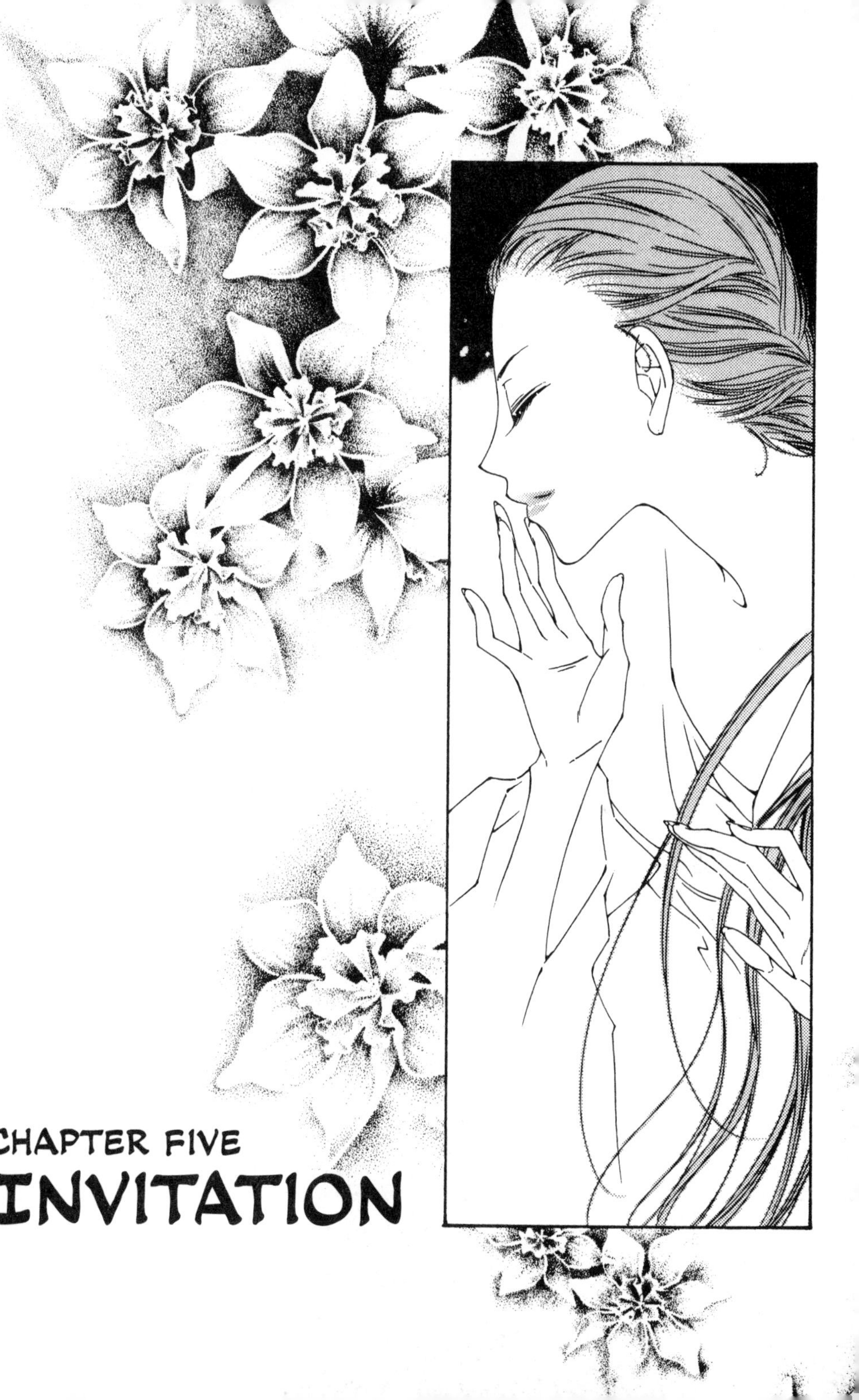

CHAPTER FIVE
INVITATION

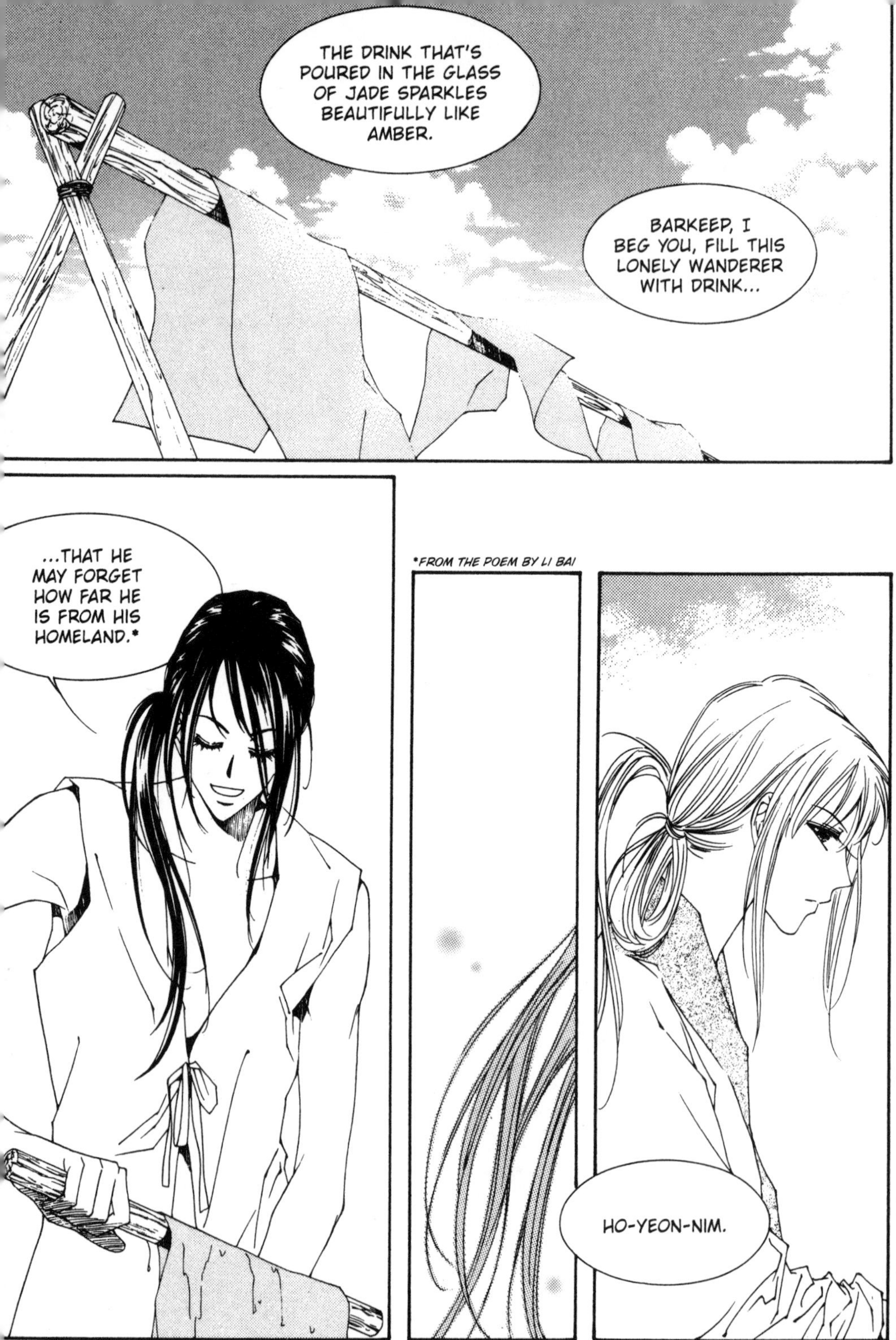
THE DRINK THAT'S POURED IN THE GLASS OF JADE SPARKLES BEAUTIFULLY LIKE AMBER.
BARKEEP, I BEG YOU, FILL THIS LONELY WANDERER WITH DRINK...
...THAT HE MAY FORGET HOW FAR HE IS FROM HIS HOMELAND.*
HO-YEON-NIM.

*FROM THE POEM BY LI BAI

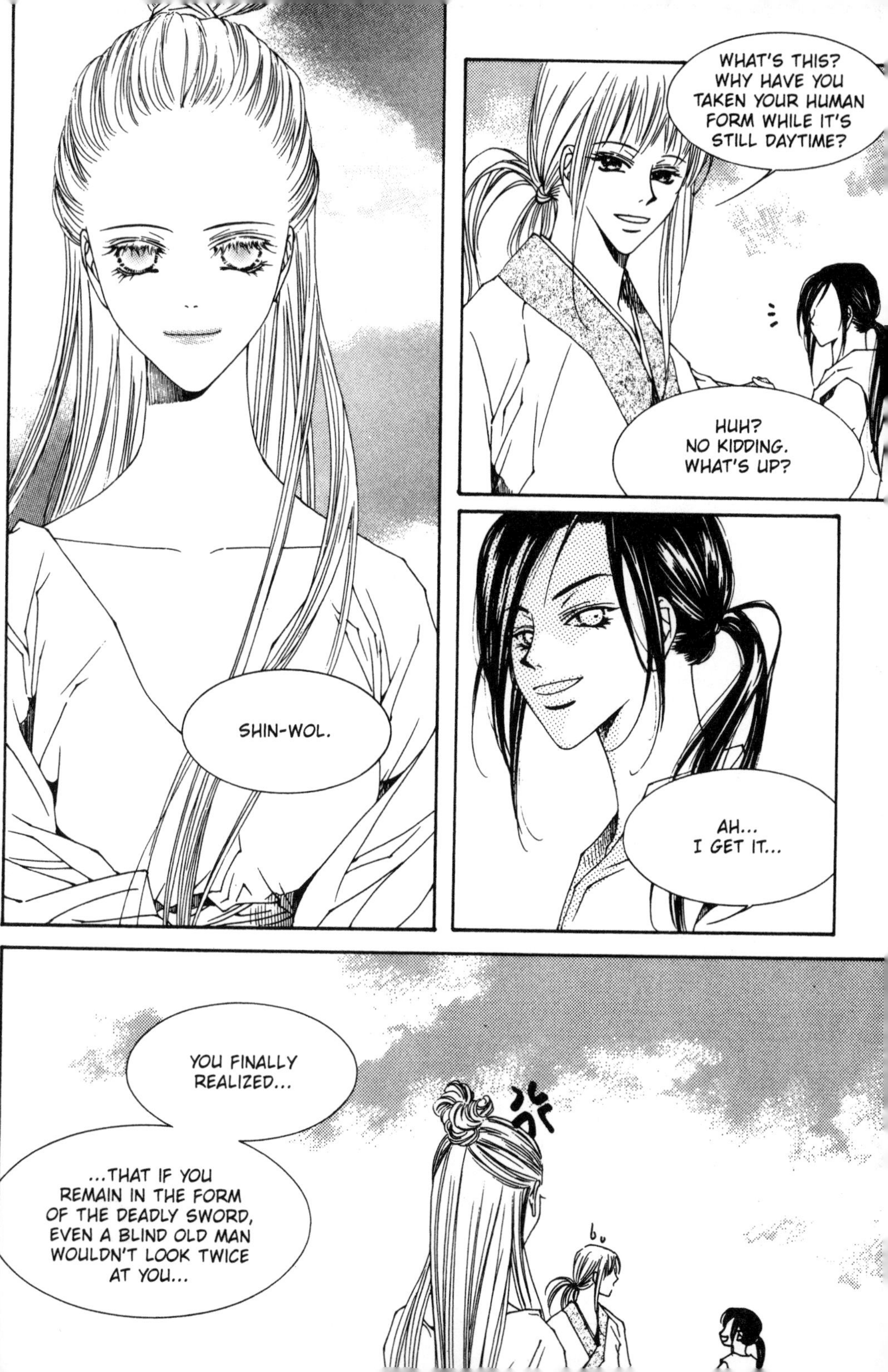
SHIN-WOL.
WHAT'S THIS? WHY HAVE YOU TAKEN YOUR HUMAN FORM WHILE IT'S STILL DAYTIME?
HUH? NO KIDDING. WHAT'S UP?
AH... I GET IT...
YOU FINALLY REALIZED...
...THAT IF YOU REMAIN IN THE FORM OF THE DEADLY SWORD, EVEN A BLIND OLD MAN WOULDN'T LOOK TWICE AT YOU...

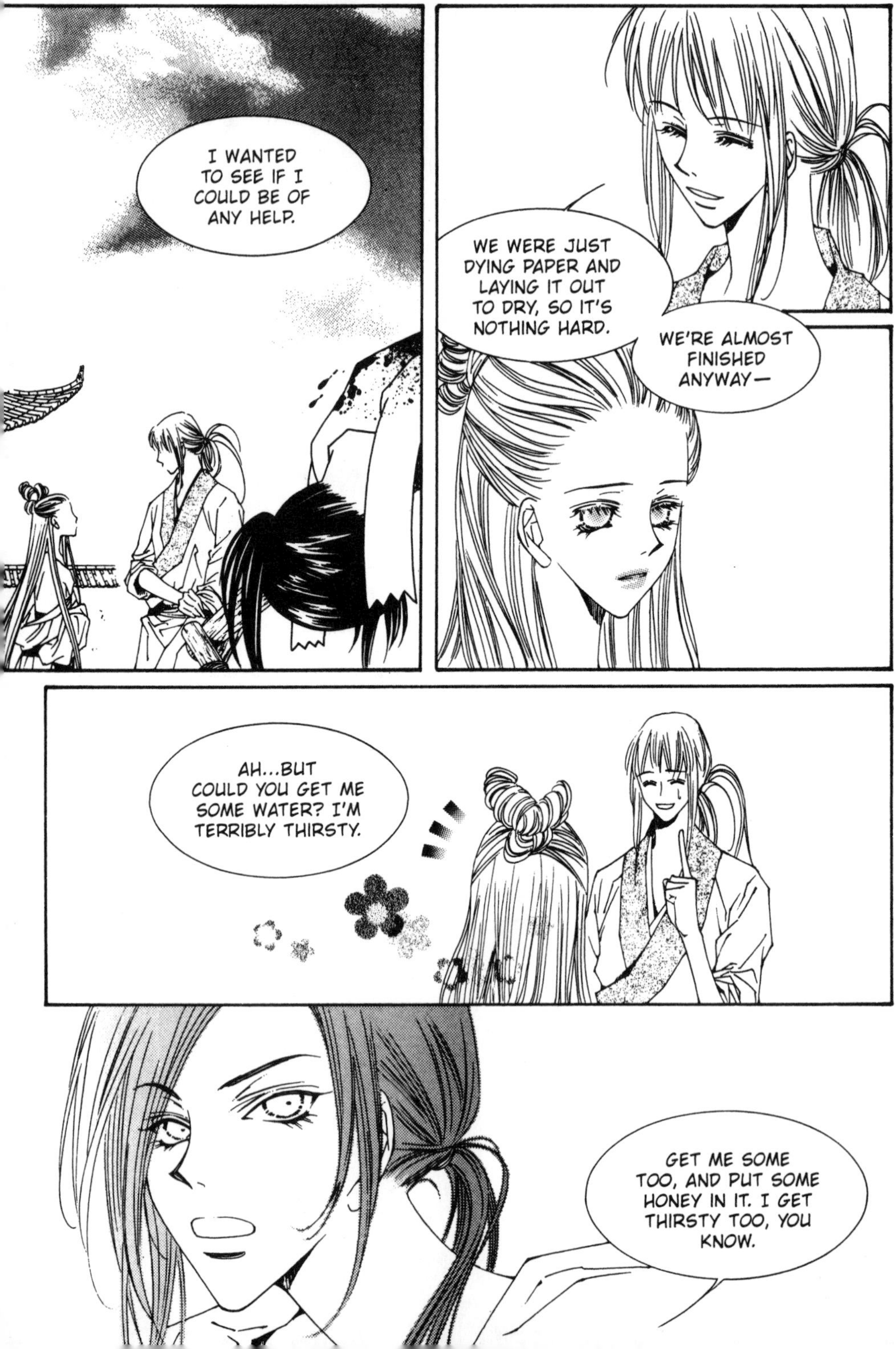
I WANTED TO SEE IF I COULD BE OF ANY HELP.
WE WERE JUST DYING PAPER AND LAYING IT OUT TO DRY, SO IT'S NOTHING HARD.
WE'RE ALMOST FINISHED ANYWAY—
AH...BUT COULD YOU GET ME SOME WATER? I'M TERRIBLY THIRSTY.
GET ME SOME TOO, AND PUT SOME HONEY IN IT. I GET THIRSTY TOO, YOU KNOW.

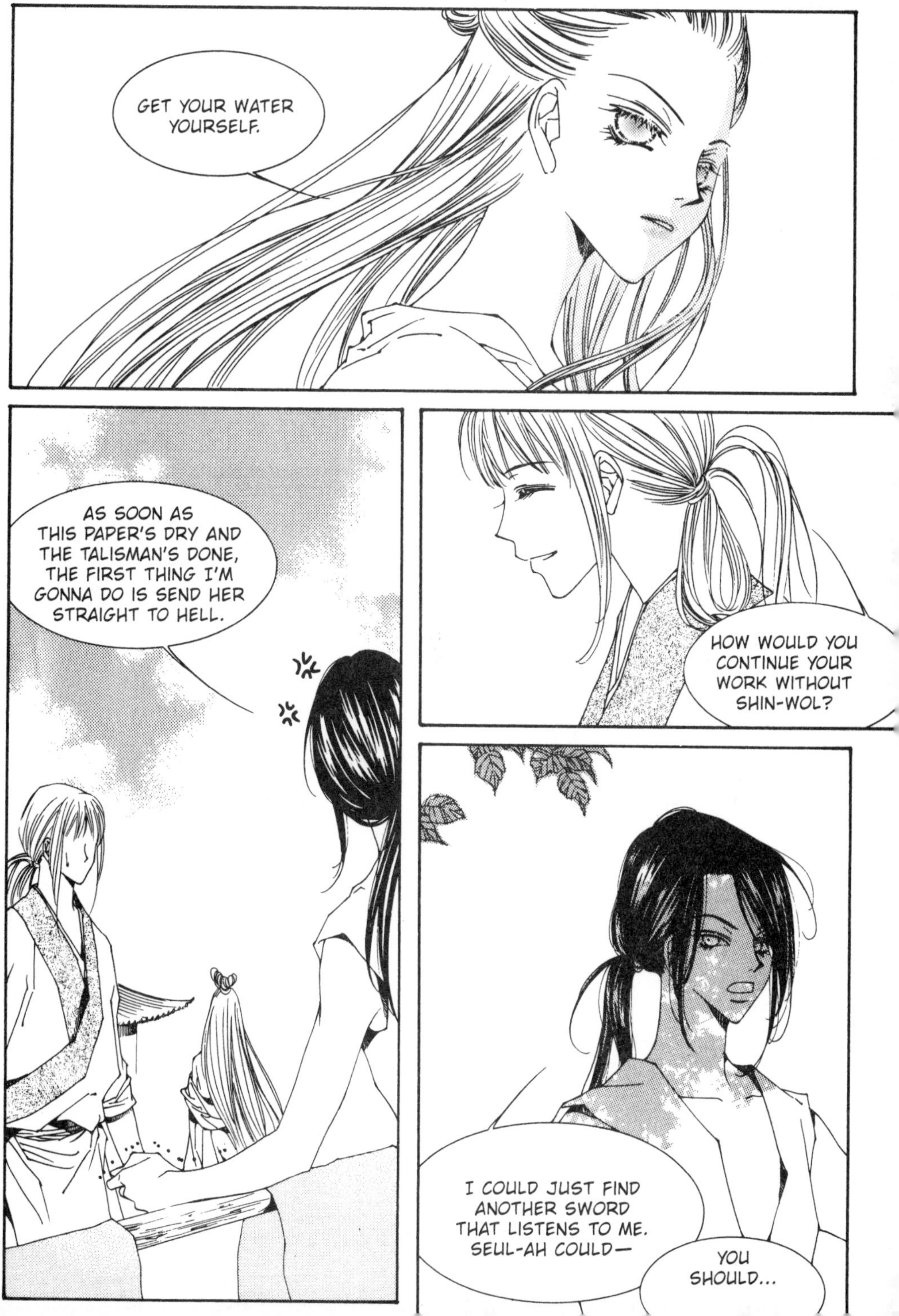
GET YOUR WATER YOURSELF.
AS SOON AS THIS PAPER'S DRY AND THE TALISMAN'S DONE, THE FIRST THING I'M GONNA DO IS SEND HER STRAIGHT TO HELL.
HOW WOULD YOU CONTINUE YOUR WORK WITHOUT SHIN-WOL?
I COULD JUST FIND ANOTHER SWORD THAT LISTENS TO ME. SEUL-AH COULD—
YOU SHOULD...

...MAKE THE SERVANTS DO THIS KIND OF WORK. DON'T YOU HAVE ANY PRIDE?

I MAKE A LIVING HUNTING GHOSTS. HOW MUCH PRIDE COULD I POSSIBLY HAVE, MOTHER?

READ THE REST OF CHAPTER 5, INVITATION IN VOLUME 2!

TIME
AND
AGAIN

Afterword

*ABOUT *TIME AND AGAIN* (PA-HAN-ZIP)

THE MEANING OF THE ORIGINAL TITLE IS "BOOK THAT SHATTERS THE TRANQUILITY," REFERRING TO A BOOK BY IN-RO LEE OF THE SAME NAME. IT IS PRIMARILY COMPRISED OF THE POEMS OF IN-RO LEE, A LITERARY FIGURE FROM THE GORYEO DYNASTY. IT ALSO CONTAINS PERSONAL ANECDOTES, REVIEWS OF POEMS, AND THOUGHTS ABOUT LITERATURE. BASICALLY, THE BOOK IS ABOUT THE VALUE OF HIS OWN LITERATURE. I FEEL BAD FOR BORROWING THE TITLE OF SUCH A RESPECTED BOOK, BUT THERE WAS NO WAY TO GET PERMISSION FROM THE HONORABLE IN-RO-NIM. ^^;;

*ABOUT THE SETTING OF THE BOOK

THE BOOK IS MAINLY SET DURING THE REIGN OF EMPEROR XUANZONG OF THE TANG DYNASTY. HE WAS THE WISEST EMPEROR IN CHINESE HISTORY, BUT LOST EVERYTHING BECAUSE OF HIS CONCUBINE YANG YUHUAN. HE BECAME THE EMPEROR AFTER CALMING THE CHAOS THAT WAS CAUSED BY QUEEN WU ZETIAN. HE ESTABLISHED THE MOST PEACEFUL ERA IN CHINA BUT CAUSED HIS OWN SHARE OF CHAOS AT THE END OF HIS REGIME. I DECIDED TO USE EMPEROR XUAN-ZONG BECAUSE HIS STORY WAS LIKE THE WHEEL OF LIFE IN BUDDHISM. THIS BOOK IS NOT HISTORICAL BUT RATHER A FANTASY BOOK (ALTHOUGH I BORROWED SOME ASPECTS FROM ACTUAL HISTORICAL FACTS), SO I DON'T MENTION ANY SPECIFIC TIME-LINES, SO DON'T THINK TOO HARD ABOUT THE PARTICULARS. HOWEVER, I WILL SOMETIMES MENTION ACTUAL HISTORICAL FACTS OR PEOPLE, SO PLEASE KEEP AN EYE OUT FOR THOSE DETAILS.

*THE NECESSITY OF AFTERWORD PAGES

IS THIS BOOK SET DURING THE TANG DYNASTY?

HUH? YEAH.

HOW CAN READERS TELL?

THAT'S EASY— THE CHARACTERS ARE WEARING CLOTHES FROM THE PERIOD.

YOU KNOW THAT AS THE CREATOR, BUT HOW WILL READERS KNOW WITHOUT EXPLANATION?

SHE'S RIGHT!

DO READERS HAVE TO KNOW CHINESE HISTORY, THEN?

I'M SUCH AN AMATEUR.

THE CHRONOLOGICAL HISTORY OF XUANZONG OF THE TANG DYNASTY

YEAR 712   **XIANTIAN YEAR 1**   LI LONGJI (XUANZONG) BECOMES THE EMPEROR.

YEAR 713   **KAIYUAN YEAR 1**   GETS RID OF THE SUPPORTERS OF PRINCESS TAIPING. CHANGES THE NAME OF THE CHRONOLOGICAL ERA TO KAIYUAN. THE PEACEFUL ERA OF KAIYUAN BEGINS.

YEAR 724   **KAIYUAN YEAR 12**   DETHRONES EMPRESS WANG.

YEAR 734   **KAIYUAN YEAR 22**   LI LINFU BECOMES CHANCELLOR. YANG YUHUAN BECOMES A CONCUBINE OF LI MAO, PRINCE OF SHOU, SON OF EMPEROR XUAN-ZONG.

YEAR 737   **KAIYUAN YEAR 25**   DETHRONES AND KILLS THE CROWN PRINCE LI YING AND TWO OTHER PRINCES, LI YAO AND LI JU.

YEAR 738   **KAIYUAN YEAR 26**   LI HENG BECOMES CROWN PRINCE.

YEAR 740   **KAIYUAN YEAR 28**   YANG YUHUAN BECOMES AN IMPERIAL CONCUBINE AND STARTS LIVING IN THE PALACE.

YEAR 742   **TIANBAO YEAR 1**   CHANGES NAME OF CHRONOLOGICAL ERA TO TIANBAO.

YEAR 745   **TIANBAO YEAR 4**   APPOINTS YANG YUHUAN TO "GUIFUI" (HIGHEST RANK FOR A ROYAL CONCUBINE).

YEAR 747   **TIANBAO YEAR 6**   HOLDS WELCOME PARTY FOR AN LUSHAN AT THE PALACE. YANG YUHUAN MEETS AN LUSHAN FOR THE FIRST TIME.

YEAR 748   **TIANBAO YEAR 7**   SISTERS OF YANG YUHUAN BECOME ROYAL LADIES, AND HER RELATIVES ARE APPOINTED TO IMPORTANT GOVERNMENT POSITIONS.

YEAR 752   **TIANBAO YEAR 11**   YANG YUHUAN'S COUSIN, YANG GUOZHONG, BECOMES CHANCELLOR.

YEAR 755   **TIANBAO YEAR 14**   AN LUSHAN STARTS AN UPRISING IN FANYANG IN ORDER TO GET RID OF YANG GUOZHONG. (AN SHI REBELLION)

YEAR 756   **ZHIDE YEAR 1**   AN LUSHAN TAKES OVER LUOYANG AND APPOINTS HIMSELF EMPEROR. EMPEROR XUANZONG FLEES CHANG'AN FOR SAFETY. YANG YUHUAN IS KILLED DURING THE ESCAPE. THE CROWN PRINCE BECOMES THE NEXT EMPEROR.

YEAR 757   **ZHIDE YEAR 2**   AN LUSHAN KILLED BY HIS SON, AN QINGXU. XUANZONG RETURNS TO CHANG'AN AFTER TAKING BACK LUOYANG AND CHANG'AN.

YEAR 759   **QIANYUAN YEAR 2**   SHI SIMING KILLS AN QINGXU AND STARTS A REVOLT.

YEAR 760   **SHANGYUAN YEAR 1**   SHI SIMING TAKES OVER LUOYANG.

YEAR 761   **SHANGYUAN YEAR 2**   SHI SIMING IS KILLED BY HIS SON SHI CHAOYI.

YEAR 762   **BAOYING YEAR 1**   XUANZONG DIES. (TEMPLE NAME IS XUANZONG AND POST-HUMOUS NAME IS EMPEROR MING.)

*FROM *THE PEACEFUL ERA OF KAIYUAN* BY GUM-MIN JO.

YOO JU
FAMILIAR NAME: BAEK-ON

HE GOT HIS TALENTS FROM HIS FATHER, A FAMOUS EXORCIST, AND CONTINUES THE FAMILY BUSINESS. HE SHOULD PRACTICE MARTIAL ARTS AND SWORDSMANSHIP SINCE HIS JOB PUTS HIM IN DANGEROUS SITUATIONS, BUT AS HE'S TOO LAZY, HE FORCES HO-YEON TO PROTECT HIM INSTEAD.

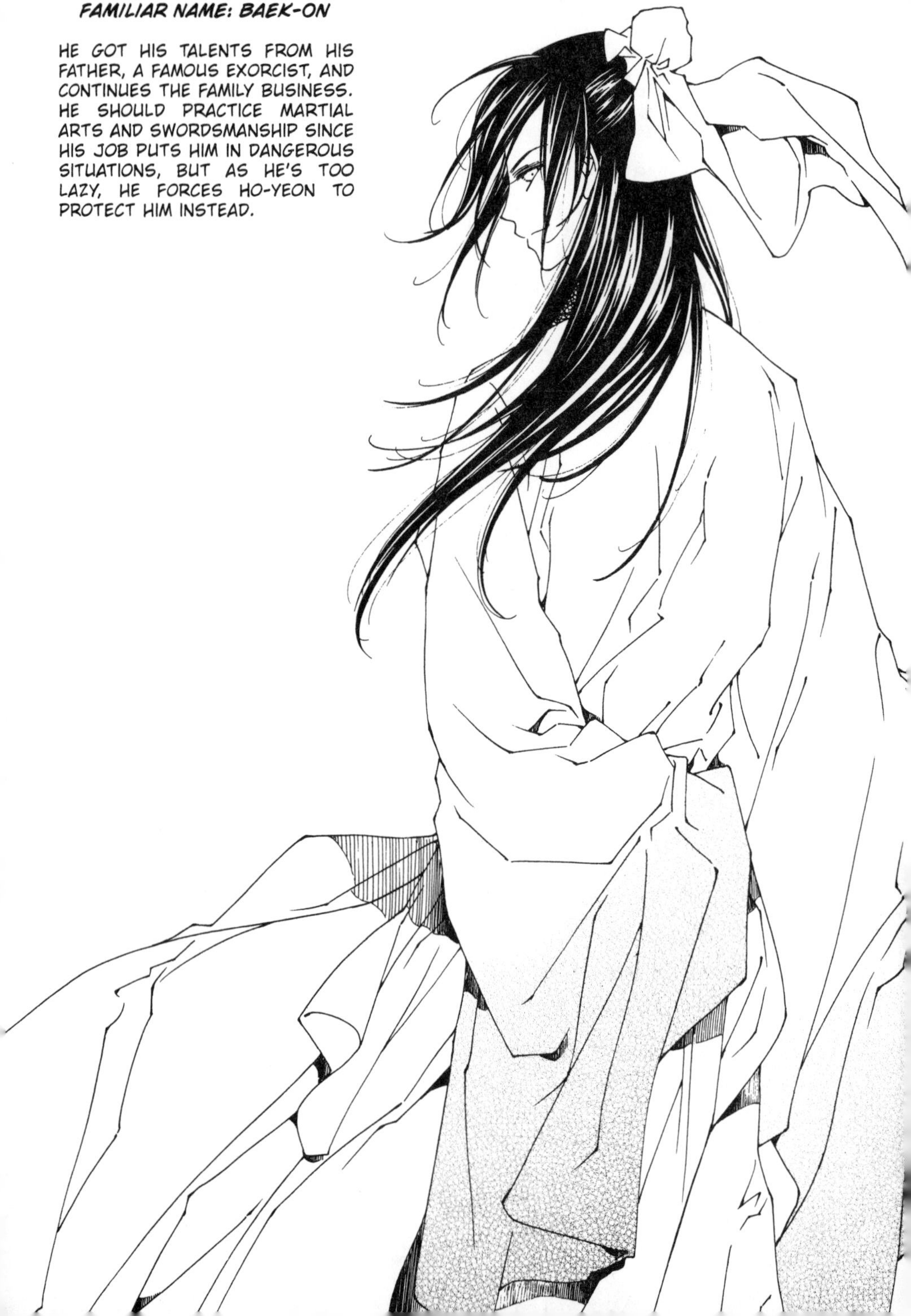

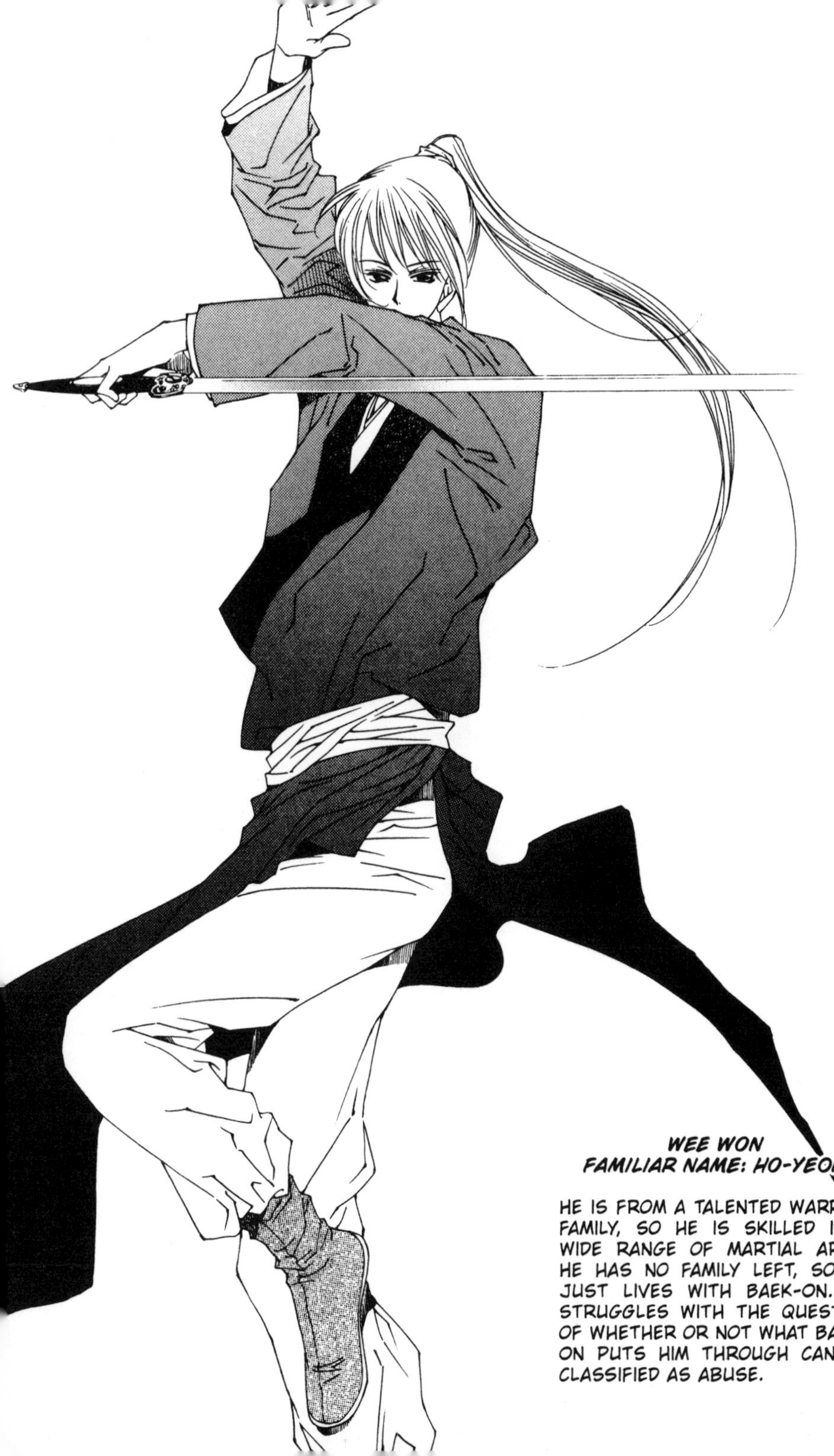

WEE WON
FAMILIAR NAME: HO-YEON

HE IS FROM A TALENTED WARRIOR FAMILY, SO HE IS SKILLED IN A WIDE RANGE OF MARTIAL ARTS. HE HAS NO FAMILY LEFT, SO HE JUST LIVES WITH BAEK-ON. HE STRUGGLES WITH THE QUESTION OF WHETHER OR NOT WHAT BAEK-ON PUTS HIM THROUGH CAN BE CLASSIFIED AS ABUSE.

CHAPTER ONE

NUMBER ONE CHARACTER THAT I DREW WITH THE GREATEST CARE: THE MAN WITH BIG CHEEKS.
NUMBER TWO. MRS. SADAKO CRAWLING OUT OF THE WELL.
NUMBER THREE. THE CHICKENS' PLUMP BACKSIDES.
WHAT ABOUT US?!!
WELL...

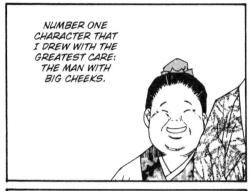

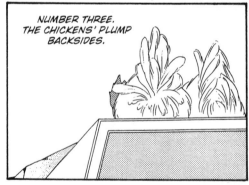

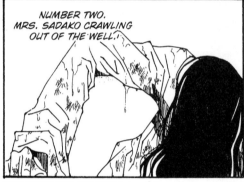

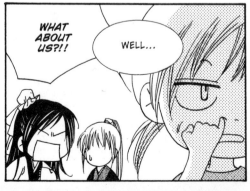

THE GRUDGE IS A VERY IMPORTANT FACTOR IN GHOST STORIES. IT'S A HUGE PART OF THE ASIAN PSYCHE AS WELL, SO I THINK IT WILL COME UP A LOT IN THIS BOOK.

CHAPTER TWO

I MEAN YOU NO HARM.

PLEASE LET ME HAVE JU-RANG.

THE YAN YUE DAO (LITERALLY "RECLINING MOON BLADE") FIRST APPEARED IN THE MING DYNASTY, AND IT DIDN'T EXIST DURING THE TANG DYNASTY. IT WAS ALSO TOO HEAVY TO BE USED IN REAL COMBAT.

COMICS ARE VISUAL!!

SHUT UP!!

BEGGING FOR A LONGER LIFE IS A COMMON THEME IN OLD STORIES. I THINK LIVING A LONG LIFE ISN'T THE SAME AS LIVING A HAPPY LIFE. TO A PERSON WHOSE MOTTO IS "LIVE FAST, DIE YOUNG," A LONGER LIFE DOESN'T MEAN IT WILL BE A HAPPIER LIFE.

CHAPTER THREE

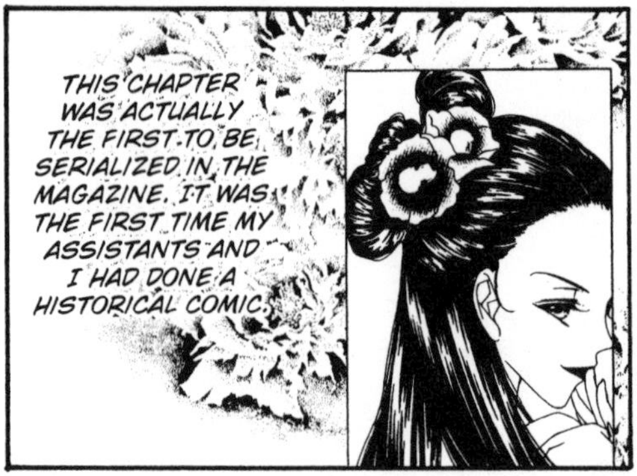
THIS CHAPTER WAS ACTUALLY THE FIRST TO BE SERIALIZED IN THE MAGAZINE. IT WAS THE FIRST TIME MY ASSISTANTS AND I HAD DONE A HISTORICAL COMIC.

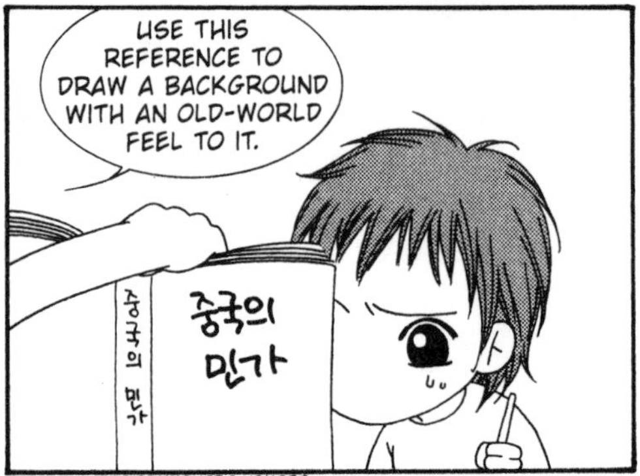
USE THIS REFERENCE TO DRAW A BACKGROUND WITH AN OLD-WORLD FEEL TO IT.
중국의 민가
중국의 민가

BOOK: CHINESE COMMONERS HOUSES

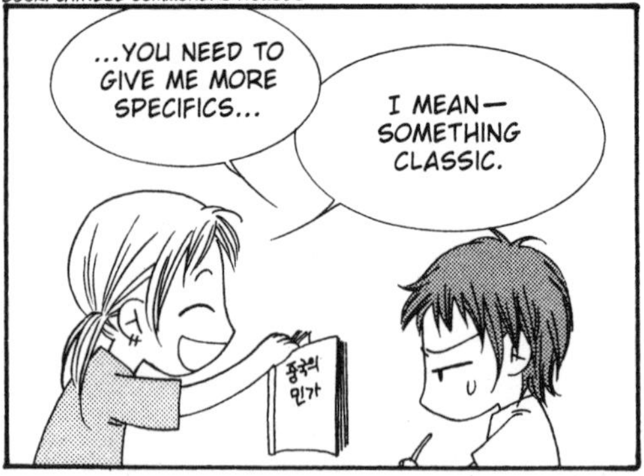
...YOU NEED TO GIVE ME MORE SPECIFICS...
I MEAN—SOMETHING CLASSIC.
중국의 민가

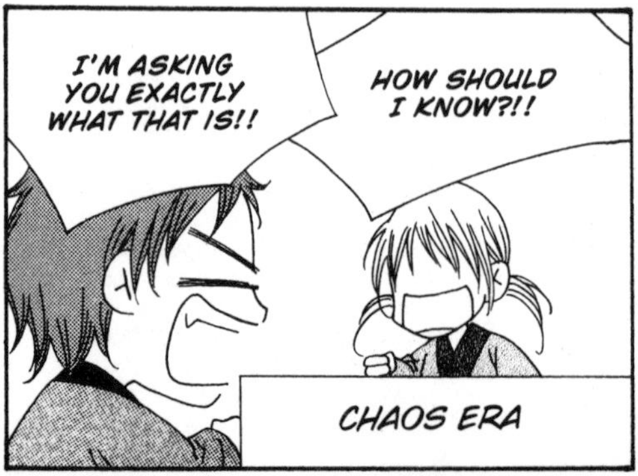
I'M ASKING YOU EXACTLY WHAT THAT IS!!
HOW SHOULD I KNOW?!!
CHAOS ERA

THIS CHAPTER'S INSPIRATION IS FROM "THE TONGUE-CUT SPARROW." I THINK THE REAL VILLAIN IS THE SPARROW WHO LIED AND STOLE FOOD. WHAT DID THE OLD LADY DO WRONG?

CHAPTER FOUR

MY SKILLS ARE NOTHING TO BOAST ABOUT...

...SO FORGIVE ME THAT I CANNOT GUARANTEE YOUR SAFETY.

HEY, JERK!! YOU SHOULD'VE ASKED ME AT LEAST ONE MORE TIME!!

DON'T YOU KNOW A KOREAN ASKS AT LEAST THREE TIMES?

KOREAN?

SINCE CHINA IS SO HUGE, I NEEDED TO BUY A MAP FOR REFERENCE. THE PROBLEM IS, THERE HAVE BEEN MAJOR CHANGES IN WHAT AREAS WERE CALLED BACK THEN VERSUS NOW. IF I MAKE A MISTAKE EVERY NOW AND THEN, PLEASE TELL ME DISCREETLY OR JUST SMILE AND MOVE ON.

OF COURSE THE GOVERNOR IS A MADE-UP CHARACTER, AND I DON'T EVEN KNOW WHAT KIND OF PERSON HE WAS IN HISTORY! (PLEASE UNDERSTAND ME...)

CHAPTER FIVE

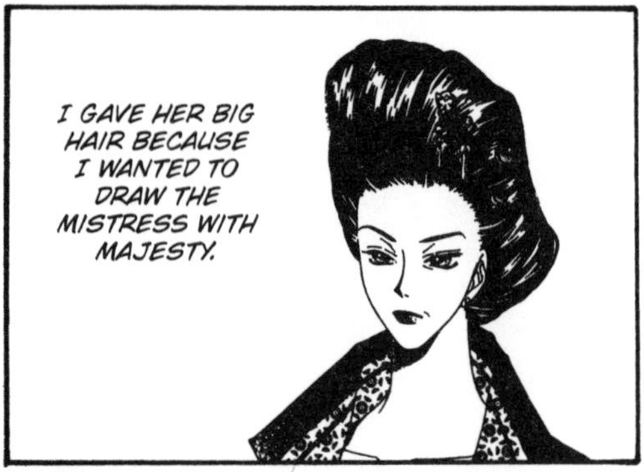
I GAVE HER BIG HAIR BECAUSE I WANTED TO DRAW THE MISTRESS WITH MAJESTY.

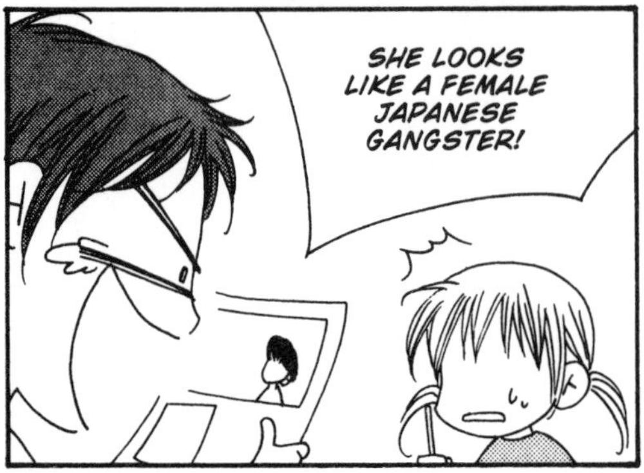
SHE LOOKS LIKE A FEMALE JAPANESE GANGSTER!

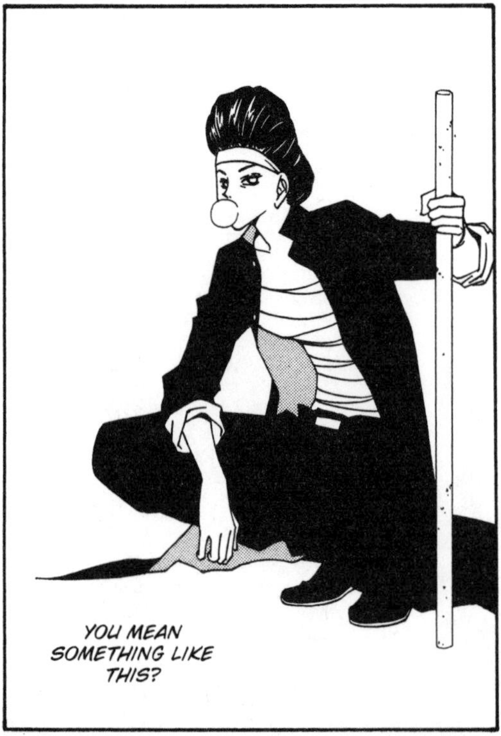
YOU MEAN SOMETHING LIKE THIS?

THIS IS LI BAI'S POEM "WRITING IN A STRANGE PLACE."

OH GLORIOUS NECTAR OF LANLING WITH THE SWEET FRAGRANCE OF GINGER,
THE DRINK THAT'S POURED IN THE CLASS OF JADE SPARKLES BEAUTIFULLY LIKE AMBER.
BARKEEP, I BEG YOU, FILL THIS LONELY WANDERER WITH DRINK,
THAT HE MAY FORGET HOW FAR HE IS FROM HIS HOMELAND.

TRANSLATION NOTES

Page 9
The Korean suffix *-nim* is used to convey respect, similar to *-san* or *-sama* in Japanese.

Page 10
In Asian history and culture, a certain value was placed on a person's given name, so it was considered rude to use it too often. Thus, when a person married or reached a certain age, he or she would be given another name to be used more commonly. This is why Yoo Ju and Wee Won refer to each other as Baek-On Ju and Ho-Yeon Won respectively.

Page 15
Yuan was the ancient currency used in China and Korea.

Page 19
Sadako is the name of the ghost that emerges from the well in the famous Japanese horror film *Ringu*. This film was remade as *The Ring* for American audiences.

Page 41
The suffix *-rang* is used to refer to someone else's son.

Page 60
The **Two Stars** refers to the South star and the North star. The South star controls life, and the North star controls death.

Look for more Time and Again in
YEN⁺ Plus
a monthly manga anthology from Yen Press

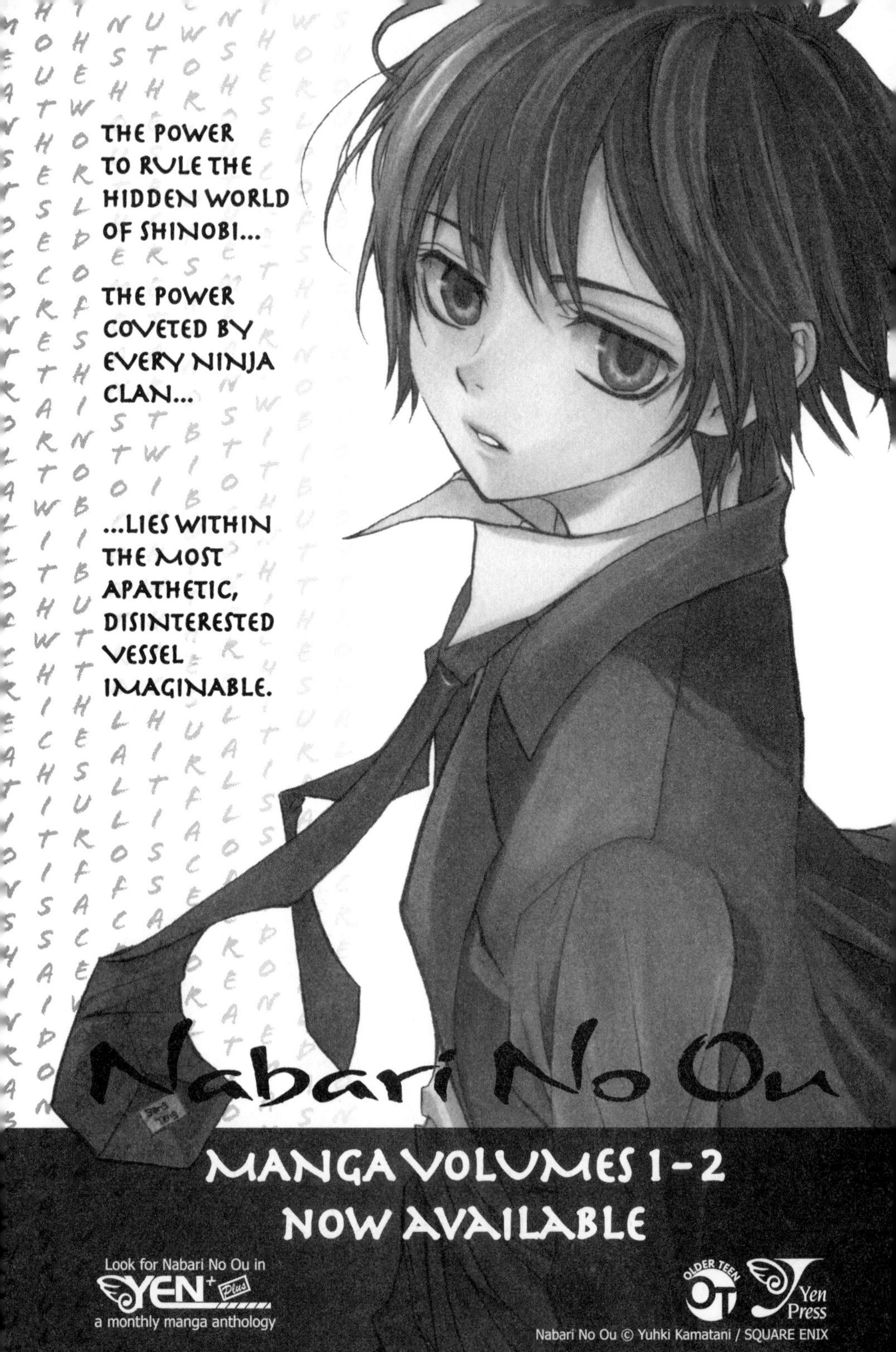
THE POWER TO RULE THE HIDDEN WORLD OF SHINOBI...
THE POWER COVETED BY EVERY NINJA CLAN...
...LIES WITHIN THE MOST APATHETIC, DISINTERESTED VESSEL IMAGINABLE.
Nabari No Ou
MANGA VOLUMES 1-2 NOW AVAILABLE
Look for Nabari No Ou in YEN+ Plus
a monthly manga anthology
OLDER TEEN OT
Yen Press
Nabari No Ou © Yuhki Kamatani / SQUARE ENIX

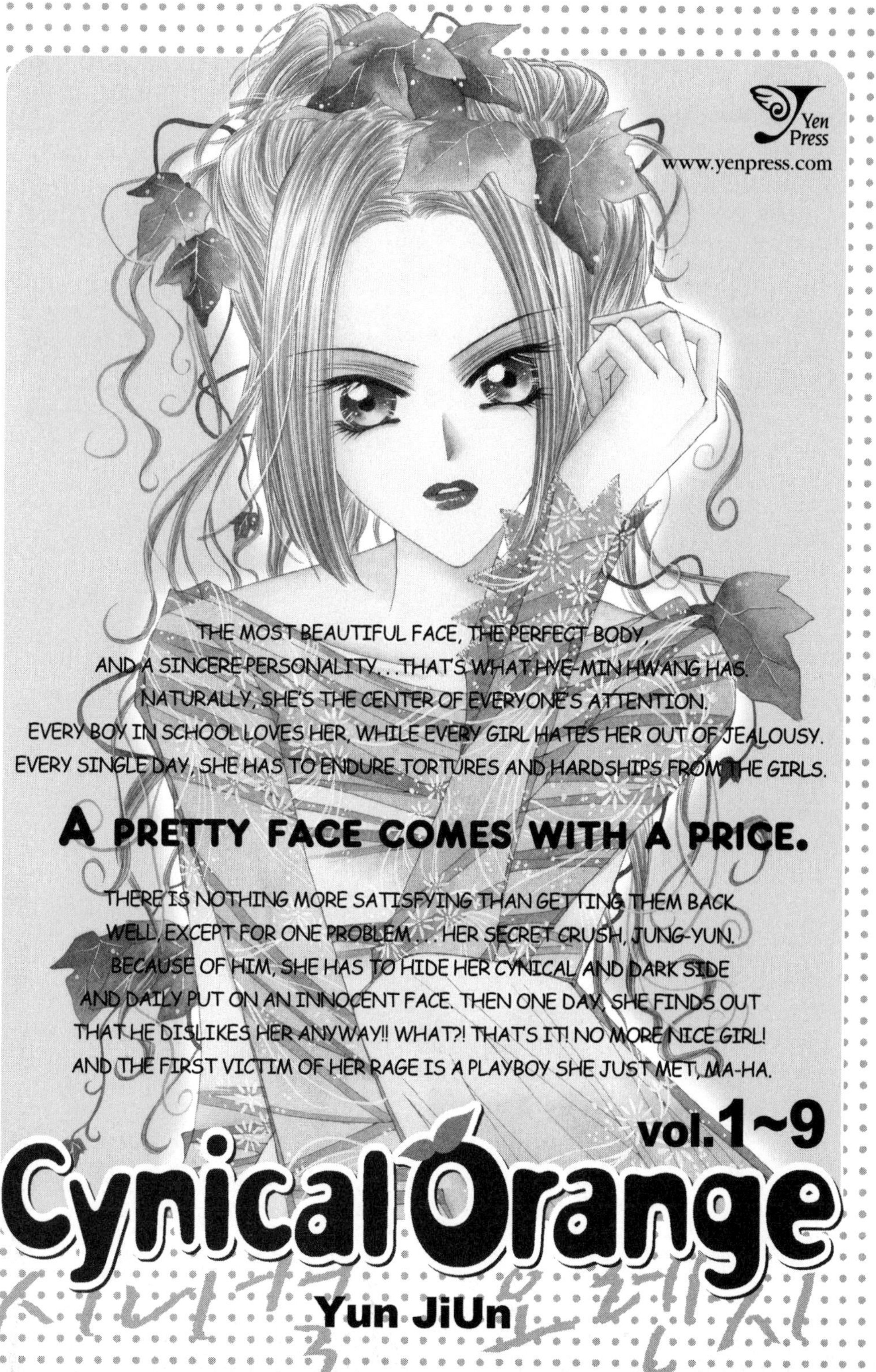
Yen Press
www.yenpress.com
THE MOST BEAUTIFUL FACE, THE PERFECT BODY,
AND A SINCERE PERSONALITY. . .THAT'S WHAT HYE-MIN HWANG HAS.
NATURALLY, SHE'S THE CENTER OF EVERYONE'S ATTENTION.
EVERY BOY IN SCHOOL LOVES HER, WHILE EVERY GIRL HATES HER OUT OF JEALOUSY.
EVERY SINGLE DAY, SHE HAS TO ENDURE TORTURES AND HARDSHIPS FROM THE GIRLS.
A PRETTY FACE COMES WITH A PRICE.
THERE IS NOTHING MORE SATISFYING THAN GETTING THEM BACK.
WELL, EXCEPT FOR ONE PROBLEM . . . HER SECRET CRUSH, JUNG-YUN.
BECAUSE OF HIM, SHE HAS TO HIDE HER CYNICAL AND DARK SIDE
AND DAILY PUT ON AN INNOCENT FACE. THEN ONE DAY, SHE FINDS OUT
THAT HE DISLIKES HER ANYWAY!! WHAT?! THAT'S IT! NO MORE NICE GIRL!
AND THE FIRST VICTIM OF HER RAGE IS A PLAYBOY SHE JUST MET, MA-HA.
vol.1~9
Cynical Orange
Yun JiUn

A totally new Arabian nights, where Scheherazade is a guy!

Everyone knows the story of Scheherazade and her wonderful tales from the Arabian Nights. For one thousand and one nights, the stories that she created entertained the mad Sultan and eventually saved her life. In this version, Scheherazade is a guy who disguises himself as a woman to save his sister from the mad Sultan. When he puts his life on the line, what kind of strange and unique stories will he tell? This new twist on one of the greatest classical tales might just keep you awake for another ONE THOUSAND AND ONE NIGHTS!

Yen
Press
www.yenpress.com

Available at bookstores near you!

One thousand and one nights 1~9

Han SeungHee · Jeon JinSeok

TIME AND AGAIN ①

JIUN YUN

Translation: JuYoun Lee, HyeYoung Im

Lettering: Abigail Blackman

Time and Again, vol. 1 © 2006 by YUN Ji-un, DAEWON C.I. Inc. All rights reserved. First published in Korea in 2006 by DAEWON C.I. Inc. English translation rights in USA, Canada, UK and Commonwelth arranged by Daewon C.I. Inc. through TOPAZ Agency Inc.

Translation © 2009 by Hachette Book Group, Inc.

Yen Press
Hachette Book Group
237 Park Avenue, New York, NY 10017

www.HachetteBookGroup.com
www.YenPress.com

Yen Press is an imprint of Hachette Book Group, Inc. The Yen Press name and logo are trademarks of Hachette Book Group, Inc.

First Yen Press Edition: December 2009

ISBN: 978-0-7595-3058-4

10 9 8 7 6 5 4 3 2 1

BVG

Printed in the United States of America